Amid the mountains surrounding Keswick; and beside the placid waters of Lake Derwentwater, Convention visitors find many a quiet spot for communion with God.

The Keswick Week
1946.

KESWICK REPRINT LIBRARY
CHRISTIAN SUPPLY, INC.
303 East Wood Street
Spartanburg, South Carolina 29303
1-800-922-7506 (Inside SC)   (803) 585-5436 (Local)   1-800-845-7618 (Outside SC)

CONTENTS.

WEDNESDAY, JULY 17th.
Pressing Home the Message.

THURSDAY, JULY 18th.
The Secret of Victory.

FRIDAY, JULY 19th.
Saved to Serve.

Forward.

BY THE REV. RON DUNN, LIFESTYLE MINISTRIES

James Stewart once said, "Behind every pulpit from which the Word is faithfully proclaimed there stretches the august pageant of the gathering ages." And nowhere is this more true than from the pulpit of the Keswick Convention. When I stood for the first time in that pulpit I was overwhelmed by the thought that I was standing where men like Andrew Murray, Handley Moule, R. A. Torrey, A. T. Pierson, Griffith Thomas, S. D. Gordon, G. Campbell Morgan, F. B. Meyer and Graham Scroggie had stood. It was both thrilling and encouraging to realize that no preacher ever stands alone in the pulpit — his presence and preaching are backed up and reinforced by those who have preceded him. He is surrounded by a cloud of witnesses and is part of God's continuity of Proclamation and Redemption. I remember speaking one Sunday evening during the convention at a little Brethren church in the village. Introducing me, the chairman said with a smile, "Mr. Dunn isn't the first Baptist to preach in our church. A number of years ago another Baptist fellow preached here — Spurgeon was his name, I think." It is this sense of holy history that makes the Keswick Convention unique.

But it is much more than that. Stronger than the sense of history is the sense of "Oneness in Christ" that permeates the Convention. Although they have come from different countries, cultures and denominations, they are from the same family whose Father is God and they look upon one another, not as Baptists or Methodists or Anglicans, but as brothers and sisters in Christ. The basis of fellowship is sonship.

And then there is the obvious hunger for the Word of God. What delights me most about speaking at Keswick (and perhaps only a preacher would appreciate this) is the congregation's attentativeness to the Word. After all, it takes good listening to make good preaching. And the folk at Keswick listen good!

Keswick has always had its critics, of course. And continues to have them. But, thankfully, they have been unable to persuade God to withraw His blessings and thousands still gather every year, as they have done for over a hundred years, to a little village in northern England called Keswick to hear the Word of God and learn more of their Saviour.

Ron Dunn
LifeStyle Ministries
Irving Texas

O Light of light,
Up in Thy face we look. Poor clay are we,
Rough rocks and withered grass, woods fresh or dry
According to the touch of life on us,
Canst Thou make aught of us? Renew our will,
Should it decay by fraud of foe, or malice,
Or by our frailty. God, whom vapours praise,
And mysteries hid in fire, and hail, and snow,
By these Thy secret things men live to Thee,
In all these things is very life of spirit.
And we, recovered by Thee, are the living :
The living, yea, the living, he shall praise Thee,
As I this day. To the stringed instruments
Of all creation setting my song, I praise Thee :
With all the music of the world I praise Thee :
With all her pageantry of colours, praise Thee :
With all her glooms and glories, worship Thee.

AMY WILSON CARMICHAEL.

Introduction.

By the Rev. W. H. ALDIS, Chairman of the Council.

SEVEN years had passed since God's people had gathered at Keswick—years full of horror, suffering and sorrow such as the world has never known before—and it seemed almost like a dream to be walking once again the streets of this little lakeside town. Yet there was the tent, and there were the gathering crowds of happy Christian folk beginning to throng the streets, greeting one another with a thrill of joy that once again they found themselves in this place of so many hallowed memories.

The Conveners of this Convention may have had a little questioning in their minds as to the response with which their invitation would be met. Much had happened since the Convention was last held in 1939. Many new movements had been born, and the war had in many respects changed men's outlook, so that there seemed a possibility that Keswick might not occupy the place that once it did in the minds and affections of God's people. But if there were any such questionings they were dispelled at the very first meeting, and right through the Convention it was again and again impressed on all present that Keswick has still a place in the purposes of God for the encouragement, the inspiration and the empowering of His people. No one could look from the platform in the large tent over the sea of eager faces without realising that God had gathered them together with a deep longing in their hearts to know more of the wondrous things which He has prepared for them that love Him. How they listened with an intentness that could be felt as the Word of God was expounded in the Bible Readings, and as the Convention messages were given—heart-searching, convicting, wounding, healing, restoring, challenging, commissioning! How they sang those hymns which have so many sacred associations with Keswick; hymns that seem to lift the soul right into the eternal Presence. You only have to hear that great congregation sing Dr. Fullerton's magnificent missionary hymn to the familiar "Londonderry Air," to know what singing in the Spirit really is! And what a place of prayer Keswick is! Are there any other prayer meetings in the world quite like those early morning gatherings in the tent and the Pavilion? What a world vision you get in the missionary prayer meetings, as those warriors of the Cross pour out their hearts in earnest, impassioned intercession for the countries from which they have come. The whole meeting seems to throb with the divine compassion for a lost world.

No one could fail to be impressed by the number of hands held up indicate those who were at the Convention for the first time. atform it seemed that almost 75 per cent. were first attenders. vention which is all on a very high level, it is difficult to y peaks, but probably it would be true to say that the great eeting on the Friday morning is regarded as the climax ntion, and as providing unchallengeable evidence of the ... of the Spirit of God during the week. Those missionary gatherings in years gone by have been memorable in the lives of thousands, and this year the same moving scene was witnessed as the call and challenge of the Lord was sounded out. Had we any doubts as to whether the young people of to-day would respond to the call to a life of whole-hearted devotion to the service of their Lord ? If so, those doubts will have disappeared as we saw that fine crowd of young men and women standing before us in token that they were ready to go anywhere and be anything for Jesus Christ.

And what a glorious ending to the Convention is that never-to-be-forgotten Communion Service—so reverent, so quiet, yet so joyous. Is there any deep hush quite like it anywhere else ? Is there any greater evidence of the truth of our motto : " All one in Christ Jesus ? " The late Dr. Fullerton going out of the tent some years ago after the Communion Service, said in subdued voice and with a tone almost of awe, " The veil was very thin tonight "—and all must have felt the same this year as we partook of the Broken Bread and the poured out Cup, and were reminded that " As often as ye eat this Bread and drink this Cup ye do shew the Lord's death

Till He Come."

The Convention of 1946 is over, but its results will be found in the very ends of the earth.

This book contains the messages given, and all have been revised by the speakers ; and it is our prayer and expectation that God will speak through the printed page as He spoke through the human voices from the platform. As we read the pages may our prayer be

> Master, speak ! and make me ready
> When Thy voice is truly heard,
> With obedience glad and steady
> Still to follow every word.
> I am listening Lord for Thee :
> Master, speak, oh, speak to me !

SATURDAY,
July 13th, 1946.

8.30. p.m.—*Opening Meeting.*

WELCOME TO KESWICK!
THE REV. W. H. ALDIS.

THE SECRET OF VICTORY.
THE REV. W. W. MARTIN.

After Six Years !

WITH what eager expectation the Keswick Convention was anticipated this year, after the long interval of the six war years ! Keswick ! The name spells, for countless thousands, the world over, the place of their first tryst with God, of their response to His claims upon their lives, of renewal in spirit and upbuilding in faith. For six years the holding of the Convention, with all its attendant blessings, had been impossible ; now at length the tents were to be put up once more, and the week of convocation enjoyed.

Not by any means all who hoped to attend were able to do so ; accommodation in the town was still severely limited, but over 3,000 Convention visitors were able to secure some accommodation in or near the town, and it was with joy of realised hopes that they travelled to Keswick. Nearly all came on the Saturday, so it was arranged that the opening meeting should be held that evening at 8.30.

How good it was to see the huge tent once again ; and still more, to see it filled with happy Christian people. The first act of the vast congregation was one of worship, in singing " Praise, my soul, the King of Heaven." Then the Rev. W. H. Aldis, presiding, suggested that Psalm 145 be read responsively, he and the congregation reading alternate verses. Dr. W. Graham Scroggie and the Rev. Guy H. King led in prayer ; then the Chairman gave his message of welcome. After glancing back to the last Convention in 1939, and alluding briefly to all that has transpired since then, Mr. Aldis mentioned some of the Convention's leaders and speakers who had been called Home, and went on to speak of what the present Convention might mean to all who would listen and respond to the voice of God.

Another favourite Keswick hymn, " Full Salvation," was sung before the Chairman introduced the Rev. W. W. Martin to give the address. Mr. Aldis said that a few months previously he had stood beside Mr. Martin's bed in hospital, and had thought he would never take part in a Convention again ; but God had raised him up wondrously to fulfil his ministry, as at so many Conventions in years gone by.

This " elder statesman " of the Convention began by asking his hearers how they had stood the test of the war years, spiritually, and went on to tell, out of his unrivalled experience of the movement, what is the message and purpose of Keswick. He showed that the holiness of life to which it calls Christian people is nothing merely theoretical, but is essentially practical. Then on a note of challenge to put first things first, Mr. Martin closed the meeting with prayer.

11

Full salvation ! Full salvation !
Lo, the fountain opened wide,
Streams through every land and nation
From the Saviour's wounded side.
Full salvation !
Streams an endless crimson tide.

Oh, the glorious revelation !
See the cleansing current flow,
Washing stains of condemnation
Whiter than the driven snow :
Full salvation !
Oh, the rapturous bliss to know.

Love's resistless current sweeping
All the regions deep within :
Thought, and wish, and senses keeping
Now, and every instant, clean :
Full salvation !
From the guilt and power of sin.

Life immortal, Heaven descending,
Lo ! my heart the Spirit's shrine :
God and man in oneness blending,
Oh, what fellowship is mine !
Full salvation !
Raised in Christ to life divine !

Care and doubting, gloom and sorrow,
Fear and shame are mine no more :
Faith knows naught of dark tomorrow,
For my Saviour goes before :
Full salvation !
Full and free for evermore !

Welcome to Keswick!

By the Rev. W. H. ALDIS.

AS we gather once again in this hallowed spot it is surely with hearts full of " wonder, love, and praise," and at the same time with a sense of solemn awe as we realise to some little extent the condition of the world around and the need of the Church, and as we contemplate the judgments of God which have been abroad in the earth.

It was my privilege in 1939 to stand here and voice the welcome of the Trustees in that momentous year, and as I did so I referred to the way in which the nations were piling up armaments, and how the clouds were gathering and increasing. I went on to say that it seemed sometimes as though the storm must break and sweep away in a destructive flood millions of precious lives. The storm did burst and raged for six years, bringing destruction and desolation in its train. Six terrible years they were, and although God in His great mercy brought us through, very many precious lives were sacrificed, and all of us are feeling in greater or lesser degree the wounds and strain of war.

And so we come to this sacred place to meet with God, many for the first time, and others who have been before, and it is my glad responsibility to offer to you, in the Name of our adorable Lord and Master, and on behalf of the Council, a welcome to the Convention of 1946.

It is probably not known to many how at one time it seemed that it would not be possible to hold the Convention this year. Difficulties seemed almost insuperable ; but, in answer to many prayers, and through the indefatigable labours of Mr. Bradley, through the kind co-operation of the local authorities in Keswick, who have been most helpful throughout, and last, but not least, the good offices of one gentleman in London, who is, I believe, present in the tent, the difficulties were removed, and finally the excellent work of the contractors, Messrs. John Laing and Son, has provided us with this floor for our tent. For all these tokens of divine favour we desire to give God thanks.

We welcome you all, but if there are those to whom we should like to offer a specially warm welcome, it would be first to the missionaries on furlough. Many of you have had a hard time. Quite a number have spent three years in internment camps in the hands of the enemy. No, for you proved that the final word was that you were " prisoners of Jesus Christ." May Keswick be to you each one a place of refreshment and renewal.

And if there are others who should be singled out for a special welcome it must be the men and women from the Services, and I imagine there must be many of you here. For some of you life has been full of peril to spirit, mind, and body, and you have felt the strain—may you find here just what you need, as you bring your lives under the skilful and loving touch of the God of peace.

I do not suppose there are many visitors of other nationalities, owing to the difficulty of travel, but if there are such I do hope that you will be very happy in our midst, and that you may feel that our motto, " All one in Christ Jesus," is a great reality. I shall be grateful if any nationals from other countries would kindly make themselves known, as we should like, if possible, to arrange a little gathering when we might get to know one another.

And so we come to meet with God, here in the quiet of this beautiful spot—we come to seek His face, and we believe we shall not seek in vain— we come to open our hearts to Him that He may search us and know us, and see if there be any wicked way in us—we come for cleansing, for healing, for renewal, for restoration, for the adjustment of our lives to His perfect will, for a deeper experience of a life of victory, for an infilling of His Holy Spirit, and for a recommissioning for His blessed service. This may be humbling, it may be costly, it may be painful, it may be breaking, but if it means that we shall be more Christlike and more usable men and women, surely we shall be more than willing to pay the price.

Now, if the Lord's purposes for this Convention are to be fulfilled, one thing is essential, and that is, that we shall seek to be much alone with Him. This is not easy in the uncomfortably crowded state of many of the houses, yet, if we are desperately in earnest, we shall find a way, and given fine weather there are many quiet spots where we can really be alone with God, as I know from experience. We need to be on our guard lest Keswick drift into becoming merely a spiritual picnic, and in an age in which even religious experiences are apt to be rather light and shallow it is all the more necessary that we should be watchful. I venture to repeat a brief story, first told by the late Dr. Charles Inwood in a welcome message many years ago. He said : " A friend of mine was invited to come and listen to the King speak over the radio, and a number of others were also invited ; but they were chattering all the time, so that my friend did not hear one word of the King's message." And he added : " Don't let the chatter of friendly voices prevent you from hearing God's voice in the Convention."

Even in the natural and perfectly rightful joy of meeting friends here once again, there is a danger which we shall readily perceive. I am sure that the fellowship one with another is very precious and is a part of the ministry of the Convention, but we must find time to get alone with God. We sing, " Speak, Lord, in the stillness, while I wait on Thee," and I think the Lord might well say to some of us, " Yes, I want to speak to you, but you are never still." I do believe it is so important that after a solemn meeting, as we leave the tent, we should avoid all needless chatter. That is not infrequently the devil's way of hindering the work of God's Spirit in our own or another's life.

We cannot gather here after this lapse of seven years without being reminded of gaps in our ranks, and it is fitting we should remember them with thanksgiving. It would be impossible to mention all, but a few surely must be recalled to memory. And the first must be our late beloved Chairman, Mr. J. M. Waite, whose genial personality and Christlike bearing won our deep affection, and made him such an outstanding exemplification of the Keswick message. Then there is dear Mr. Walter Sloan, for so very many years the devoted Secretary of the Keswick Convention Council, and a greatly respected speaker at the Convention. Those who knew about his closing days on earth would, I think, feel inclined to say, " Let my last end be like his." Another name which seems to call for mention is that of our honoured brother, Mr. George Goodman—a very prince of expository teaching, and whose Bible Readings on Romans 6, 7 and 8 stand out as some of the finest Bible Readings we have ever listened to from this platform. And yet another, who has spoken from this platform in years gone by, and of whom it could be truly said, " O man greatly beloved." I refer to the late Rev. Barclay Buxton, who so recently went in to see the King. Yet one more must be named, who served the Convention so devotedly, not as a speaker, but in a very important and helpful way. I am thinking of the late Sir Francis Outram, who superintended the stewarding in that quiet, efficient way which so characterised all he did. For all these, and many others who cannot be named, who have departed this life in the faith and fear of the Lord, we give Him heartfelt thanks.

I suppose the Keswick Convention has done more than any other movement in the Churches to call men and women to the mission field. Probably we should be amazed if would could question missionaries from all lands as to how the Lord's call came to them at the number who would reply " at the Keswick Convention." Many of us are deeply concerned about the needs of the mission field. There are thousands less missionaries overseas from this and other countries than there were ten years ago. The war is largely responsible for this—but the need of more labourers is an exceedingly urgent one, and it must be our prayer that Keswick, 1946, may have a vision of a world of need, and of the unfinished task which faces the Church of God, that many lives may be laid at our Lord's feet for His use anywhere He wills.

When we last met in 1939 the burden in our hearts was the urgent need of revival, and that burden is no less to-day. It may be difficult for us to appraise the spiritual condition of our land to-day, but whilst we thank God for all that has been done during the years of war we feel that nothing that has happened could be called revival. There is a grave danger lest we " heal the hurt of the daughter of My people slightly," to use the word of the Lord to Jeremiah. We need a deep work of God.

It cannot be that our cry to God has been unheeded, and I think one little sign of this may be seen in a new sense of need which is coming to the Churches, surely a prelude to revival. One evidence of this sense of need is provided by that startling book, " Towards the Conversion of

15

England." We may not by any means agree with all the conclusions or proposals of that book, but we shall agree that it is a striking evidence of that sense of need which does seem to precede all true revivals.

Oh, that there might come to us all during the Convention such a conviction of the truly desperate spirtual need of our land as shall afresh drive us to our knees and keep us there until God in His mercy and sovereignty breaks in afresh, as He has done before.

> O Breath of Life, come sweeping through us,
> Revive Thy Church with life and power.
> O Breath of Life come, cleanse, renew us,
> And fit Thy Church to meet this hour.

The Secret of Victory.

BY THE REV. W. W. MARTIN, M.A.

KESWICK ! After six years we are again allowed to gather at this place. What memories it will call up in every part of the world, to thousands of people who, in past days here, got such a vision of God that it has changed the whole character of their lives. What is it that makes this spot so dear to them ? It is not its outstanding beauty alone, though that conspires ; it is not the friendships which were made, though they were very precious ; it is something far removed from that. It is a place where they met with God, where revelations of their own need were made, where the potentialities of Christian life were revealed, where the secret of victory was discovered, and where the experience of the abundant life began. Not that there is anything magical about the tent or the place ; it is quite true that in days gone by this town has been hallowed more than any other in the world, yet God is not confined to this beautiful spot, though He be a God of beauty.

There is that tragic instance in God's Word in which our Lord, having again and again referred to " My House," yet at the end of His life described it as " your house," no longer Mine. If in this place we did not continue seeking God's glory, it might be that the candlestick would be removed and the blessing associated with its yearly gatherings disappear.

You old attenders who have been here so often, look back tonight : How have you stood the test of those awful, weary, tragic times of war ? Has your life stood out as triumphant, and when it was tested, calm and radiant ? What an opportunity we have had ! Or have your nerves become strained and your life become fretted ? Look back and ask yourself : What about my life in these years when I had not the inspiration that comes from our yearly gatherings together in this place ?

May I say a word to new attenders. How very gladly we welcome you ! It may be that you have come from all sorts of motives, perhaps from curiosity, to find out the secret of how life change comes to be. Or it may be you have come here conscious of some lack in daily life ; as a defeated man or woman, longing to know the secret of victory. Or it may be you are an unsatisfied Christian. A worker among young people told me that the two great problems which he discovered among the student life of our land were, first of all, sex ; and secondly, unsatisfaction. God grant if either of these has been the problem of any of you, you may learn that solution in the light of the guidance of God's Spirit.

Keswick ! At this opening meeting we do well to explain something of the design of the Convention, because it differs from all other kinds of gathering in which we may take part in Christian life.

First of all, it is not designed for the purpose of evangelism. It pre-supposes that every man and woman who comes to this Convention already has the assurance of forgiveness of sins ; you will not get any other blessing until that original experience is yours. The urgency of it is beyond mention—" Escape for thy life, look not behind thee," " to-day is the day of salvation." Delay is fatal. The Devil is always saying " tomorrow " ; God is always saying " to-day." So if there are in our midst those who have never known that great fundamental truth and entered in by the door into the path which leads to glory, will you not face up to it on this very night ?

There is something else. This is not a Convention whose theme is the whole realm of religious experience. It has to do with one phase of Christian life, partly in connection with sin, and partly with victory over sin. We do not gather here simply to hear addresses. Nor is the emphasis on numbers, as it is in church worship ; the emphasis is on the individual. It is as though God and you are the only persons concerned. It may be likened to a consulting room of a physician. It is not healthy to be always feeling our spiritual pulse, but there are occasions when we ought to get alone with God, go into God's great consulting room and ask Him to overhaul us, to find if there is any spiritual disease or any want of adjustment, or any amputation which has to be performed. God can do it. He is so wonderful in His wisdom and power that we do not need to go one by one into the consulting room. We can all enter together, and yet have the personal experience of individual dealing with Him. I wonder what the Great Physician will point out and put His finger upon in men and women here tonight ?

What is the object of Keswick ? It is to make men and women what the Bible calls perfect, better translated " full grown." It is to teach how we may become consistently victorious, happy witnesses for Jesus Christ. Its object is to inspire us to crown Jesus King. In other words, it is to promote scriptural, practical holiness by faith.

It is scriptural. The whole basis of any remarks by any of our brethren on the platform will be scriptural. We emphasise that by the very fact that we have our Bible Readings as the first meeting of the day. It will all be founded on Scripture, that will be the final court of appeal.

It will be practical, because holiness is not simply an idealism which we cannot attain. The holiness for which Keswick, and indeed the Bible, stands, is one which is intensely practical, having to do with the details of daily life, and can be obtained on terms by every Christian of every type, and in every position and in every experience of life. It is not the prerogative of the few, it is possible and obtainable by every Christian if he will count the cost and follow Christ.

Holiness. I think we can illustrate it by the fact that the word " holiness " comes from an Anglo-Saxon word which means " whole." A holy man means a whole man, a man who has every part of his tripartite nature whole—brain, spiritual life, physical life, whole in every part of his being.

Is our *spiritual* life holy ? That part of life which only God and our own selves know about, that part by means of which we hold communion with God ; our thought-life—" Without holiness shall no man see the Lord." " As a man thinketh . . . so is he." What about your thought-life, that life about which no outsider, not even your truest friend can ever know anything ? Is that pure ? Is that clean ? Is there jealously in thought ? Is there envy ? It will spoil your communion with God. Then, holiness in relation to our *bodies*. What emphasis the Bible puts on the sanctity of this vehicle of our soul and personality, our body, this wonderful, marvellous complex organism created by God— " Know ye not that your body is the temple of the Holy Ghost ? " Is that body of yours kept for the Lord, or is it used for base and impure things ? Let us face up to it to-night.

Then, holiness has to do with our attitude toward others. Maybe some of you will not get the blessing for which Keswick stands unless reparation is made for wrongs done to others. The Bible is very full of that—" Leave there thy gift before the altar, and go thy way ; first be reconciled to thy brother." Before the Old Testament sacrifice of the trespass offering could be made, any wrong done to any fellow man had to be estimated by the priest of that day, and one-sixth added and paid before the offering could be made. I wonder whether some letter has to be written before what you seek will become an actuality ? Years ago a young woman came to me and said, " I cannot get what has been spoken about. . . You are talking about victory and joy and holiness, but there is a memory in my life. When I was a schoolgirl we used to go to a sweetshop, and when the person behind the counter was not looking we used to take a sweet here and there. Whenever I kneel down God says to me, ' What about those sweets you stole ? ' " I said, " You have got to get that matter of the sweets put right before you will get any further in this matter of holiness. How much do you think you stole ? " She said " About a shillingsworth." I replied, " If you want to get right with God and experience blessing, go the Post Office tomorrow, buy a Postal Order for half-a-crown—that is compound interest—and send it with a letter to the proprietress of the shop, and use the word ' stole.' " She said " I do not like the word ' stole,' it is humbling." When I met her the next morning she told me she had sent the letter and the Postal Order, and I could see by her face that the peace of God had come into her soul. God puts tremendous emphasis on the fact that wrong must be put right before we can enter into blessing. I want to stress this : you will not enter into all that God has for you as long as there is any sin harboured in your life. Neither will you obtain all that God wants for you in this Convention if there is any doubtful thing in your life. Nor will you get blessing if there is a controversy between God and yourself—I am speaking to Christians of course—about any part of your life. I said " any doubtful thing, any sin harboured." It has nothing to do with how other Christians

19

act ; you and I have to stand before the judgment seat of Christ and this is a personal matter between God and ourselves. I know a girl in whom there was a controversy between herself and God about one thing in her life, which went on for three years, until one night as the clock struck midnight she surrendered all to God, the controversy came to an end, and she entered into the full blessing.

Then, holiness has to do with the daily life. We can do everything to the glory of God. It has to do with our family life. Oh mother, in these days when young people are causing such tremendous anxiety, remember that the first years of your child's life are of supreme importance. They are the anchor which will hold your child in future days. If you are too busy to listen to the story of your girlie's broken doll, you must not expect her later on to bring to you the tale of her broken heart. Mothers, seize these opportunities, especially now when so early in life these young people assert themselves and your influence will largely go.

Fathers, be very sure about your life. A man going out in the snow to a public-house, making deep impressions in the snow with his feet, suddenly heard a voice say, " Daddy, take care, I am walking in your footsteps." Many a boy and girl is saying : " Daddy, take care, I am walking in your footsteps." In these desperate days, are you living a holy life, father ?

Ministers of the Gospel, suffer a word from one of yourselves. There are great movements on foot just now among young people. The tragedy is that God seems to be largely by-passing the ministers of the Gospel in this work, of which they should be the leaders, and God is raising up lay people to do it—thank God they are there. It is not enough to be orthodox and correct. A lady writing from the West Coast of Africa not long ago said, " My husband is panting as much for souls as ever." That is the sort of thing that will attract life. Is that a characteristic of your ministry ?

This Convention may mean a transformation of hundreds of lives. Are you prepared to face up to whatever God has for you, and by whatever means ? Are you really desirous of finding out God's will about your life ? ·Are you prepared to spread your life out before God, for Him to put His finger upon anything not in harmony with His will ? Are you prepared to count the cost ? It *will* cost ; in the past it has cost in money and life, and in many other ways. Remember that there is no short cut to holiness, yet right down through the history of this Convention lives have been transformed and transfigured in men and women who dared to face up to God's challenge. Remember that Keswick with all its teaching is only a portal to a fuller life. Crisis here must mean progress hereafter. The act by which I crown Jesus King must mean a continual attitude. Surrender here must mean continual obedience in the future. Crowning Jesus King means uncompromising loyalty.

Are you prepared to put first things first ? There will be wonderful fellowship with other Christians. There will be the making of many new friends, there will be the inspiration which comes from the beauty of our surroundings, there must inevitably be a certain amount of spiritual emotion such as comes with the singing of such a hymn as " Full Salvation," but that is all evanescent ; we are here for spiritual adjustment. We are here to have our lives reviewed by the Holy Spirit. We are here to be searched through and through. Will you face up to that ?

May I doubly underline what the Chairman has said : get as much alone with God as possible. In the old days on hillsides, in the park, and down by the lake people could be seen with their Bibles open, alone with God. I wonder whether there is as much of that as formerly. There is no need to do what a friend of mind did who wanted to make the great surrender of himself to God. He climbed one night up the slopes of Skiddaw by himself, and there built a stone altar, and after a night of wrestling such as Jacob had, as dawn was breaking he stretched himself upon that altar and consecrated himself to God. I met him as I was going to the early morning prayer meeting, tired, haggard and wet through, but the light of Heaven was beaming in his face. You need not do that, but your surrender must be just as real.

Now to sum up. If you and I are to enter into blessing, sin, doubtful things, and controversy with God must be faced, reparation must be made, and total surrender to God's will. Remember, Spirit-filled is always Spirit-ruled. Are you prepared for that ? Or shall you go down from Keswick disappointed—thrilled with the crowd, yes, but when you get back into the rough and tumble of life, shall you be disappointed ? Are you prepared to face up to everything and anything, determined at all costs to learn the secret of joyous, glad, victorious living, so that from henceforth this Convention shall be *the* occasion in which this great transformation took place ?

The God of love my Shepherd is,
  And He that doth me feed ;
While He is mine, and I am His,
  What can I want or need ?

He leads me to the tender grass,
  Where I both feed and rest ;
Then to the streams that gently pass,
  In both I have the best.

Or if I stray, He doth convert,
  And bring my mind in frame ;
And all this not for my desert,
  But for His holy name.

Yea, in death's shady black abode
  Well may I walk, not fear ;
For Thou art with me, and Thy rod
  To guide, Thy staff to bear.

Nay, Thou dost make me sit and dine,
  E'en in my enemies' sight ;
My head with oil, my cup with wine
  Runs over day and night.

Surely Thy sweet and wondrous love
  Shall measure all my days ;
And as it never shall remove,
  So neither shall my praise.

—GEORGE HERBERT.

SUNDAY,
July 14th, 1946.

9:15 a.m. *Broadcast Service.*
THE UNCHANGING CHRIST.
THE REV. W. H. ALDIS.

11 a.m. *Forenoon Meeting.*
FALLEN INTO GRACE.
DR. DONALD G. BARNHOUSE.

3 p.m. *Afternoon Meeting.*
GOD'S THREEFOLD CONDITION FOR A
THREEFOLD BLESSING.
PREBENDARY COLIN C. KERR.

6.30 p.m. *Evening Service.*
THE CALL AND CHALLENGE OF CHRIST.
DR. W. GRAHAM SCROGGIE.

Worship and Witness.

SUNDAY was the first full day of meetings—and it had this added significance this year, that it was the only Sunday of the convention, since problems of accommodation made it impossible to continue over the second week-end as was customary before the war. Very fittingly, the day began at the throne of grace, with the two prayer meetings. Despite heavy rain goodly numbers gathered in the small tent, where intercession was made for all Gospel witness that should be borne that day ; while in the Pavilion prayer was offered for the Continent of Europe and the stricken Jewish people.

Other than the prayer meetings and the open-air meeting, the day began and closed with broadcast services. Before the war the evening Convention meeting had been, for some years, broadcast, and this proved of untold blessing to listeners both at home and abroad. This year, however, the B.B.C. could not arrange for any service to be included in the Home programme ; but a special short service was transmitted on the overseas wavelength at 9.15 a.m., and an half-hour of hymn-singing, in the General Forces programme, for Service men abroad, at 9.30 p.m.

It seemed singularly appropriate that the first gathering in the large tent on this first day of the week, should be one in which friends of Keswick in all parts of the earth could join ; and all who took part in it were very conscious of " the tie that binds our hearts in Christian love " to all who are one with us in Christ Jesus. The service began with the singing of the metrical version of Psalm 23, " The Lord's my Shepherd." Then the Rev. Guy H. King led in prayer, and the Chairman, the Rev. W. H. Aldis, gave a brief but moving address on " The Unchanging Christ," in which he presented clearly and convincingly the central truths for which Keswick stands. The fervent singing of " Jesus, Thou joy of loving hearts " brought an impressive and heart-warming service to a triumphant close.

According to custom, Convention speakers occupied the pulpits of churches in Keswick, so that visitors were scattered among all the congregations. Especially large numbers gathered at St. John's, which has been so intimately connected with the Convention ever since it was founded by Canon Harford Battersby.

Despite this partial dispersal, the tent was nearly filled for the morning service, which was conducted by the Rev. W. H. Aldis. It began upon the note of praise with the singing of " Oh, for a thousand tongues," and after Mr. H. J. Jaeger, of the *Sunday School Times* of Philadelphia, had led in prayer, Dr. Donald G. Barnhouse preached a stimulating sermon on the age-old problem, " Can a Christian fall from Grace ? "

25

—which he answered firmly by saying that he can do so only by forsaking grace for law : when a Christian sins, he falls not *from* but *into* grace. This thought-provoking message was followed most appropriately with the singing of " Grace, 'tis a charming sound."

In the afternoon, Preb. Colin C. Kerr gave a challenging message on " God's Threefold Condition for a Threefold Blessing," based on the familiar words of Malachi, " Prove Me now herewith, said the Lord of Hosts, if I will not open you the windows of Heaven, and pour you out a blessing, that there shall not be room enough to receive it." At the same hour a children's meeting was held in the small tent, led by the Rev. Gordon M. Guinness. The children sang choruses heartily, and the Rev. Guy H. King gave an address on six virtues, each beginning with the letter " P," which he illustrated with cut-out letters suitably painted.

The evening service began with the lovely hymn, " At even ere the sun was set." Then the Rev. W. H. Aldis led the congregation to the throne of grace, and read the story of blind Bartimaeus, which was the subject of a characteristically lucid sermon by Dr. W. Graham Scroggie.

The first of four instructional meetings for young people was held in the small tent at 9 p.m., and at the same hour, as the rain had stopped during the evening, the first of the open-air meetings was held in the Market Place. Attendances at both of these was affected by the desire of most visitors to take part in the broadcast hymn-singing. This was an outstanding success. Mr. Aldis, in a brief introductory talk, described the tent and its lakeland setting ; and he was able, in a word or two, to commend the Gospel in which the Convention rejoices. Then the vast crowd sang heartily several of the best-loved hymns from " The Keswick Hymn Book "—" Oh, worship the King," " Let me sing, for the glory of Heaven," " I heard the voice of Jesus say," " Like a river glorious," " For My sake and the Gospel's," " Oh, for a heart," and finally, " When I survey." These all were interspersed by explanatory comments by Mr. Aldis ; and the whole half-hour was so arranged as to lead up to the note of dedication. The hymns were worthily sung, and were indeed a most attractive presentation of Keswick's message.

Thus the day was brought to an exhilarating close, in praise to God and witness to a vast unseen host of listeners, exiles from home, to whom the hymns doubtless brought both blessing and challenge.

The Unchanging Christ.

By the Rev. W. H. ALDIS.

IT is not easy for me to find words to express adequately the joy we are experiencing as, after a lapse of six years, we gather once again in the tent at Keswick, a place of many sacred and precious memories. Already at our opening meeting last night we have been made very conscious that the Lord Himself is here in the midst, and we anticipate during the week such an unveiling of Himself to our hearts that we shall be bowed before Him in penitence for our many failures, in rejoicing over His pardon and cleansing, and in renewed and adoring consecration to Him and His glorious service. It is our prayer that all who are here, and those who listen to my voice this morning, may enter into a deeper experience of victory in life, and into the meaning of being " filled into all the fullness of God." It is a privilege, through the kind arrangement of the British Broadcasting Corporation, to send over the air a message to the many friends of Keswick overseas, and in the Name of our Lord and on behalf of all present here in the tent, I send you loving greetings.

A summer morning in Keswick is always a joy, and Keswick hasn't changed. Skiddaw is there in her majestic beauty, the lake is there with its calm serenity, and the little town is just the same as you have known it ; for unlike so many devastated towns and cities of our land, Keswick has come through the war unscathed, so far as its buildings are concerned. These six years of war have brought bereavement, sorrow, and loss to tens of thousands of families, and our rejoicing this morning is tempered by the thought of the many homes where there is a blank which can never be filled. To any of you to whom war has brought the anguish of the loss of a dear one, we should like to offer our deep and loving sympathy.

We are being constantly told that the war has changed everything, that the world has entered on a new era and that nothing can be the same in this " atomic age." But whatever truth there may be in these statements, we are glad to think that there are some things which remain unchanged. The message of Keswick is unchanged, and yet it is as relevant as ever it was, because the need it sets out to meet is unchanged, and the One who is the centre of Keswick's message is also unchanged— " Jesus Christ, the same yesterday and to-day and for ever."

It has ever been the desire and aim of Keswick to exalt the Lord Jesus Christ, and to make Christ crucified, Christ risen, Christ glorified, Christ ever present, with all that these truths mean for us of pardon and peace and purity and power and victory, as the dominant theme of the Convention. So for the few minutes at my disposal this morning I want very simply to emphasize the glorious fact of the unchanging Christ.

> Yesterday, to-day, for ever,
> Jesus is the same,
> All may change, but Jesus never,
> Glory to His Name.

There are all kinds of ideas abroad as to why Christ was manifested—" God manifest in the flesh "—and many of these are widely divergent from the statements of Holy Scripture.

We believe and declare that He, the Sinless One, was manifested " to take away our sins," and that " He put away sin by the sacrifice of Himself," and we rejoice that this truth is unchanged, that Jesus Christ, the Eternal Son of God, was made sin for us on Calvary, that " He made there a full, perfect, and sufficient sacrifice, oblation, and satisfaction for the sins of the whole world." It is still true.

> I hear the words of love,
> I gaze upon the blood,
> I see the mighty sacrifice,
> And I have peace with God.

" Peace through the Blood of His Cross," " Peace with God through our Lord Jesus Christ." This may be called old fashioned by some, but it is never out of date. It is the unchanging message of our redemption through the atoning sacrifice on Calvary.

Again, we remember that when the birth of Jesus Christ was announced by the angel, it was said " Thou shalt call His name Jesus, for He shall save His people from their sins." This, too, is unchanged, for not only has He dealt finally and completely with the guilt and condemnation of sin, but He has broken its power and domination, so that " sin shall not have dominion over you " is still the glorious charter of our liberty. We are saved—being saved day by day—by His life, and we rejoice to know and to proclaim that He, the risen Christ, " is able to save unto the uttermost all who come unto God by Him, seeing He ever liveth . . ."

It is still true that anyone, saint or sinner, who comes to God through Christ, can be utterly freed from the bondage of sin. By faith we can accept our identification with Christ in His death, in His resurrection and in His session at the right hand of God, as the great secret of victory in life. As our Keswick hymn expresses it,

> Risen with Christ, my glorious Head,
> Holiness now the pathway I tread,
> Beautiful thought, while walking therein
> He that is dead is freed from sin.
>
> Living with Christ, who dieth no more,
> Following Christ, who goeth before,
> I am from bondage utterly freed,
> Reckoning self as dead indeed.

Yes, that great and glorious fact of our deliverance from the power of sin is still unchanged, because He, our living Saviour, is the same to-day as yesterday.

And yet again, we proclaim the unchanging Christ as the One who by His abiding presence as our risen, victorious Lord is able to guard us from stumbling, to give victory in the hour of temptation, to bestow upon us grace sufficient for every emergency of life, and daily by His Spirit, who indwells and infills us, to enable us " to will and to do of His good pleasure."

Finally, He is unchanged in His sovereignty. " He is Lord of all," says St. Paul. We look out over a world which seems chaotic, and hopelessly perplexing, where statesmen are baffled and the best schemes of men so often appear to fail utterly to achieve any permanent good. Then we lift up our eyes away from it all, and like Isaiah of old we see also " the Lord sitting upon a throne," the Sovereign of the Universe—not unconcerned and indifferent about the world and its need, but deeply and infinitely concerned and eagerly anticipating the day when the hour shall strike for the final manifestation of His sovereign power—for " He must reign," and in the meantime He is ordering, guiding, restraining, and controlling, making even " the wrath of man to praise Him " and moving majestically toward the consummation of His glorious purposes.

In His gracious condescension He permits us to be " workers together with Him " in the carrying out of His purposes, and at this Convention we are being faced again with the challenge to an unreserved surrender to His Lordship over our lives.

All around us is a world of overwhelming spiritual need, and that need can, and can only, be met by Jesus Christ, the unchanging Saviour and Sovereign. Are we willing that God should use us to give this message to the world, whenever and wherever He wills, and to give it because it is our own personal experience of His saving, keeping and liberating power ? If so, let us in unreserved consecration hand over these lives of ours to Him and say :—

> In full and glad surrender
> I give myself to Thee,
> Thine utterly and only
> And evermore to be.

Fallen into Grace.

By Dr. DONALD G. BARNHOUSE.

" (God) called you into the grace of Christ."—*Gal.* 1 : 6.   " Ye are
fallen from grace."—*Gal.* 5 : 4.   " What then ! shall we continue
in sin, that grace may abound ? "—*Rom.* 6 : 1.

IN our consideration of the three texts that lie before us this morning,
I propose to ask and answer four questions from the Word of God.
First, What is the grace of Christ, into which God has called us ?
Second, How can a Christian fall from grace ? Third, Where does a
fall into sin bring the Christian ? Fourth, Shall we continue in sin against
abounding grace ?

There can be no doubt as to the answer to the first question : What
is the grace of Christ ? The whole of the New Testament proclaims
the flaming response. It is the grace of God which bringeth salvation
that has appeared to all men (Titus 2 : 11). When our love moves
upwards toward God, it is adoration. When loves goes out to man on
our own level, it is affection. When God's love stoops to us, it is grace.

I confess readily that I am totally unable to treat a word like this in
the fashion of the great oratorical preachers. During these past days I
had opportunity of reading Alexander Gammie's new book on the
great preachers he had heard over the course of the years. As I read essay
after essay a note of doubt about my own preaching crept into my thinking,
for the characteristic which had singled out these preachers to the author
was frequently the exalted and stately periods of their oratory which
had gripped him as a thing of sheer beauty. One instance will suffice.
He spoke of a moment in a sermon by a famous preacher that had enthralled
the audience. It was a paragraph on grace. I pass on the paragraph,
not for its doctrinal or spiritual content, which it undoubtedly possesses,
but for an illustration in method of approach. The orator spoke as
follows :—

" There is no word I have wrestled so much with as grace. It is
just like expressing a great American forest by a word. No phrase can
express the meaning of grace. Grace is more than mercy. It is
more than tender mercy. It is more than a multitude of tender
mercies. Grace is more than love. It is more than innocent love.
Grace is holy love, but it is holy love in spontaneous movement
going out in eager quest toward the unholy and the unlovely, that by
the ministry of its own sacrifice it might redeem the unholy and the
unlovely into its own strength and beauty. The grace of God is
holy love on the move to thee and me, and to the likes of thee and me.

30

It is God unmerited, undeserved, going out toward the children of men, that He might win them into the joy and brightness of His own likeness."

I know I could never produce minted coins like that. My metal comes pouring from the furnace in a hot torrent, sometimes spattering its greying drops outside the mould. Rather must I say that there is such a thing as the grace of God, and that I know it, first of all because God has commended His own love for us in that while we were yet sinners Christ died for us. And secondly, like a forlorn child who has known the wanderings that come from being lost, and who has known the yet sobbing calm of the haven of its mother's arms, we who have been overtaken by the grace of God can merely tell you who have not known it that therein have we found our peace. And if you will let yourself go, the irresistible undertow, the grace of God, will take you into the great depths and you will know and feel the love that passeth knowledge and the peace that passeth understanding.

This grace is eternal grace. It takes the one who becomes the child of God out of the pit of the past, into the power of the present and guarantees the future glories that are our inheritance, incorruptible and undefiled and that fades not away. But at this point someone asks if the inheritance of grace is really incorruptible and unfading. Is it not possible, they ask, to fall from grace ? This brings us, then, to our second question : How can a Christian fall from grace ?

The phrase " fallen from grace " occurs but once in the Bible, and its clear context teaches us that it has nothing whatsoever to do with the sins of the believer. I propose, in fact, to show that a believer cannot fall from grace by sinning, but that falling from grace is entirely a theological matter.

The only way that a Christian can fall from grace is by falling into law. The Galatian Christians fell from grace by adding to the Gospel circumcision as a practice necessary for salvation. Against the whole legalistic plan of law-works, Paul inveighed heavily. The entire epistle to the Galatians is written to show that a Christian is not bound by the ceremonial law. The Judiastic party claimed that even the Gentiles had to observe the ritual of the law in order to be saved. Paul says that when he confronted the leaders of that party concerning the matter he did not give place by subjection, no, not for a single hour. It was concerning this that he resisted blame-worthy Peter to his face. He called the Galatians foolish for thinking that, having begun by the grace of God, they could keep on by their own doings. Clearly they had fallen from grace by falling into law.

In our day the method and the result of the fall are the same. One falls into law and thereby falls from grace. The Romanist falls from grace by adding ceremonies and works to the process of salvation. If original sin is removed by the waters of baptism, daily sin by the non-bloody sacrifice of the mass (and we must not forget that the Council of Trent said, " Let him be accursed who saith that sins are not removed by the non-bloody sacrifice of the mass ") ; if venial sins are removed by the oil of extreme unction, and other sins by the fires of purgatory, it can well be seen that there is not much left to be removed by the bleeding sacrifice of the Cross of Calvary. Where water, bread, oil and fire remove sins, what does the blood do ? If so much is done by works, little is done by grace. A friend of mine once wrote a booklet on the subject of our redemption to which he gave the long, but true and thought-provoking title, " Salvation by Grace through Faith plus Nothing." That is the reality of the Christian Gospel. Adding to Christ destroys the doctrine of free and sovereign grace.

The Seventh Day Adventist has fallen from grace by adding the false doctrine of Sabbath-keeping as a necessary element of salvation. They say that keeping Sunday is the mark of the beast, and that anyone who fails to keep Saturday is thereby lost. They may talk of salvation by grace, but they have fallen from grace by falling into law. We could paraphrase our text and write, truly, Behold, I say unto you that if you keep the Sabbath (as a part of the means of salvation), Christ shall profit you nothing. For I testify to every man that is thus a Sabbatarian that he is debtor to do the whole law. Christ is become of no effect unto you, whosoever of you are (in any part) justified by the law ; ye are fallen from grace.

The Christian who believes that it is possible to lose salvation after it has been received has fallen from grace. Failure to believe in the eternal security of the believer is really the doctrine of, Christ saved me, but I must keep saved by what I do. This is legalism. This is death. This is falling from grace into law.

The man who believes that only some inner circle of believers will be taken up at the coming of Christ, and that the rest must pass through the tribulation, has fallen from grace. He makes the glorification of the believer dependent upon something in the believer instead of something in the Saviour. And it is an interesting fact that those who have fallen from grace into some form of legalism are always sure that the works which they are doing are enough to meet the demands of God, and that they are in the group that, though they could be lost, are nevertheless saved, or that though some could be left behind at the coming of the Lord, they are sure that they will go up. To have fallen from grace into law may thus be seen to be an immense stimulus to human pride.

We come, now, to our third question, Where does a fall into sin bring the Christian ? We dare to reply that a fall into sin brings a Christian into the grace of God. No born-again man, a new creature in Christ Jesus, ever fell from grace by sinning, but every stumbling believer has found that he has stumbled into the grace of God.

God never punishes a believer ; He chastises a believer. Punishment, by its very etymology, is punitive. Hell and the lake of fire are punishment. This punishment the Lord Jesus Christ has taken for us, and God cannot demand satisfaction from the Saviour and then demand further satisfaction from the sinner. The death of the Lord Jesus Christ—and we believe that this is the most important thing that could ever be spoken concerning the redemption provided by our Lord—the death of our Lord Jesus Christ absolutely satisfies all the demands of a just, righteous and holy God. But the child of God is oftentimes chastised in the grace of the Father. " For whom the Lord loveth, He chasteneth, and scourgeth every son whom He receiveth. If ye endure chastening, God dealeth with you as with sons ; for what son is he whom the father chasteneth not ? " (Heb. 12 : 6, 7). And the chastening of the grace of God into which the believer falls when he sins, " yieldeth the peaceable fruit of righteousness " when the believer is exercised thereby (Heb. 12 : 11).

A charming anecdote comes to us from the life of one of Britain's most famous artists, to illustrate the truth of my answer to this third question. Sir Edward Burne-Jones, in his later years, went one day to his daughter's home for tea. His little grand-daughter, Angela, was allowed to come to the tea table. During the course of the meal the child did something for which her mother told her to leave the table and go and stand with her face to the wall in a corner of the room. The quiet dignity of the child and her evident sorrow greatly touched the heart of her doting grandfather. He said nothing, but early the next morning he returned to the house with his box of brushes and paints. On the walls of the chastisement corner he painted a mural which became the most precious spot in the room. A flight of birds adorned the wall, and a kitten played with the tail of its mother.

Every true child of God who has ever fallen into sin has discovered that there is marvellous grace in the chastisement which the Lord has inflicted upon him. Let us call some of the witnesses from the Word of God.

Moses ! You fell into sin. Did you fall from grace ? And Moses would answer us. Oh ! the grace of God. I played the fool, grew fat with pride, unleashed my angry passions and killed a man. I got put into the corner—and my corner was forty years in the desert. But God came and painted pictures on my wall. I met Him in that desert. On the wall He painted for me a burning bush, and when I stood there I took my shoes from my feet and learned His Name and the holiness of His being, and He brought me back out of the corner and put in my hands the tables of stone where I read, " Thou shalt not kill ! " These words God gave to the race by my blood-stained hands. Oh ! I fell into grace, and such grace.

David ! You fell into sin. Did you fall from grace ? And David would answer us : Oh ! the grace of God ! I played the fool. I idled at home in the days when kings go forth to battle. My lusts seized me and I yielded to them. I took another man's wife, and murdered the man to hide the foul deed. I got put into the corner—and it was as though all the bones of my soul were broken, and I lost the joy of my salvation. But God came and painted pictures on my wall. There were green pastures and still waters, and a table spread with royal dainties. And there He taught me to sing my sweetest psalms, until I could cry, " Blessed are they whose iniquities are forgiven, and whose sins are covered. Blessed is the man to whom the Lord will not impute sin " (Psa. 32 : 1, 2). I fell into grace, and such grace !

Peter ! You fell into sin. Did you fall from grace ? And Peter would answer us : Oh ! the grace of God. I played the fool. I, a fisherman, buckled on a sword and thought that I was a soldier. I boasted to the Lord that He could count on me, and then I denied Him with oaths and cursings. I got put into the corner—and my bitter tears were hot upon my face, and I thought that I was no longer one of His disciples. But my Lord came and painted pictures on the wall. There were lambs and sheep. And there He taught me to look away from myself and to point to His own all-knowledge as the proof that I loved Him ; and there, He told me that I was to feed His sheep, and that I was to feed His lambs.

And you ! And I ! We fell into sin. Did we fall from grace ? And our hearts must answer : Oh ! the grace of God. We played the fool, and not twice or thrice. He knows the sordid details, as He knows our frame and remembers that that we are dust. And oftentimes we have been in the corner. And there, on the wall, our Lord has painted pictures for us :—

> . . . there a precious fountain,
> Free to all, a healing stream,
> Flows from Calvary's mountain.

What then ? Shall we continue in sin that grace may abound ? Here we are at our last question, and our renewed hearts cry out, thunderingly. God forbid ! Out in Nigeria a black preacher was expounding the sixth of Romans to his congregation. The first verse was his text, " What then : shall we continue in sin that grace may abound ? " His audience was composed almost entirely of folk who had never worn shoes in their lives. Even the children run with fleet step over the rocky fields and paths. It is a country of many thorns, and it goes without saying that every foot has been pierced some time or other. One of the great desires of every man is to possess a type of steel prod that is sold in the markets and that is very useful for dislodging any thorn or splinter that has pierced the foot. The evangelist spoke of a man who longed to possess the steel, who saved his money and finally purchased the implement. " Did he then cry out, ' Now I can run in thorny paths with impunity. It makes no more difference, for I now have a prod with which I may remove the thorns that may pierce my feet ? ' " And the preacher concluded, " What then ? shall we continue to walk freely upon thorns in order that we may use a steel to remove those that pierce us ? God forbid ! " For the thorn-wound may become infected, and may leave a scar, and may leave us lame in our walk. God forbid !

The love of Christ constraineth us. The love that painted forgiveness on the walls of our chastisement constraineth us. The same voice says to us to-day, " Neither do I condemn thee. Go in peace, and sin no more."

God's Threefold Condition for a Threefold Blessing.

By the Rev. Prebendary COLIN C. KERR, M.A.

IN Malachi 3 : 7 we have God's three-fold condition for a three-fold blessing : " Return unto Me " (v. 7) ; " Bring ye all " (v. 10) ; and " Prove Me now herewith " (v. 10). Return—bring—prove. Now let us look at the three-fold blessing : " If I will not open the windows of heaven, and pour you out a blessing, that there shall not be room enough to receive it. And I will rebuke the devourer for your sakes, and he shall not devour the fruits of your ground ; neither shall your vine cast her fruit before the time in the field. . . . And all nations shall call you blessed, for ye shall be a delightsome land, saith the Lord of Hosts " (vv. 10-12). Return unto Me, O Israel—return unto Me.

As you read through this prophecy of Malachi, one of the first things which impresses you is the fact of God's passionate desire to bring His people back from a state of spiritual devastation into a life of blessing. It would seem as though His chief concern was not His own sovereign rights, nor indeed His personal glory. It is not that He should have, though it is His due, the worship of mankind ; it would seem as though His chief concern is that His people should come back into the pathway of blessing ; that those devoured, as a land stripped by locusts, should come back into spiritual plenty.

The marvel of God's grace ! I cannot help thinking of Saul on the road to Damascus (Acts 9). With the blood of Christian victims upon his hands, hatred in his heart, but a strange and growing disturbance in his conscience, he was arrested by the heavenly voice : " Saul, Saul, why persecutest thou Me ? It is hard for thee to kick against the goad." How well we might have expected something that would have cut right through Saul's conscience in quite a different way. Jesus Christ might have reminded him from the glory of what he was doing to His disciples, of the homes that he had split and the hearts he had broken ; He might have spoken of the hurt being done to the little Church ; and how supremely He might have spoken of His own anguish of soul. But no ; " Saul, it is hard *for thee* " just as though the only person that mattered to God the Son was Saul, the blood-stained murderer, who was despising the sacred Name, who spat on the ground at its very mention. Oh, the grace of God !

So when you come to this prophecy of Malachi there is a passion permeating the whole story which is the passion of God, who knows no greater longing than that all people who have been devastated and devoured should come back

35

into the place of blessing before they lose their chance. We sometimes sing that lovely old hymn:—

> 'Tis His great delight to bless us
> Oh, how He loves !

Mercy and grace embrace every opportunity for blessing man.

In this prophecy of Malachi we see, in four short chapters, the story of an insensitive people—actively religious, yet absolutely insensitive to their lost spiritual condition and to their lost prestige among the peoples to whom they should have been a blessing. And not merely insensitive, but—a fact which follows hard on the heels of insensitivity—they have become a people spiritually stripped, as stripped as fields by locusts ; they have been devoured.

In these four chapters you find the inspired answer to eight questions which are not so much being asked the people, as being hurled at God by this insensitive people. These eight questions nearly always find their place in the lives of those whose love for God has grown cold. The questions might have been written yesterday, and not 400 years before Christ.

First of all, they almost snarl, " Wherein hast Thou loved us ? " (1 : 2). They ask the question with cynicism and scepticism, with a curl of the lip ; they have ceased to be sensitive to the love of God. God lovingly rebukes them and says, " You have despised My name." They ask, " Wherein have we despised Thy name ? " (1 : 6). And the reply comes—why, you have been offering polluted things, and you should know it, and you would not do it were you not so insensitive. Then they ask a third question : " Wherein have we offered Thee polluted things ? " (1 : 7). Well, says God, " You have offered me the blind and the lame ; the thing that was unwanted and unsuitable, for which you no longer had need." We come to the fourth question : " Why hast Thou not regarded our offerings ? " (2 : 14). Here they were doing what many have done since, perhaps some are doing to-day. Had you gone to their Temple you would have seen the ritual, the sacrifices and their offerings ; but had you gone to their homes you would have heard them say, " God does not answer, God is not there, God is distant." They never stopped to ask what moral obstacle stood in the way of God regarding their offerings. They never stopped to deal with the one thing He actually mentions, the adultery of their home-life, as also their spiritual adultery. They simply said, " Why does not God answer ? "

Then there was a fifth question : they were crying out, " Where is the God of judgment " (2 : 17), and asking why evil is blessed and good seems to be cursed. Pass on to 3 : 7, and the sixth question is found. God says that, if they return to Him, He will gladly receive them ; and with a superiority which you can sense in the very Scripture, they reply, " Wherein should we return ? " —we. They do not realise the distance they have slipped away ; they do not realise the deadness of their insensitive nature. But God again pleads with them, to deal with their spiritual robbery. They have been robbing Him. They cry out once more, with almost a tinge of anger in their voices, " Wherein have we robbed Thee ? " And the last question that is dealt in these four chapters you will find in 3 : 13, where God says, " You have spoken against Me." How insensitive they have become that they could speak against God whose passion is so real, whose longing to get them back into blessing is so apparent. And the answering of these questions forms really the texture of this great prophecy of Malachi.

"Insensitive." "Devoured." Has this anything to say to us to-day ? Surely this, at any rate : how easy it is for the most favoured people to become insensitive. I wonder how many such people have come to Keswick ? They are religious, as was Israel; they are offering sacrifices to God, though they do not realise that they are polluted, because offered by unholy lives. They have come here with intent, because they realise the loss of something, yet they are insensitive to their real needs.

I wonder whether there are any such, insensitive of the *low level of their spiritual life*. I doubt not there are many in this gathering who have been coming to Keswick year after year, yet are hardly aware of some things which their own friends, not unkindly, are thinking about them. The low level of their Christian life is a comment of the critic and a sorrow to the friend, but never seems to occupy their own serious concern. How many have become insensitive to the presence in their lives of things that God has condemned, and still condemns, though the sense of condemnation has long since passed away? They are now insensitive to things which once troubled them not a little. When I was watching Niagara Falls I was impressed by the presence of shops and houses within the proverbial " biscuit toss " of those great Falls, and I wondered how anybody could live near the incessant and ceaseless roar of the mighty flood ; but they did. You can get used to almost anything. How easy it is to become quite insensitive to things in the life which once cried out with a challenging voice ! To-day we have got used to them.

Again, how easy it is to become insensitive to the fact that *we have two standards of life*. I refer to the Christian who allows one standard for himself, but demands an entirely higher standard from everybody else. We permit ourselves just a little more licence than we are prepared to tolerate in one we take it upon ourselves to judge.

How easy it is to become insensitive to the *loss of spiritual vision* which once we had, of spiritual voices which once we understood. Like Philip, we knew when the Spirit of God told us to join ourselves to the chariot. Like the Apostle of old, we knew when a man of Macedonia came with the call, " Come over and help us." Like Peter, we knew what it was to be led from our housetop of prayer along the roadway of life to help some seeking Cornelius. But to-day we do not seem to understand the voices, if indeed we hear them. We sit down in our chair, so to speak, and say " Everything is pointing to the hour when the Lord draweth near, and I suppose for such reasons I have not the experiences I once had." We are insensitive to the fact that we have lost things we never need have lost, and we have allowed to slip through our fingers things which God meant us to hold tenaciously, and the more so in the light of what may be the near coming of His Blessed Son.

How easy it is to become insensitive to our *soul's responsibilities*. I would call it soul-guiltiness. Poor David, he cries out with a bleeding heart, " Deliver me from blood-guiltiness," and those who know the background of the Psalm are sympathetic with a man who has behaved as he had behaved. Should he not cry out " O God, deliver me from blood-guiltiness " ? Was not the blood of a husband whose wife he had wronged upon his soul ? Do not misunderstand me. How can any man ever appear to belittle immoralities of such a kind. But I put it to you deliberately. Is the sin of a murderer, the sin consequent upon physical immorality, any greater in God's sight than the sin of the Christian who is allowing people to walk over the edge into eternity ; as of one who is flirting with the world and the Devil, and who seems not to care the proverbial twopence for the fact that he is living in the midst of men and women who are without Christ ? How easy it is to be insensitive ! God maybe is using this old-time prophecy to remind us of the fact that one of the experiences of Christian life, if that life is not carefully watched and prayerfully preserved, is that it gradually becomes insensitive to the most important things.

The people of Malachi's day had become insensitive, and that which follows insensitivity had followed : they had been devoured. " I will rebuke the devourer," says God. What is in His mind ?

Here is a field, and in my imagination I am walking with its owner, who walks with the stride of satisfaction. He speaks with an air of security. His farm is prosperous, his way is happy, and all is well. A rich harvest lies around him ready to be gathered in within a few days. As I talk with him I suddenly sense and see that he pulls himself up and stands erect. I look at his face. It is horror-struck as he points and cries out, " Look ! Look ! " He knows full well that what he sees in the distance will soon spell complete disaster and devastation to all that he has, and to the hopes of a moment ago. In a minute the sky is clouded and the mid-day sun is darkened. It is a cloud of locusts, millions, billions of them, and they are passing over the land. Now turn back and see what has happened. The land is stripped, every vestige of green has gone. The harvest which was ripe for the gathering has disappeared ; the locusts have eaten all. The man stands heart-broken, dumb, facing the devastation of his fields.

Maybe the devastation is following hard on the heels of an insensitivity into which the world, the flesh or the Devil, or all three, have led some of my hearers, and they stand this afternoon devoured, stripped. No man going from Jerusalem to Jericho, from the House of God to the city of the cursed, has been more man-handled than you. No man has been more definitely stripped, or to use the figure, devoured. Your *influence* has been devoured. You are like Lot of old, when he stood up to speak to the people of the city of which he never should have been a citizen but to which should have been a preacher. When he stood up to preach, his own household refused to listen, and we read " He seemed like one that mocked unto his sons-in-law." Lot was a devoured man, his influence had gone.

It may be I am talking to Christian workers, or even sadder, Christian parents, and if you did but know it your influence in your own home toward those you love as only parents can love, has almost disappeared. There was a time when the little boy watched father with an admiration he could not explain. There was a time when your daughter loved to come to you with her troubles. You had a wonderful influence, and could you have heard your child speaking you would have heard something like this : " If my mother is not a Christian, then I have yet to find one." " If father is not a Christian, then I do not understand the word." They would have done anything for God for your sake. And they would have done anything for you. But to-day it is not so ; your home-life has been devoured ; family prayers have gone, or have become simply an unwanted formality. Conversation about spiritual things has long since disappeared, and given place to talks about jazz or the cinema, or the theatre, or other things which may be quite right, but the spiritual atmosphere has gone, or is going, and you know it. Why ? The home has been devoured, and other things you have prized.

Take conscience. Conscience is not an infallible guide. Paul himself gives testimony : " I thought I ought to do many things contrary to the name of Jesus, which things I also did," and he was quite wrong. It is only as the conscience becomes informed that it can in any sense have a final authority in your life, and when you cease to keep it healthy and informed, conscience becomes corrupt and the real power disappears ; the conscience, too, is devoured.

It may be that *character* has followed, and you no longer are the person you once were. You have been stripped of the glorious dress of a real consistency, of real holiness. You have been devoured.

I may be talking to a few who have even *lost hope*, hope has been devoured. Some may have said, " I am going to Keswick, it is my last attempt to get right ; it is my last chance to get spiritually fit." You have said that because hope has all but disappeared from your horizon, as it has long since nearly gone from your heart. Life is devoured, character has suffered, and hope seems almost to have left you.

Now, what had God to say to these insensitive, devoured people ? He had three very definite things to say : First, " Return to Me " ; Second, " Bring all to Me. . . into my storehouse " ; Third, " Prove Me now herewith." God always says those same things where lives have become insensitive and are in danger of spiritual devastation.

" Return to Me." " Against Thee and Thee only have I sinned," cried the Psalmist ; and the prodigal of old as he sat in the field with the swine said, " I will arise and go to my father." When Jehovah was speaking through Hosea to people under very similar conditions to those of Malachi's day, He said, " Return unto me, O Israel, take with you words." Returning to God is something very precise, very real. It does not consist in coming in a pious way and saying " O God, I have failed," it means I return to God, taking with me words. I say : " Father, I have sinned, I have been a liar, I have been a thief, I have been unclean, I have gone back on my promises, I have turned from the vision I had when I heard Your voice, I have been deceitful, I have been slothful, I have lived a double life, I have required a different standard from everybody else from the standard I have required of myself, I. have brought Thee polluted offerings though people did not know it, and I have questioned both Thy love and Thy judgment. God, I return to Thee." The second thing God says is, " Bring all," for an honest repentance will ever express itself in a full surrender, and if there is not a full surrender you can be perfectly certain there has not been honest dealing with God. We were singing a while ago, " Thou art the Potter, I am the clay." That picture suggests a piece of clay *in its entirety* put into the hand of the Potter for His disposal—Bring all.

The third thing God says is, " Prove Me now herewith." Return to Me—Bring all to Me—Prove Me now herewith. Will you do it ?

Then come the three most glorious promises, or if you would have it, the three-fold promise : " I will open the windows of heaven and pour you out a blessing." More than that : " I will rebuke the devourer," the Devil who was behind so much that spelt devastation in your life. The mighty Lord and Saviour who rebuked the Devil in the Garden, saying, " Get thee behind Me " will rebuke the devourer in your life. He will also hold back the other things that have spelt destruction and devastation. " I will bless" and " I will rebuke," and then the last part of the promise, " Ye shall be a delightsome land, and people shall call you the blessed of the Lord." Men and women, is it not worth it ?

Return, bring all, prove me; I will bless, rebuke, transform, and ye shall be called the blessed of the Lord.

One very practical question : do you want this three-fold blessing ? Do you want it sufficiently to meet the three-fold condition ? Will you return, bring all, will you in faith put God to the test, and go from this tent singing :

> Out of my bondage, sorrow and night,
>> Jesus, I come ! Jesus, I come !
> Into Thy freedom, gladness and light.
> Jesus, I come to Thee !
> Out of my sickness into Thy health,
> Out of my want and into Thy wealth,
> Out of my sin and into Thyself,
>> Jesus, I come to Thee !

The Call and Challenge of Christ.

By the Rev. W. GRAHAM SCROGGIE, D.D.

AFTER a long break in the sequence of these gatherings we meet again, but the circumstances have entirely changed. During the intervening years the world has seen the most desolating war in all history, and the end is not yet.

Many who attended former Conventions in this hallowed place will never come again, and, no doubt, it is true of many who are here, that their hopes and plans before the war are now lying withered in the dust. Disillusionment and perplexity have taken the place of confidence and certainty, and at the moment the map of life is crumpled up.

Many of us here, perhaps most of us, have suffered much, and a tremendous strain has been put upon our pre-war faith. It may even be that under that strain the faith of some has entirely collapsed, and you have come here wondering whether it is a temporary or a fatal collapse.

I cannot but believe that the future course of very many who have come up to this Convention will be determined this week.

This story of blind Bartimæus (Mark 10 : 46-51) is full of spiritual suggestions, showing the successive steps into and in the Christian life. There is, first of all, the man's *pitiable condition*, blind, poor, and miserable ; then his *consciousness of need*, expressed in his cry for mercy ; his *readiness for blessing*, for as soon as he had the chance he came to Jesus ; his *hold on opportunity*, evidenced in his defiance of the rebuking crowd, conscious as he was, that it was then or never ; his *simple faith* in the power of Jesus to give him what he needed and wanted ; his *instantaneous cure*, " immediately he received his sight " ; and his *grateful discipleship*, " he followed Jesus in the way, glorifying God."

For our present purpose let us consider the call and challenge of this man by Christ. The people said to him, " Be of good cheer ; rise, He calleth thee." And when he came, Jesus did what he wanted Him to do for him. May it be that in this call and challenge of long ago, we shall hear the voice of the Lord calling and challenging us.

Let us consider first of all, THE CALL OF CHRIST. There is nothing more certain, momentous, or wonderful than that Christ calls people to Himself. Many voices, and contradictory, are heard to-day, and it is little wonder if we are perplexed ; yet, clear above them all is the voice of Christ, calling us to spiritual life, to holy fellowship, and to joyful service ; and we may be quite sure that if we fail to possess that life, to enjoy that fellowship, and to render that service, it is not because Christ has not called us, but because we have not heard Him, or, having heard, have not obeyed.

The inviting voice of Christ is never silent. He calls us in the morning of life, when wondrous powers are stirring within us, when love, and hope, and ambition fill our hearts. At such a time He calls us to the realization of a life better than our brightest dreams.

And He calls us in the noontide of life, when, with developing powers and growing responsibilities, we bend to our tasks beneath the burning sun ; when, also, we feel most keenly the impact of temptation on our souls. At such a time, if we will but listen, we may hear Him calling us to courage and endurance.

And also He calls us in the evening of life, when the shadows are gathering, and our powers are beginning to fail, when interests are declining, and when we have to make room for others. Christ does not leave us then but calls us to a new and rich experience of Himself as able " to save to the uttermost."

As He calls us at all times, so also He calls us in many ways. His voice may reach us by force of circumstances, as in the case of Moses, who little thought when he killed the Egyptian that God was thereby calling him to a new discipline, and to preparation for a great mission.

And Christ may call us by sudden illumination, as in the case of Saul of Tarsus. In one brief moment all the past was seen in a new light, and all the future took on a new significance. What has not happened in a millennium may happen in a moment, and what through half a lifetime may have been dark may suddenly be flooded with light.

God's call to us may come also by growing conviction, as it did to Timothy who, from his youth, was taught to listen to the divine voice. In these and other ways God calls us, men and women, young and old ; and He does so because He desires to have us, delights to save us, and designs to use us.

Nothing is more certain than that He has a place and a use for each of us. It may be as minister, doctor, lawyer, artist, writer, teacher, tradesman, or something else ; but what will give any and all of these their chiefest significance, and secure success in the pursuit of them, is that, in God's plan, they are not merely employments, but vocations.

And now, in the second place, let us consider THE CHALLENGE OF CHRIST to each of us : " What wilt thou that I should do unto thee ? " This question is much more profound and penetrating than at first it may seem to be, and I will endeavour to disclose its significance.

First of all, *Christ designs to awaken in each of us a definite sense of need.* " What wilt thou that I should do unto thee ? " If we have no need, there is nothing that Christ *can* do for us. But, of course, the need of all of us is great, and yet we may not be conscious of it. There were some to whom Christ said : " He that is whole has no need of a physician but he that is sick." Christ did not mean that there were people who were spiritually " whole," but that there were some who thought they were. Again, when He said : " I came not to call the righteous, but sinners to repentance," He did not imply that there were any who were

42

" righteous," but that some thought they were. I need not, however, stress this point, for our presence here, from all over the country and the world, is a loud expression of our consciousness of need.

In the next place, then, *Christ declares that the greatest human need is a personal matter.* " What wilt *thou* that I should do unto *thee* ? " Christ comes to people of every nation, and class and age. Race and colour, distinctions of position and accomplishment, youth and old age, in no wise effect the basic needs of men, but everywhere and always the challenge is a *personal* one. Christ comes to us now not as a multitude, but as individuals. Though we are all together, in Christ's view we are all separate, we stand apart, a unit of human need. Whatever fellowship we have in our common consciousness of need, it will be well for us to remember that in the last analysis we are alone. Christ's appeals always were, and always are made to individuals. Isolate yourself for the purpose of blessing.

The next thing we should notice in this challenge is that *Christ makes it plain that no one can meet his own need.* The blind man is not asked or told to do anything. He is not told that he is blind, for he knows that, but what Jesus would bring home to his consciousness is that unless something is done for him by Another, he will be forever blind. There are many things that we can do for ourselves, and these Christ never offers to do for us, but in the realm of the soul we are impotent to help ourselves, to meet the deep-seated need which sin has created.

We shall never fall back upon Omnipotence until we realize our own impotence. The tragedy of all religions, except Christianity, is that men are trying to do for themselves what only God can do for them. We have made progress when we have learned where our ability and responsibility end. Not even Christian people can meet the need of others. A man in great distress about his lunatic boy said : " I brought him to Thy disciples, and they could not cure him." It is not Keswick that can meet the need of each of us here, but Christ. Let us apprehend this truth at the beginning of the week, and it will prevent disappointment later on.

Once more, in this statement we see that *Christ claims the power to meet our need.* " What wilt thou that *I* should do unto thee." Right at the heart of the Christian Gospel is the claim of Christ to do for man all that he needs to have done. It is a tremendous claim, and perhaps familiarity with it has blunted our sense of its greatness. " Come unto Me, all ye that labour and are heavy laden, and I will give you rest. Learn of Me, for I am meek and lowly in heart, and ye shall find rest unto your souls. Take my yoke upon you ; it is easy and it is light." Such words as these will fail to impress and capture us until we realize who it is that utters them, for the value of Christ's claim is rooted in His Person. All true experience has a doctrinal basis, and so what Christ does arises from what He is.

Let anyone deny or doubt the perfect humanity and true Deity of Jesus Christ, and he will not see the point or feel the power of such a question as this : " What wilt thou that I should do unto thee ? " But let anyone believe that Christ is what He claimed to be, and such a question begets hope in the soul, and opens up a vista of unlimited possibility. It is the Christ of the New Testament who is asking each of us what He can do for us.

But this challenge has more to tell us ; it shows us that *Christ makes a definite appeal to the* will *of the needy one.* " What *wilt* thou ? " But if Christ has all power, cannot He bless me whether I will or not ? No, for Omnipotence has set limits to His own power. " How often would I have gathered thy children together . . . and ye would not." " He did not many mighty works there because of their unbelief." " Ye search the Scriptures because ye think that in them ye have eternal life, and these are they which bear witness of Me, and ye will not come to Me, that ye may have life." God has made us moral and rational beings, and He will not do for us what our will rebels against. Man can frustrate the purpose of God for his salvation, or his sanctification. If Bartimæus had not willed to see, he never would have seen ; and if this week you do not will to be blessed, most certainly you will not be blessed.

Christ is saying to each one of us, " What wilt thou ? " He will not leave us to ourselves, but gets astride our path and challenges us. Professor Gaston Frommel, the Swiss theologian, has described his own religious experience in this way : " I was following out my life, pursuing my own desires, when Christ advanced to meet me, placed Himself before me, and barred my way. He stopped me. He made a silence in my heart. And then He held with me a solemn interview in which He spoke as He alone can speak."

And so, finally, let it be said, *Christ would have us know that for our need this is an hour of crisis.* When Bartimæus asked what was happening, the people said that " Jesus of Nazareth passeth by." Let us not think that we need to wait till the end of the Convention to receive what we need ; indeed, that may prove to be too late, for " Jesus of Nazareth is *now* passing by." Like Bartimæus, cast away every hindrance, and come with your need to Christ now. Tell Him what you believe to be your most urgent need, and let Him come into your life to control and direct it.

It has been pointed out that, in Holman Hunt's great picture, " The Light of the World," the feet are not turned toward the door, but toward the roadway. If Christ does not get admission, if there is no response from behind the sealed portal at which He is knocking, He will pass on. But if the door is thrown open now, the divine supply will come into our human need, and the soul will take a leap forward into peace and power. This may well be for many an hour of crisis. On this Sabbath evening if the Lord Jesus comes into us, we shall enter into rest.

> Come in, Oh, come ! the door stands open now ;
> I knew Thy voice ; Lord Jesus, it was Thou ;
> The sun has set long since ; the storms begin ;
> 'Tis time for Thee, my Saviour, Oh, come in !

44

Alas, ill-order'd shews the dreary room ;
The household-stuff lies heap'd amidst the gloom,
The table empty stands, the couch undress'd ;
Ah, what a welcome for th' Eternal Guest !

Yet welcome, and to-night ; this doleful scene
Is e'en itself my cause to hail Thee in ;
This dark confusion e'en at once demands
Thine own bright presence, Lord, and ord'ring hands.

I seek no more to alter things, or mend,
Before the coming of so great a Friend ;
All were at best unseemly ; and 'twere ill
Beyond all else to keep Thee waiting still.

Come, not to find, but make this troubled heart
A dwelling worthy of Thee as Thou art ;
To chase the gloom, the terror, and the sin :
Come, all Thyself, yea come, Lord Jesus in.

Joined to Christ in mystic union,
  We Thy members, Thou our Head,
Sealed by deep and true communion,
  Risen with Thee, who once were dead—
Saviour, we would humbly claim
All the power of This Thy name.

Instant sympathy to brighten
  All their weakness and their woe,
Guiding grace their way to lighten,
  Shall Thy loving members know :
All their sorrows Thou dost bear,
All Thy gladness they shall share.

Make Thy members every hour
  For Thy blessed service meet :
Earnest tongues, and arms of power,
  Skilful hands, and hastening feet,
Ever ready to fulfil
All Thy word and all Thy will.

Everlasting life Thou givest
  Everlasting love to see :
They shall live because Thou livest,
  And their life is hid with Thee.
Safe Thy members shall be found,
When their glorious Head is crowned !

—FRANCES RIDLEY HAVERGAL.

MONDAY,
July 15th, 1946.

10 a.m. **_Bible Reading._**

FOUR CHAPTERS OF CHRISTIAN EXPERIENCE.

(*i*) A CHAPTER OF FOUNDATION—ISAIAH 53.

THE REV. GUY H. KING.

11.45 a.m. **_Forenoon Meeting._**

PRACTICAL HOLINESS.

THE REV. J. DUNLOP.

SAINTS IN THE MAKING.

PREBENDARY COLIN C. KERR.

3 p.m. **_Afternoon Meeting._**

THE " GEOGRAPHY " OF THE HEAVENLIES.

DR. DONALD G. BARNHOUSE.

7.45 p.m. **_Evening Meeting._**

SUPER-ABUNDANT BLESSING.

THE REV. GORDON M. GUINNESS.

PURPOSING AND ACCOMPLISHING.

DR. W. GRAHAM SCROGGIE.

Firm Foundations.

L ITTLE of the attractiveness of Keswick's encompassing mountains could be seen on Monday morning, for they were enshrouded in low-hanging clouds, and rain was falling steadily. Quite good numbers attended both prayer meetings, however ; though in the small tent the noise of rain on the canvas was somewhat distracting.

It was with keenest anticipation that a congregation which practically filled the tent, gathered for the first Bible Reading. The Rev. Guy H. King is one of the best-loved of the present speakers at the Convention, but this was the first time that the important responsibility of the Bible Readings had been committed to him. Mr. King excels at making the deep truths of the Christian Faith clear and plain, and is especially effective as a speaker for young people. Now a very contrasting ministry was to be his. Those who had heard him talking so delightfully to the children on Sunday afternoon listened with yet greater wonder to his sparkling studies of " Four Chapters of Christian Experience." He proved himself a masterly expositor, and, of course, the addresses abounded in alliteration. He prefaced each study with the reading of the chapter with which it was to deal. The first of these was " A Chapter of Foundation "—Isaiah 53, which he described as a " Symphony in B-saved ! " Continuing this simile, he divided the chapter into three " movements " of the " symphony "—the perplexity, publicity and prosperity of the saving sacrifice. Mr. King was obliged, through pressure of time, to abbreviate what he had intended to say under the third heading, but it appears in full in this report.

The other outstanding ministry of the Convention this year was that of Dr. Donald G. Barnhouse, of Philadelphia, in the afternoons, when he gave five addresses on the Epistle to the Ephesians. Attendances were unusually large for afternoon meetings, and there was no sign of somnolence—which is not unknown in the tent on oppressive afternoons ! Dr. Barnhouse kept his hearers alert, however, and made these gatherings as memorable and rewarding as any.

The rain had stopped by the time of the evening meeting, but the sky remained overcast. There was no dullness in the meeting, though ; the singing was excellent, and the addresses were listened to with closest attention. The Rev. Gordon Guinness—who this year was taking part in the Convention for the first time—spoke on the same passage in Malachi as had Preb. Colin C. Kerr on Sunday afternoon (3 : 10). His message was quite different from that of the Prebendary, however, and caused us to remark how wondrous is the Book which is ever fresh, and from which there ever breaks forth new light.

Dr. W. Graham Scroggie gave the closing address of the day, on Gen. 12 : 5—" They went forth to go into the land of Canaan ; and into the land of Canaan they came." He spoke first of the divine revelation of which the passage speaks—the land which God promised to show them. Following upon the revelation was a momentous resolution ; leading to a joyful realization. All this, Dr. Scroggie showed, is a parable of spiritual experience ; and he pressed home the challenge to his hearers, personally, as to whether or not it was true of them that " into the land of Canaan they came."

Ah ! give me, Lord, the single eye,
Which aims at nought but Thee ;
I fain would live, and yet not I—
But Jesus live in me.

Like Noah's dove, no rest I find
But in Thy ark of peace ;
Thy cross, the balance of my mind ;
Thy wounds, my hiding-place.

In vain the tempter spreads the snare,
If Thou my keeper art ;
—Get thee behind me, God is near,
My Saviour takes my part !

On Him my spirit I recline,
Who put my nature on ;
His light shall in my darkness shine,
And guide me to His throne.

Augustus M. Toplady.

Four Chapters of Christian Experience.

(i) A Chapter of Foundation—Isaiah 53.

By the Rev. GUY H. KING.

THE chapter and verse divisions of our Bible are not inspired, of course. Indeed, the former task did not get done until A.D. 1207 or so, when Archbishon Stephen Langton accomplished it. He was the same man that, as you remember, drew up Magna Carta for King John's signature. So all Englishmen are in his debt ; while all Bible-men are thus double indebted to him. Nearly 350 years more rolled on before a certain printer, named Robert Stephens, broke up the Archbishop's chapters into verses, in the year 1551. Almost all scholars are by now of the opinion that the distinguished prelate's judgment in this regard was not always infallible, and it seems to be almost universally held that our chapter 53 of Isaiah should have begun at 52 : 13. We shall confine our study at this time to the chapter as it stands in our Bible ; but, for all that, we are not unaware of its link with those previous three verses.

Perhaps we may put it that these verses are a sort of overture or prelude to the main theme of our great Drama of Redemption. God has a wondrous saving plan for the world ; and, as the late Sir George Adam Smith said, " The purpose of God is identified with a Minister or Servant, whom He commissions to carry it out . . ." In Isaiah there are several " Servant " passages which are specifically concerned with Him and His work : 41 : 8-20 ; 42 : 1-7 ; 18ff. ; 43 : 5-10 ; 49 : 1-9 ; 50 : 4-10 ; and crown and climax of them all, 52 : 13—53 : 12.

" Behold, My servant . . ."—on that note our overture begins ; and it goes on to tell us that He " shall deal prudently," act wisely, or with knowledge. He knows what He is doing. Others may understand little or nothing of Him—astonished at the very idea of a suffering Messiah ; but He knows that beyond, even because of, the suffering shall come the exaltation, with all that is included and involved. " So shall He startle many nations "—not " sprinkle." The great Hebraist, A. B. Davidson, says : " It is simply treason against the Hebrew language to render ' sprinkle.' The interpreter who will so translate will do anything." Indeed will the nations be startled, when, contrary to all they have seen or heard before, they find Him who so suffered " extolled and very high " ; no wonder that even " kings " shall gaze open-mouthed at the sight ! Well, He knew all this, knew that His work would " prosper," as R.V. margin translates the " deal prudently " of our version. Hebrews 12 : 2 has the idea, " Who for the joy that was set before Him endured

51

the cross, despising the shame, and is set down at the right hand of the throne of God."

Here, then, is the introduction to our Chapter of Foundation. All our hope of eternal salvation, all our chance of personal daily victory, all our possibility of Christian experience, are founded, based, upon the truth and the fact adumbrated in this chapter. After the overture comes now the unfolding of the great theme, a divinely inspired symphony in B-saved; there are three movements—Perplexity, Publicity, and Prosperity.

I. THE PERPLEXITY OF THE SAVING SACRIFICE.

We note that—(i) *He is introduced.* What is the identity of this " Servant " who is to undertake the work of our redemption ? Dr. George Adam Smith has no doubt : " About five hundred and fifty years after this prophecy was written a Man came forward among the sons of men— among this very nation from whom the prophecy had arisen ; and in every essential of consciousness and of experience He was the counterpart, embodiment and fulfilment of this Suffering Servant and his Service." Or, listen to this, from a very different mind, the late Dr. Joseph Parker : " No man known to history, but one, can carry this chapter in all its verses and lines and particles. Here and there some other man may come in and partially appropriate a word, a hint, a suggestion ; but has any man ever seized the whole chapter and said, That is mine ? . . . Yet there is one Man in history who would fit the occasion . . . the happy and sacred realisation of the marvellous forecast." Yes ; but let us go to the New Testament account of the matter : Acts 8 : 32-35 will give us what we seek. There we find the Ethiopian Chancellor reading a part of Isaiah, our verses 7-8, probably in the Septuagint Version, a copy of which he had secured in Jerusalem, to read on his journey back to North Africa. He could not make head nor tail of the bit where he was until Philip joined him, " and began at the same Scripture, and preached unto him Jesus." When He was introduced as the " Man " concerned, things became plain. So often that is the key to the understanding of a difficult passage : put Jesus there, see Him there, and all is clear. I remember so well an old printed puzzle, in which were depicted a garden lawn and paths and tools, beds and bushes, flowers and fruit trees—all very delightful ; and, on the picture, these words, " Puzzle : Find the gardener." After a careful scrutiny you found first one line, then another, until the man's face was seen peering out at you from among the foliage. There he was : and whenever you looked at the scene again, you spotted him at once : you just could not get away from him. So it is with this chapter of ours : once, like Philip, you see Jesus in it, the whole passage becomes illuminated and irradiated by His presence there—once find Him there, you will never be able to miss Him.

" The Arm of the Lord " (v. 1) is the Name by which He is introduced ; the Executive of the Godhead. It is a favourite figure with Isaiah— " Be Thou their arm . . . our salvation " (33 : 2) ; " He shall

52

gather the lambs with His arm " (40 : 11) ; " O arm of tho Lerd " (51 : 9). He was the divine arm or agent in creation, for " all things were made by Him " (John 1 : 3) ; He was the divine arm or agent in recreation, for it was He who " obtained eternal redemption for us " (Heb. 9 : 12). What a witness and testimony were to be borne to the arm of salvation—yet, as the prophet looked on down the centuries he saw that such a multitude refused to believe the " report " ; a fact sadlv corroborated by the apostle who speaks, in 1 John 5 : 10, of those who believe not the " record " that God gave of His Son. To none such will the almighty, saving efficacy of the arm be " revealed." The world's maxim is that seeing is believing ; but God's order is that believing is seeing—" Said I not unto thee that, if thou wouldest believe, thou shouldest see . . . ? " (John 11 : 40). Only those who, believing the report, come to trust on that Arm, will ever know the strength, the solace, and the salvation of that Arm.

But what is the reason for this tragic unbelief ? There, surely, must be some explanation ? Indeed, there are probably many causes ; but one in particular rises out of the chapter before us.

(*ii*) *He is misunderstood.* " For "—so opens our verse 2 : we are to be offered an account of the source from which arises the strange refusal of the Arm of the Lord. The language is prophetic : hundreds of years afterwards it was literally and exactly fulfilled. If we take our stand at the period of time when our Lord Jesus Christ came, we find ourselves in an atmosphere of expectancy. Many, like Simeon, were " waiting for the consolation of Israel " ; many, like Anna, " looked for redemption in Jerusalem " (Luke 2 : 25, 38). All through the years they had been brought up to believe in the coming of Messiah. From their study of the Old Testament they knew that He would come in power, and in glory, and in victory. Nevertheless, there was something puzzling in the fact that there were other passages of a quite opposite character. Indeed, this led a few of the Rabbis to teach that there would be two Messiahs— one suffering and the other triumphing. This was not at all widely accepted. We know, of course, that the answer to the perplexity lay in the fact that there were to be, not two separate Messiahs, but two separate comings of the one Messiah. However, that first coming in humility did not at all fit in with the prevailing idea of the Jewish nation concerning their great Deliverer, so they conveniently dismissed it from their minds, and concentrated all the ardour of their expectancy upon the coming of a mighty monarch, conquering and to conquer.

And now, " when the fullness of the time was come," He arrived upon the scene (Gal. 4 : 4) : a certain unknown Jesus of Nazareth announcing Himself as the Christ, proclaiming Himself as the long-foretold Messiah. But—who was this ? Surely this was not—could not be—the promised One. The rulers and teachers of the people were thrown into uttermost perplexity. Here was a Being clean contrary to all they had anticipated ; but it was just as our chapter had predicted of Him.

(*a*) " *He shall grow up before Him as a tender plant.*" Did they expect that their Messiah should descend full grown from Heaven, that this was

53

part of their stumbling-block ? Surely they remembered their Genesis 3 : 15, that He was to be the " seed " of a " woman," " made of a woman," as our Galatians verse above has it. In very truth, if He is to be our representative, He must begin where we begin ; and so, when " a Son is given," " a child is born " (Isa. 9 : 6), there is nothing incongrous, but everything proper, in Messiah being born a babe, and growing up, like a tender plant, from frailty to maturity—the Christ in a cradle. Yes ; but what a cradle !

(b) " *As a root out of a dry ground.*" In what an uncongenial soil it was that the tender " plant of renown " (Ezek. 34 : 29) grew : born, not in a palace, but in the stable of an inn ; brought up, not in an influential family, but in a lowly household ; bred, not in a helpful atmosphere, but in a world riddled with vice ; beginning, not in some honourable town, but in a city so despised that it had become proverbial, " can there any good thing come out of Nazareth ? " (John 1 : 46); breaking forth, not at a time of religious healthfulness, but when spiritual things were at a low ebb, when under the dead hand of the scribes, the repressive conservatism of the Pharisees, the unsettling liberalism of the Sadducees, the political materialism of the Herodians and Zealots, religion became, for the majority of the people (always excepting the few earnest souls who remained spiritually alert and alive, to whom we referred earlier), a thing dead, and dull, and dry, and dreary. Says Dr. W. P. Paterson, in One Volume Hasting's Dictionary of the Bible, " The condition of the Jews at the birth of Christ may be summarily described as marked by political impotence and religious decadence." Speaking humanly, this " root of Jesse," as Isaiah 11 : 10 describes Him, owes nothing to His native soil—it was " dry ground " indeed : bone dry. And so—

(c) " *He hath no form nor comeliness* . . . *no beauty that we should desire Him.*" It is sometimes said that we do not really know what our Lord looked like ; but I am inclined to think that the usual pictures of Him are a true likeness of His general physical appearance. The late Dr. J. C. Carlile, in the introductory chapter of his " Portraits of Jesus " says : " Miniature paintings and portraits were then at their zenith ; bronze and marble statuary was very common. . . In the catacombs there are little pictures of Christ that have been carved upon the walls . . . all of them possessing some things in common." Probably, then, the traditional presentment of Him—varied in detail, but persistent in main features—is an authentic portrayal. Was there actual beauty in His face ? I do not know. The Gospels give us scarcely any hint of this kind. There is one passage that may be significant—" Thou art not fifty years old " (John 8 : 57). How came they to mention such an age when actually He was only a little over thirty ? Did He look so much older than his real age ? His had been a strenuous and suffering life : did He show it in His face ? Certainly, Pilate found His physical demeanour disconcertingly at variance with His regal claim, when he asked, " Art thou a king then ? " All the emphasis, I believe, is on that " thou "— " thou " ? ! But, even if His face and figure bore all the marks of virile strength and perfect symmetry and unruffled calm and exquisite beauty, still it would have no attraction for His enemies, so bitter was their animosity, so venomous their hostility.

These are the things that unravel the perplexity of why—

(*iii*) *He is rejected.* He anticipated their rejection when He made the men of His parable say, " We will not have this man to reign over us " (Luke 19 : 14) ; and sure enough, when Pilate offered Him to their choice, they said, " Not this man, but (even such a creature, by preference, as) Barabbas " (John 18 : 40).

(*a*) " *He is despised and rejected of men* "—the haunting melody of Handel has helped to engrave the poignant words on our hearts.   The " men "—upon whom He expended all the wealth of His matchless love, for whom He suffered all the agony of His measureless sacrifice, to whom He offered all the blessings of His great salvation, turned their backs on Him, indeed, turned all the violence of their hatred on Him.   Is it any wonder that we go on to read,

(*b*) " *A man of sorrows, and acquainted with grief* "—not, I think, a sorrowful Man.   He Himself speaks of " My joy," in John 15 : 11, even at such a time ; and Hebrews 1 : 9 says that " God hath anointed Thee with the oil of gladness above Thy fellows."   Yet, what sorrows came upon Him, what grief He was acquainted with !   And deepest sadness, perhaps, of all—

(*c*) " *We hid our faces from Him* "—we " cut Him dead."   We who should have " esteemed " Him " the chiefest among ten thousand," and " altogether lovely " (Song of Solomon 5 : 10, 16) account Him among men and things " despised."   I say " we," following upon the prophet's vocabulary ;   but let me press the pronoun for one moment—" we " ; you and I.   Is there anyone amongst us who has accorded Him little recognition, afforded Him little place ?   Even if we are not of the company of the historic inn-keeper, who could find " no room " for Him (Luke 2 : 7) are we guilty of giving Him but little room in our lives, or, out of deepest gratitude, have we offered Him chief room ?

> The Head that once was crowned with thorns
> Is crowned with glory now ;
>   *   *   *
> The highest place that heaven affords
> Is His, is His by right.

In Heaven—yes, indeed ; then, surely, in our hearts and lives.   But, to return to our passage, He was to be rejected—and hundreds of years afterwards He was rejected, just as had been foretold.

What tragic perplexity occasioned it—the perplexity of a suffering Saviour.   They expected one so gloriously different from that ; and yet both here in this chapter, and in scores of other Old Testament places it was written plain for all to see.   They were obsessed with the idea that He would be garbed with royalty, not with humility.   One day, in the reign of our late beloved King George V, a certain hospital in London was informed that His Majesty proposed making an informal visit.   It may well be imagined what excitement was caused ; and not least in the children's ward. How eagerly the little patients watched the entrance of their ward, to see the king come in. One small fellow could scarcely contain himself in his pleasurable expectation. Throughout the afternoon of the promised visit, many people passed in and out of the place. About four o'clock quite a party of people came—matron brought them in ; and one of the gentlemen was ever so kind ; he came and patted the small boy's head and spoke so nicely to him. Then the group disappeared ; and presently others arrived and departed, but the king hadn't come. After a bit the time came for the little patients to settle down for the night ; and our little friend was so bitterly disappointed. "Sister," he said, " the king hasn't come." " But, sonny," she answered, " don't you remember a kind gentleman who came and patted your head, and spoke so nicely to you, and you loved him so ? " " Yes," " Well, that was he." The small eyes opened wide in wonderment, the small brow puckered in bewilderment: " But, Sister, he hadn't his crown on ! " That's just about how it was with those Jews. The coming of the Messiah, their King, was promised and expected. He came ; but He went unrecognised ; they still say He did not come. You see, He had not His crown on. Or, wait a moment—

> Hath He diadem as monarch,
> That His brow adorns ?
> Yea, a crown, in very surety,
> But—of thorns.

That was the (needless) cause of all the perplexity.

Now we turn to listen to the second movement of our salvation symphony.

II. THE PUBLICITY OF THE SAVING SACRIFICE.

I remember reading the story of a man who, at considerable risk, dived into the sea to rescue someone who was drowning, but who, after his deed of fine courage, slipped away without giving his name, or leaving behind any clue to his identity. I expect you will think that was rather splendid ; but it could not be like that with this One who, in the words of I Timothy 1 : 15, " came into the world to save sinners," drowners in the sea of sin. In this case, it is not just the act that is to be emphasized, but the person who performed the act—it is the nature of the Person that gives adequacy and efficacy to the deed. You will have noticed how, in the Epistle to the Hebrews, before the inspired writer (whoever he is) deals with the work of our great High Priest, he discusses first His worth— it is this latter which gives acceptance of the former. So we must be quite sure of the identity of our Redeemer ; and our passage seems to meet that need of the situation when it opens its fourth verse by saying, " Surely." There is no doubt about who He is, and what happened to Him, although, we reiterate, the words here were uttered all those hundreds of years previous to the event, yet they " surely " shall come to pass, as, indeed, they " surely " did—all was plainly and literally fulfilled, for all to see.

Do you recall how, when Paul was pleading his cause before Festus, and was speaking of the death and resurrection of the Lord Jesus, he said, " this thing was not done in a corner " (Acts 26 : 26)—He died under the gaze of a multitude ; there was a fore-ordained publicity about the whole affair. This same apostle has a remarkable word to the like effect, when in Galatians 3 : 1 he writes, " before whose eyes Jesus Christ hath been evidently set forth, crucified among you." That " evidently set forth," one word in the Greek, means " placarded "—and this Isaiah chapter is one of the early placards. Whether the actual deed itself, or whether the prophetic description, or whether the Gospel declaration— in every respect, and in every sense, the whole matter was accomplished in public and unfolded in public. " Surely," we say, as we proceed to the remarkable predictions of the familiar verses.

Here is set out for us something of (i) *His Life.* Already, in the previous verses, much has been said concerning the nature of His experiences in the days of His flesh, and still the sad tale goes on. (a) *" He hath borne our griefs, and carried our sorrows."* The late Professor David Smith said that these words of A. V. are scarcely a true rendering of the original, the word for " griefs " being rather physical then mental, grief ; and he stated that Matthew, the Jewish evangelist, familiar as he was with the Hebrew text, is more accurate, quoting this passage in 8 : 17, " Himself took our infirmities and bare our sicknesses." Well, now, when and where did Christ bear our sicknesses ? I Peter 2 : 24 leaves us in no doubt that He bore our *sins* " on the tree " at Calvary ; but Matthew says that, for instance, He bore our sicknesses at Capernaum. It was in His death that He bore our sins, but in His life that He bore our sicknesses. Further, it seems likely that Isaiah is referring to spiritual sickness, that is, to sin— and so he uses for " bear " the substitutionary word ; and, indeed, whenever he speaks of " health " or " healing," the prophet has spiritual, and not physical, health in mind—Isaiah 19 : 22 ; 30 : 26 ; 53 : 5 ; 57 : 17, 19. Matthew uses the Isaiah passage as an *illustration* of Christ's bearing of our physical sickness—as is evident, I think, by the fact that he deliberately alters the word used for " bear." The evangelist, unlike the prophet, used a word never linked with atonement, but employed to express sympathetic bearing, as when it occurs in Galatians 6 : 2, " Bear ye one another's burdens," and in Romans 15 : 1, " Ye that are strong ought to bear the infirmities of the weak." Who authorised Matthew to make such a change in the vitally important word unless he was guided by the Holy Spirit his inspirer ? For my own part I am, therefore, persuaded that our verse 4 is referring to the compassionate way in which the Master did atone for all our *spiritual* sickness, and that Matthew is led to apply the thought to the compassionate way in which He entered into all our *physical* sickness. With what tender sympathy He dealt with both— and at what an enormous expenditure to Himself. In his life of Henry Drummond, George Adam Smith tells of how one came upon the Professor, after one of his University mission meetings, leaning with his head bowed on the mantlepiece, looking into the fire, with a worn and haggard face. When asked if he were very tired, he said, " No, not very ; but oh, I am sick of the sins of these men. How can God bear it ? "

57

But the words of this verse have a still wider application to His wondrous fellow-feeling with all our troubles and anxieties. Whatever that may mean His was no sheltered life. In His humble circumstances He knew only too well the buffetings of the workaday world. Even out of His own experiences " Jesus knows all about our struggles," as the hymn says ; and as the-inspired Hebrews 4 : 15 records, " We have not an high priest which cannot be touched with the feeling of our infirmities." (b) " *He was taken from prison and from judgment,*" says verse 8—from " oppression," says R.V., and verse 7 has the same word ; from " judgment," such as it was : a cruel travesty and mockery of true justice. How little we can conceive the weight of impact upon His wholly innocent soul, His utterly sensitive spirit, of the treatment that He received during the brief years of His ministry, and especially in the last days of his life. (c) " *Who shall declare His generation ?*—His seed. To have many children was the highest ambition of Hebrew parents, and their most coveted honour—" Happy is the man that hath his quiver full of them," says Psalm 127 : 5. But Christ was to have none of them, and was to suffer thus discredit in the eyes of men. Yet He was to have " seed " of another sort, as our chapter shall presently disclose. (d) " *He was cut off out of the land of the living* "—that was to be the end of His human life on earth. There was to be no thought of His slipping quietly and peacefully off, like the majority of folk. " Cut off " suggests a violent finish, a premature end ; and so indeed it proved to be. Thus, by the medium of little hints, and almost disjointed phrases, we are shown something of what that life, in all the sharp detail of its public performance, was destined to be.

And then, with inexorable footsteps, with inevitable logic, it moves on tragically to (ii) *His Death.* Let it be said straight away that He was (a) *A Victim*—" we did esteem Him stricken, smitten of God." If, for the first time, we had heard of His death, and knew nothing whatever of the circumstances, we might have asked, "Who killed Him ? " And what different answers we might, quite reasonably, get—each true, in its way. *The soldiers killed Him*—it was they who actually nailed Him to the Cross ; it was a duty to which they had become largely accustomed, for cruci-fixions were all too frequent in those days ; but never had they heard one pray, as He did, " Father, forgive them, for they know not what they do " (Luke 23 : 34), and, at the end, they were forced, having heard His enemies repeat, " *If Thou be* the Son of God," to exclaim, along with their officer, " Truly this *was* the Son of God." Yes ; but *Pilate killed Him*— he didn't want to do it, he knew he oughtn't to do it, he tried all kinds of expedients for escaping from doing it, but at last somebody mentioned " Cæsar," and that frightened him into an unwilling acquiescence, and having ostentatiously and dramatically washed his hands of the matter, " he delivered Him to be crucified " (Matt. 27 : 24-26). Ah, but *the Jews killed Him*—it was they who harried the Roman Governor to this foul deed of injustice ; they perpetrated that strange contradiction in terms when they " killed the Prince of Life," they made their extra-ordinary choice in that they " denied the Holy One and the Just, and

58

desired a murderer "—almost unbelievable preference ; and so it remains to stain their escutcheon for ever, " Whom ye slew and hanged on a tree " (Acts 3 : 14, 15 ; 5 : 30). Yet, there was a sinister personality behind these Jews, *the Devil killed Him*—it had been predicted so, right away back in the very first day of sin, "thou shalt bruise His heel" (Gen. 3 : 15), and now, in the course of time, it has been brought to pass, though in very truth Satan overreached himself, for his own head was mortally bruised on that great day of salvation.

Every one of these was, in varying measure and degree, responsible for the death of Christ ; but our chapter takes us deeper yet : *God killed Him.* " He was smitten of God " ; " He hath put Him to grief," says verse 10 ; " it pleased the Lord to bruise Him " : that is, it was the fulfilment of God's wish and purpose. So greatly did God love us that He permitted the stroke of His wrath to fall upon His only begotten Son— to such a plan God " gave " Him up (John 3 : 16). A " plan," yes, for it was no sudden outburst of sentiment, no whim of the moment, for the shedding of the Lamb's precious Blood " verily was fore-ordained before the foundation of the world " (I Pet. 1 : 20). That word "foundation" means, roughly, the architect's plan, so that the implication is that, just as the architect thinks out his prospective house and then puts all his thoughts down in the plan, to meet the needs of those who shall afterwards live there, so the Great Architect of the universe thought, and then planned, the meeting of all man's requirements : among them, chiefest of them would be the need of redemption—may we reverently say, what gracious ingenuity was demanded to satisfy this necessity ; how humanly hopeless it would be to devise a scheme that would enable God, in the face of all the implications of the sin problem, not only to save sinners, but, at the same time, to safeguard His own holy character—in other words, that He might be both " just and the Justifier " (Rom. 3 : 26). Thank God, in the council chamber of the triune God such a plan of salvation was produced as met all the necessities of the case—the plan which is summed up in Paul's phrase, " Christ crucified," and which he goes on to indicate as displaying, not only " the power of God," but also " the wisdom of God " (1 Cor. 1 : 24). We remember Newman's words :—

> Oh, loving *wisdom* of our God !
> When all was sin and shame,
> A second Adam to the fight
> And to the rescue came !

Not that we must ever forget that, while it is true that God killed Him, it is nevertheless equally true that the whole triune God was in this act of redemption. The justice of the transaction will never be appreciated unless we bear in mind that " God was in Christ, reconciling the world unto Himself " (2 Cor. 5 : 19), and that the Church of God was " purchased with His own blood " (Acts 20 : 28). As Professor W. M. Clow put it, " If there was a cross in the place which is called Calvary, there was a cross also in Heaven. If a sword pierced the heart of Christ, a sword pierced the heart of God."

To return to our chapter, " the Lord hath laid on Him the iniquity of us all " (v. 6). That word " laid " is a very interesting one : they tell me that the Hebrew means " made to meet." The Cross stands central in the long course of human redemption—all before it looks forward to it, in blessed prospect ; all after it looks back to it, in blessed retrospect ; all meet there. From that first sin in Eden, all sin, and every sin, before Golgotha, was by the great plan brought to that place to be ultimately dealt with—being meanwhile " covered " (which is what " Atonement " means) by the divinely ordained sacrifices : " for it is not possible that the blood of bulls and of goats should *take away* sins " (Heb. 10 : 4) ; it could only cover them, until the Cross, which alone could take them away. Is that not the meaning of Romans 3 : 25, with its account of the manner in which the " sins that are past " were dealt with ; and of that other word, in Hebrews 9: 15, which details the way of redemption for " transgressions that were under the first testament " ? Believers under the old dispensation will be saved, just as we are, " through the blood of His Cross "—because all their sin was there " laid on Him." Moreover, all after-Calvary sin, right up to the end, is, in the eternal plan, as it were, brought back to be borne and dealt with in the same way. All the penalty, and power, and problem of " the iniquity of us all " were made to meet on Him.

" All " did we say ? Yes. Do you notice how the word opens and closes that sixth verse—a very prison of a verse. Look at all those prison doors. (1) *There is the door of entrance*—" all " of us go into that house of bondage ; and how can we ever get out ? Thank God (2) *There is the door of exit*—" all " may escape through the saving fact embraced, as we have seen, in that second " all." Of course, (3) *There is the door of each cell*—" we have turned every one to his own way." All different cells, but the same dread and dreary prison : all have got in, all may get out. We cannot break out, cannot force the doors ; but the God who, in Acts 12, opened Peter's prison doors, can open these and set us gloriously free from all sin. As it is true that " He only could unlock the gate of Heaven, and let us in," so is it also true that " He only could unlock the gate of sin, and let us out." My friend, let me ask you, as if you and I were the only ones here, Have you come out of prison yet ? And, if so, are you using your privilege of giving the emancipating message to others who are still bound ? For, as Isaiah 49 : 9 has it, " Thou mayest say to the prisoners, Go forth "—if you yourself are free, you are entitled to say it, expected to say it, enabled to say it.

Well, now, let us get this clear, that the saving Person of this chapter was not merely a victim, He was (b) *A Vicarious Victim*—" He was wounded for our transgressions, He was bruised for our iniquities " (v. 5). He had no sins of His own to be " bruised " for. If He had, His sacrifice would have been unacceptable, unavailing, for us. I Peter 1 : 19 reminds us that He had to be " a Lamb without blemish and without spot." You recall how carefully the Passover Lamb was scrutinised in Exodus 12 : 5, 6, not only because God requires the best, but also because *this* lamb was a type of *the* Lamb. When the time came for Him to fulfil the type, and to be " sacrificed for us " (I Cor. 5 : 7), He was, after most intensive examination, given His certificate of spotlessness—" Behold, I bring Him forth to you, that ye may know that I find no fault in Him " (John 19 : 4)—a testimony subsequently endorsed in most unlikely quarters : (1) The thief, " This Man hath done nothing amiss," and (2) The soldiers, " Certainly this was a righteous Man " (Luke 23 : 41, 47). No, He had no sins of His own, but He " bare our sins in His own body on the tree " (I Pet. 2 : 24). How beautifully does this fifth verse of our chapter correlate the " He " and the " we "—" *He* was wounded . . . *we* are healed."

Then, it is of such great importance to bear in mind that He was (*c*) *A Voluntary Victim*—" a Lamb . . . dumb " (v. 7) was He ; unresisting, unprotesting. His sacrifice would have been unjust and immoral, if it had been otherwise. His silence was one of the most remarkable—and, to His enemies, most awkward—features of His long-drawn-out trial : over and over again it is noted that He answered never a word. (1) *He said nothing to the Sanhedrin*—until the High Priest challenged Him with the most solemn of all the oaths, " I adjure thee by the Living God " (Matt. 26 : 63). (2) *He said nothing to Pilate*—until continued silence would have been construed into a denial and disavowal of His Kingship (Matt. 27 : 11). (3) *He said nothing to Herod* at all : for that personage was only concerned to slake his curiosity ; he had no right to ask any questions, and so he got no answers (Luke 23 : 9). He accepted the " cup " (Matt. 26 : 39, 42). Hear His earlier statement, as John 10 : 17, 18 records it, " I lay down My life . . . no man taketh it from Me, but I lay it down of Myself." At any moment He could have come down from the Cross ; but " how then shall the Scriptures (this chapter among them) be fulfilled ? " Even at the excruciating moment when they impaled the sacred Body, he did not resist, but " made intercession for the transgressors " (Luke 23 : 34). How amazing that those hundreds of years before the event, such exact details of it should be predicted as in this Isaiah 53 and in Psalm 22.

And so we are led on, in this precious Scripture, to think upon (*iii*) *His Burial*. All through His earthly sojourning " He was numbered with the transgressors " (v. 12). At the start, He came to dwell among sinful men ; through His ministry, He was known to be " the Friend of publicans and sinners " (Luke 7 : 34) ; toward the end, He was " in the midst " of two malefactors (John 19 : 18) ; and now, at the finish, " He made His grave with the wicked " (v. 9)—He shared the common lot of humanity, He was buried. Yet we stay to mark one very interesting point : His interment was " with the rich." How came it that a poor man received such treatment ; how came it that a Man then regarded as " evil " got such consideration ? Normally, the bodies of crucified victims were thrown ignominiously upon the fire of Gehenna outside the city, unless, for a price, some friend could secure them for decent burial. Joseph of Arimathea paid that price, and that reverence (John 19 : 38), thus atoning somewhat for his former silence of fear. So in that rich man's tomb they laid Him, little realizing, of course, that in their act of love they were fulfilling something that our prophet had been given to foretell several hundred years before. Extraordinary! We could have understood if it had been reported hundreds of years after; but it is very remarkable how truly the Bible writes history before it happened. So He was buried. We linger awhile at the place where He died: the American J. C. Whittier, shall help us—

Well may the cavern-depths of Earth
Be shaken, and her mountains nod;
Well may the sheeted dead come forth
To see the suffering Son of God!
Well may the temple-shrine grow dim,
And shadows veil the Cherubim,
When He, the chosen one of Heaven,
A sacrifice for guilt is given!

And shall the sinful heart, alone,
Behold unmoved the fearful hour,
When nature trembled on her throne,
And death resigned his iron power?
Oh, shall the heart—whose sinfulness
Gave keenness to His sore distress,
And added to His tears of blood—
Refuse its trembling gratitude!

Thus did the great transaction secure the widest publicity. It was plainly forewritten in all these many prophecies; it was tragically displayed to the festival crowds that thronged Jerusalem, at the open execution ground just " outside the city wall "; it was grimly emphasized by the three-hour darkness, and the rending earthquake; it was unforgettably recorded by those inspired to tell the wondrous story; it is now for us to give it ever-continuing and world-wide publicity, by passing on the news in every way we can. We sing with William Cowper:—

E'er since, by faith, I saw the stream
Thy flowing wounds supply,
Redeeming love hath been my theme,
And shall be till I die.

Dead and buried! Is that the end? Does the story finish there? Was it all a tragedy, a mistake, a failure? No, no; a thousand times No. Our chapter would have been strangely at variance with New Testament practice if it stopped short at His death and burial; for the Spirit-taught writers of Gospels, Acts and Epistles scarcely ever mention the Crucifixion without referring, in the near context, to the Resurrection. So shall we now give ear to the third movement of our salvation symphony:

III. THE PROSPERITY OF THE SAVING SACRIFICE.

In verse 10 is written, " *when* Thou shalt make His soul an offering for sin," and in verse 12 we read, " *because* He hath poured out His soul unto death "—in between those two statements there is given a whole gamut of happy results of His redeeming work. " When " it happened,

62

and " because " it happened, there was released a mighty river of blessing and joy for all concerned. Never before, and never since, did any person, or any work, achieve such immense prosperity.

Look, then, at the glad recital, item by item. (*i*) " *He shall see His seed.*" In John 12 : 24, our Lord said, with the double under-lining of His " Verily, verily," " Except a corn of wheat fall into the ground and die, it abideth alone ; but if it die, it bringeth forth much fruit." That applies to any believer's self-dying, as the following verse shows ; but it refers to His own self-giving, as the former verse shows. What a magnificent harvest of souls would come from the sowing into death of His own soul. Verse 8 of our chapter said, " Who shall declare His generation ? " His seed—for, as we suggested, He had none ; but of spiritual seed He has abundance. At any one point of time, at any one place on earth, always, comparatively, the " few " (Matt. 7 : 14), always a " little flock " (Luke 12 : 32), but, in the assembled aggregate of Heaven, " a great multitude, which no man could number " (Rev. 7 : 9). Of all these, as of the Galatian Christians among them, the apostle could write, " Ye are all the children of God, by faith in Christ Jesus " (Gal. 3 : 26) ; of these is Jesus the appointed Agent " in bringing many sons unto glory " (Heb. 2 : 10) ; and it is surely this great multitude of heavenly sons and daughters that entitles Him to the mysterious name in Isaiah 9 : 6, of " Everlasting Father." Down here He saw no seed ; up there " He shall see His seed." Do we all belong to it : you, my friend, do you ? That question is settled down here ; and John 1 : 12 tells us how to settle it.

Shall we look now at a second sequel of His crucifixion : (*ii*) " *He shall prolong His days.*" In verse 8 it was said, " He was cut off out of the land of the living " : how, then, shall He prolong His days ? The answer, of course, is, by His resurrection. When a wrongdoer has completed his sentence, the prison can no longer hold him ; he must be given his discharge. Likewise our Lord, having fully satisfied the Law's demands, having " finished " the sentence (John 19 : 30), was raised up from death " because it was not possible that He should be holden of it " (Acts 2 : 24). It was not that He broke out from prison by His own power : He could have done, of course, but He did not. If He had done so, we should never have known that God accepted His work of redemption as fully paying the price. So He was authoritatively released. God sent down His warders to open the prison doors of death (Matt. 28 : 2), and the Saviour stepped forth—no longer a dead Jesus, but a living Christ ; no longer a fond memory, but a living reality ; no longer a lost companion but a living Friend ; no longer a past protagonist, but a living Conqueror.

And, thank God, because " death hath no more dominion over Him," it is gloriously possible that " sin shall not have dominion over you " (Rom. 6 : 9, 14)—it *ought not*, it *need not* ; then shall we adopt God's word and purpose it *shall not* ! So that, even in the ancient prophecy, the crucifixion and the resurrection are intimately linked together—with all that is implied for us believers, in each truth separately and in both truths combined. Indeed, they must ever be held in combination :

63

the Cross, though historic fact, is tragic failure, without the empty tomb. As old Robert Herrick, the seventeenth-century poet said,

> That Christ did die the pagan saith :
> But that He rose, that's Christian's faith.

Another issue of His death now claims attention : (*iii*) " *The pleasure of the Lord shall prosper in His hand.*" When the early part of this verse said that " it pleased the Lord to bruise Him," it does not mean, of course, that God took delight in hurting His beloved Son, any more than the fathers of Hebrews 12 : 10 who " chastened . . . after their own pleasure " rejoiced in their necessary task. Dean Wickham translates this latter passage, " chastened . . . as seemed good to them "—a very different thing. So this " pleasure of the Lord " is the good of His people, His cause in the world, His kingdom among men, His loving purpose of full salvation and abundant life, for all believers. The death and rising of the Saviour was (the combination !) essential to the prosperity of His cause. And what a privilege that we are invited to take a share in the advancement of that cause, as Paul says, in 1 Thessalonians 2 : 4, " We were allowed of God to be put in trust with the Gospel . . . not as pleasing men, but God "—there you are, " the pleasure of the Lord " again ! Does this, His work, prosper in the corner of the vineyard where He has put you to labour for Him ? Let us, anyhow, do *our* part—by prayer, by gifts, by testimony, by enthusiasm, by holiness, and by joy— so that any lack of prosperity shall not be *our* fault. Never forget that we are members of an advancing cause—there may be set-backs, or dead-spots, here and there, but ours is the winning side ; here or there His army may lose battles, but it won't lose the war. Be eager to take your place. Do you remember that stern message to those who held back from God's cause away back in Judges 5 : 23, " Curse ye Meroz . . . because they came not to the help of the Lord . . . against the mighty " ? Or, what Dr. G. H. Morrison called the Unconcerned Spectator, in Obadiah 11, " In the day that thou stoodest on the other side " ? Come now, the Lord's cause is challenging you to make your choice : will you hook on, or look on ? Appropriately enough that cause is placed in His hand ; amazingly enough, He invites us to link our hand in His.

Note, next, another outcome of His Cross : (*iv*) " *By His knowledge shall My righteous servant justify many.*" By knowledge of Him—that is, in effect, by reason of our coming to know Him, trust Him, as our own personal Saviour and Lord. We may know Him in our heads, without the knowledge having any effect upon us, except, perhaps, to arouse some measure of admiration ; but this know is to know Him in our hearts— evoking our deepest gratitude, our true love, our real trust : and that faith secures our justification at the Bar of God. 1 Peter 3 : 18 says, " Christ . . . hath once suffered for sins, the just for the unjust, that He might bring us to God." When a soul (the unjust) turns, in real repentance, from his sin, and turns, in true faith to the Saviour (the Just) in the just reckoning of God a double transference takes place : the sin of

64

the unrighteous sinner is laid on Christ, and the sinlessness of My righteous Servant is accounted to the sinner. Oh, mystic, marvellous accountancy ! Now, being justified, it is, in God's sight, "just-as-if-I'd " never sinned, as the old puritan wrote. But why is He said here to justify " many," and not all ? The " all " are found way back in verse 6 : He died for all ; yet, alas, not all receive and trust Him, and so He does not save all, does not " justify " all ; but " by Him all that believe are justified from all things " (Acts 13 : 39). You find the same distinction in connection with the " ransom," another figure of His saving work. 1 Timothy 2 : 6 says, He " gave Himself a ransom *for all*," but Matthew 20 : 28 says, He came " to give His life a ransom *for many* "—the explanation is that the two " for's " are different words in the Greek : the former signifies " *on behalf of all*," all *may* receive it ; the latter signifies " *instead of* many," all do not take advantage of the grand emancipating opportunity, only the many *do* receive it. Oh, the eternal bliss, oh, the present blessing, of being among those " many." Here is a further result of His suffering : (*v*) " *Therefore will I divide Him a portion with the great, and He shall divide the spoil with the strong.*" The actual words are admittedly difficult ; but perhaps we may say that the gist of them is fairly plain. The scene is the return home of the triumphant hero of the war—in this case, " the Captain of our Salvation," as Hebrews 2 : 10 describes Him. The victorious General, coming back from his successful campaign (*a*) receives honours for himself, placing him among the great ones, and (*b*) secures rewards, out of the spoils, to distribute to his soldiers, the strong ones. It all reminds me of Psalm 68 : 18, " Thou hast ascended on high, Thou hast led captivity captive : Thou hast received gifts for men," and of Ephesians 4 : 8, " When He ascended up on high, he led captivity captive, and gave gifts unto men." Do you remember Bishop Christopher Wordsworth's great hymn—

> See the Conqueror mounts in triumph,
>
> .   .   .   .
>
> Who is this that comes in glory
>   With the trump of Jubilee ?
> Lord of battles, God of armies,
>   He has gained the victory ;
> He who on the Cross did suffer,
>   He who from the grave arose,
> He has vanquished sin and Satan,
>   He by death has spoiled His foes !

If I am not greatly mistaken, we have here, included in our ancient prediction, prophetic reference to the Ascension and to Pentecost. Because He was " obedient unto . . . the death of the Cross, wherefore God also hath highly exalted Him . . .", says Philippians 2 : 8, 9. Thus has God fulfilled the promise to dispense to Him His portion, His place, among the great, and over all the great. We see the Lamb on the Throne up there (Rev. 5 : 6), even as we shall one day see the Lord on the Throne down here (Rev. 11 : 15). And as part of His ascension triumph, He has dispensed the spoils of victory for those who follow Him—He " received " the Pentecostal gifts for men, and then " gave " them to men. It all flowed from His victory in the most titanic, and the most strategic, battle the universe has ever witnessed : His conquest at Calvary. It seems that no single aspect of His story in the flesh has been omitted from the marvellous pre-view of this wonderful chapter.

And now, to sum it all up : (vi) " *He shall see of the travail of His soul, and shall be satisfied.*" Here is, let us imagine, an athlete, who for months has been vigorously, and rigorously, training for his race. He has had to deny himself many goods that he is fond of, he has had to submit himself to a code of rules and regulations that have often proved irksome, he had had to engage in most strenuous exercise and practice. But now the race is over ; and as he gazes fondly at the prize he has won, he feels that all his " travail " has been worth while. Or, here is a father, who for years has stinted and scraped and starved and saved, that his son might have the very best of educational advantages. But now the results of the Finals are out, and as he reads the announcement of the boy's First Class degree, he feels that all his " travail " has been worth while. My dear friends, I am going to say something that I almost tremble to say, if it had not been down here in our chapter : one day the Saviour is going to look back over all His sufferings, and He is going to look over all the souls that His sufferings have redeemed, and He is going to say that He is " satisfied," that His " travail " has been worth while ! This moment was part of what sustained Him through it all, " who for the joy that was set before Him endured the cross, despising the shame " (Heb. 12 : 2).

So we have listened afresh to this age-old, familiar symphony—well known, but well loved. Whittier has a phrase, " His heart stood still to listen as his ear," and that, perhaps, is how some of us have listened to-day to this moving redemption music, which we shall ever place foremost among " These you have loved." And if words would not too greatly intrude upon our adoring worship, they shall be—

> Love so amazing, so divine,
> Demands my soul, by life, my all.

Practical Holiness.

By the Rev. J. DUNLOP, M.A.

"Like as He who hath called you is holy, so be ye also holy
in all manner of living. Because it is written, ye shall be
holy, for I am holy."—1 *Pet.*, 1 : 15-16, R.V.

NEW Testament holiness of living is set before every Christian,
not simply as an ideal, but as his personal duty. I am conscious
that holiness is something which to the average man, and even
to many Christians, does not always sound attractive, or very practical.
So let us remind ourselves that holiness of life is not something from
which to shrink, nor to be derided or despaired of. It is what God
requires and expects of every one of us.

I think our ideas of holiness have been marred by conventional
portrayals of holiness—for instance, the stained glass window idea of a
saint, rather anaemic, insipid, and unreal—and also by the teaching by
those who claim to have a monopoly of what they call holiness. But
holiness is just spiritual health, spiritual wholeness, and the lack of it
is spiritual sickness ; every truly God-pleasing Christian is a " holy "
person. The Hebrew word translated " holy " is *qodesh*, and the
Greek word is *hagios*, and both have exactly the same meaning, namely,
set apart for God, separated unto Him. For example, in the old
dispensation the vessels used in the temple worship were holy vessels ;
which does not mean that there was a special aura of sanctity about them,
so that one scarcely dared to look upon them or touch them. They
were ordinary vessels, but they had been taken out of ordinary usage
and set apart for God and the service of His House. Every Christian
is holy in that sense. Christ has chosen us for Himself, and He wants
us to be a people distinct from other people in the world, in belonging to
Him and living His life. The normal life for a Christian is that he should
be holy, set apart as Christ's, separated unto God. But many Christians
are falling short of that in its practical out-working—hence the exhortation
of our text, " Like as He which hath called you is holy, so be ye also
holy in all manner of living." The life marked out as God's should be
like God's.

Now this implies, I suggest, that the holy life has certain definite
characteristics which we may see and understand and assess. Remember,
we are not here in the realm of theory ; holiness is a very practical
thing, and the pursuit of holiness *must* be practical ; it is not a reverie
but a reality ; it is not a sentiment, but a character ; and it is based not
on theories but on facts.

What, then, is holiness of life, practically, apart from the theories about it ? The first and most obvious thing is, surely, that holiness is *purity of life from purity of heart.* And purity means cleanness from sin ; and sin is any want of conformity unto, or transgression of, the law of God. Purity is the denial of all that is contrary to the will of God for human living, cleanness from all known sins and sinfulness. The one all-embracing characteristic of God as He has revealed Himself is His opposition to, and oppositeness from, sin ; and the one who receives and shares His life will immediately begin to deny sin in his life. Definite sin in all its forms will be renounced when a man becomes holy. And that instantly sets one apart from the ordinary run of men. There *is* a difference, a decided difference, between a true Christian and a non-Christian. We have a different standard, a new standard, yea, a new incentive and power for living, and that is, the nature and character of the God who has made us akin to Himself. We are *not* conformed to the world ; our pattern is not even the standard set by the lives of other Christians (for then we might be satisfied sometimes too easily), " But as He who hath called you is holy, so be ye holy in all manner of living." Our standard is God Himself, high and lifted up ; Jesus Christ, the revelation of God in human life, is our standard, and He, the Son of God, in human life was " holy, harmless, undefiled and separate from sinners." He who lives *His* life lives a pure, sin-denying life, a life that obeys God secretly and openly, a life that, being in fellowship with God, reflects the purity of God, a life like Christ's who was God manifest in the flesh. That means : no crookedness of any kind, no dishonesty, privately or in business and social relationships, no vice, no uncleanness cherished in thought, word or act ; in a word, no conscious disobedience to God's commandments.

The important thing to notice here is that this purity of life can come only from real purity of heart, as our Saviour said " Out of the heart proceedeth murder, and lying, fornication and all uncleanness." You cannot have a life pure and righteous outwardly which is not rightly adjusted at heart.

Purity of heart. And what is heart purity ? Well, it is not sinlessness ; for none is sinless, nor ever will be this side of Heaven. A pure heart is first a penitent heart that has come to Christ, the sinless Saviour, and been forgiven by Him and cleansed through His blood. A pure heart is actually a new creation in human nature brought about by the creative work of God. As the penitent soul comes in true penitence and surrender to Christ, and humbly receives Him by faith as Redeemer, to him is given the right to become a son of God. He is born again into the family of God. His heart is cleansed and made pure, and readjusted to the life and the will of God. But it is constantly assailed by sin, which is all around us in the world, and in our old corrupt nature still within us ; and it needs constant cleansing. Purity of heart is only maintained as the Christian soul abides in Christ, in full obedience and close communion, for then the Lord keeps on cleansing from all sin. The tragedy is that many Christian people depart from this central enthronement of Christ as Lord and countenance sin and disobedience in their innermost lives, while still professing to be His. Purity of heart is not maintained, and holiness of life is missing. This is a sad, but marked phenomenon in Christian living. The Bible is full of the anomaly of sin in the believer, and it is something that must have a prominent place in our understanding of things and must be dealt with faithfully and continually.

So let us ask ourselves, Do I reach the Christian standard? Have I come to Jesus for the cleansing power, and is my heart really right with His heart? It is easy to live on the surface, and to deceive other people by our Christian profession. It is easy to be a better Christian, seemingly, at Keswick than at home or in other places; it is easy to be a seemingly good Christian anywhere; but the Lord looks upon the heart, and so He knows us, and so He judges. Do we constantly adjust our wills and affections to Christ? Do we obey in all things? And is it all issuing in purity of life, so that we are holy " in all manner of living," as Peter puts it? You see, it is to cover the whole life, " all manner of living." If it is really deep it will be broad. That is the standard: purity of life from purity of heart.

But let us go on to notice another element of New Testament holiness: *fidelity in daily life to duty.* Now, there is something very practical and something greatly needed in the present day. One great characteristic of this age is that you can scarcely get a man to do an honest day's work in any section of life; greed, graft, something for nothing, personal gain and advantage whatever the method, selfish materialism: that is the key-note. There seems to be no pride in one's job for its own sake, no idealism of service, no pleasure in work well done, and Christian people are far from being exempt from the spirit of the age, and the ordinary practice of the age, in this respect. I say unhesitatingly that if Christ were in the world to-day He would not work and live like that. When God came into human life in His Son, what was His great characteristic? His one supreme passion was to do completely the will of Him that sent Him, to be about His Father's business, to do the work which was given to Him to do while it was called to-day, " for the night cometh when no man can work." And how did He do it? For thirty out of the thirty-three years of His life He was subject unto Joseph and Mary, toiling and serving in a humble home, in a carpenter's shop; and He never did a shoddy job, and He never skimped His work. He did the will of God in absolute fidelity to that earthly duty, and He has sanctified human labour for ever. Then, when He went out into His full ministry, He never spared Himself; every minute must be filled with service true to God and His fellows; He *must* be about His Father's business." He *must* be obedient to His last breath. Fidelity in daily life to duty.

What is holiness, in part at least, for the Christian student and schoolboy? Conscientious work, no slacking. What is holiness for the Christian working man? Fidelity to duty, fidelity to his employer, no skimping. What is holiness for the Christian shop-keeper? No false measures, no sharp practice, fidelity to his customers. What is holiness for the Christian in his church work ? Fidelity to his commitments, to the work of that weekly Sunday school class, or whatever it may be. What is holiness for everyone ? Fidelity in daily life to the task given us to do. We can apply it, each to himself. That is practical holiness, the sort that the world believes in. A Christian should be a better workman, or at any rate a more conscientious and dependable workman, than a non-Christian; one who carries out his task well. God has given us our task to do in the world, and He expects us to do it with " all our might and heart, as unto the Lord." If we are enjoined to be " fervent in spirit," we are likewise enjoined to be " diligent in business," serving the Lord. And that takes the sense of constraint out of " duty " in our ordinary work ; that brings joy into it ; for it is God's appointment, it is His will and way for us in this present time, and that knowledge makes it cheerful. There is that aspect of fidelity to duty in everyday work. And there is this also : fidelity at all times to one's Christian convictions and principles ; steadfast, unmoveable, even amid strong temptations, even when left to stand alone. And it means this : Fidelity to one's promises, to the engagements that one undertakes. There is a standard raised in the Old Testament for the godly man, and the New Testament standard certainly falls no whit below it. The man of God when he has given his word " changeth not, even though he swear to his own hurt." It would often be more comfortable and less inconvenient to break one's promises and engagements, but that is not for the Christian; his word is his bond. It means also : fidelity above all to the vows made before God, obedience to the call to service ; no turning back when the road grows hard : " faithful unto death " is the word of the Revelation.

Fidelity, moreover, to the ministry of prayer. Oh, how many professing Christians have broken their early vows to God in one respect and another ! And that is where the trouble lies with their lives. Fidelity in daily life to duty. In all practical matters we are to be " workmen that need not be ashamed " as workmen, for holiness is not an indulgence, it is a work, a daily work, a hard work.

A third element of holiness I would mention is *kindliness*, a word and an idea which I am afraid has often been lacking in theories of holiness. If we are to be upright and pure in our living, that does not mean to be austere and strict and upright merely. If we are to be undeviating to principle and to duty, that does not mean doing our duty in a cold, meticulous way. New Testament holiness is the happiest, kindliest, most natural thing in the world, for a " born-again " man ; and if there is a sense of unnatural strain in your life and standard of holiness, it is not New Testament holiness.

Kindliness ! How that brings the breath of Jesus Christ really into it all ! How that kindliness radiated from Him ! He never compromised with sin, He never countenanced evil in any form, He was absolutely straight and upright, undeviating in integrity and obedience to principle ; yet sinners of all kinds flocked to Him continually from every quarter, because of His kindliness, His winsomeness, His attractiveness ; they could not keep away.

In the negative aspect perhaps the idea is conveyed best by the word " meekness," meekness under provocation. Does that sound to any Christian rather soft and weak and craven ? Jesus Christ our Lord was the most courageous man who ever lived, and He joyed in that He was " meek and lowly in heart " ; " when He was reviled, He reviled not again ; when He suffered, He threatened not." It is not weak, but divine, to forgive those who have wronged us. It is not weak, but divine, to refuse to stand up for and claim our rights oftentimes. And, in the positive sense, it just means practical kindliness ; doing kindnesses, and doing them in a kindly way. The Christian is to be given to hospitality, generous in heart and in hand, liberal, helpful, kindly. Are people glad to see us because we always lift the burden, because we always bring help instead of bringing further depression ? Kindliness means causing no offence, avoiding criticism—oh, how much there is of criticism among Christian people, and what incalculable harm it is doing to Christ's cause ! Holiness is kindliness. No wonder a little girl prayed : " O God, make all the bad people good, and make all the good people nice." So many of us who are " good " in her sense are not " nice " in her sense. Yet that is what convinces the people of the world of the reality of Christ in us, perhaps more than anything else. You know the lines—a constant rebuke and inspiration to my own heart :—

> Not merely in the words you say,
>   Not simply in your deeds confessed,
> But in the most unconscious way
>   Is Christ expressed.
>
> Is it a beatific smile,
>   A holy light upon your brow ?
> Oh no, I felt His presence
>   When you laughed just now.
>
> To me 'twas not the truth you taught,
>   To you so clear, to me so dim,
> But when you came to me
>   You brought a sense of Him.
>
> And from your eyes He beckons me,
>   And from your heart His love is shed,
> Till I lose sight of you
>   And see the Christ instead.

*   *   *

> Let the beauty of Jesus be seen in me
> All His wondrous compassion and purity ,
>   Oh Thou Spirit Divine,
>   All my being refine,
> Till the beauty of Jesus be seen in me.

71

Which brings us back to the all-important question : How is this to be accomplished ? As we face the word of the Lord, we are convicted of our sin, our own sin ; we are not holy as we have been called to be holy. How can we be ? It is well if we are in deadly earnest in asking that question. The answer is : It must be the actual life of Christ within us ; it is not our natural life, it is *His* life. He must be enthroned in our hearts in truth, and kept there ; and He must live out through our lives. The secret of holiness is God indwelling and ruling in the heart and filling the life by His Holy Spirit. But for that to be so, we must first honestly search our hearts and lives, and deal with every wrong thing that the Spirit reveals. We must seek cleansing from sin, from particular sins revealed, and from all sin ; and we must seek adjustment to the will of God in practical things ; and then in full obedience enthrone Him as our Lord. How to do that is what this Convention seeks to teach. May we be willing, constrained by His sacrificial love, and by the glory of our own high calling, to follow Him fully, as He reveals the way ; that we may " be holy in all manner of living, like as He who hath called us is holy."

Saints in the Making.

By the Rev. Prebendary COLIN C. KERR, M.A.

IF we could see behind the scenes to-day, looking upon this world and viewing what is taking place as from God's angle, we should see how His purposes for this dispensation are being most gloriously fulfilled, in spite of all that would seem to suggest otherwise. For the Holy Spirit, like the nameless servant in the day of Abraham (Gen. 24) is going out seeking a Bride for the altogether wonderful King's Son. He is going hither and thither and revealing the wonders and glories of the great Isaac, and drawing out a Bride worthy of Isaac. We should realise that throughout the world this calling-out process is going on, an *ecclesia* is being established, a Church is being built up, a holy temple of living stones, a residency of God by the Spirit is being spiritually erected ; and we should find that a called-out body is to redound to His eternal glory. We should see the work of the nameless servant, the Holy Spirit, as He draws men and women to the Lord Jesus, causing them to behold His glory, and then to fall in love with their Lover. How we should rejoice if to-day we were in Heaven and could see and appreciate the triumphs of the Gospel and the work of the Spirit, and behold the building up of this eternal edifice.

I want to suggest to you something equally glorious and perhaps more pertinent. If we could see to-day the work of the Holy Spirit in making lives holy, how encouraged we should be. We have been hearing about holiness of life, and many a prayer has arisen to the throne of grace, " O God, make me holy, I want to be holy, I ought to be holy." How indeed can my prayer be answered ? I want if possible to see how God makes men holy, how God answers the inarticulate prayer of many a saint. I want to see how God is going to make men and women in this tent this morning holy men and holy women, redounding to the glory of His Eternal Son.

My subject, then, is *saints in the making*. Do not be afraid of that word. We have been wisely reminded this morning that the conception of a saint for many is the vision in a church coloured window, or others have thought of saints as those who have attained to an unusual degree of holiness unto God. What do we mean by saints ? We simply mean those who have become attached unto God in His holiness, and to that degree detached from the world in its sinfulness. A saint is a man who has become attached by the operation of the Holy Ghost unto God in His holiness. A saint, put negatively, is a man who no longer is attached to the world by its praise and the allurement of evil. A saint is an attached

man and a detached man ; attached unto God, he has become strangely
detached from the world upon which he looks almost as from a place of
remoteness.

Saints in the making—what a subject! We may quarrel perhaps
in the outworking of it, but we shall be at one in the title. You will, of
course, want Scripture for such a glorious and pertinent subject, and you
shall have it. In 2 Corinthians 3 : 18 you have (*i*) *a principle in operation :*
(*ii*) *a person at work*, and (*iii*) *the perfect product*. The man of God made
perfect, throughly furnished unto all good works, redounding to the
glory of His Redeemer, and demonstrating the power of the indwelling
Spirit of the living God. " We all, with unveiled face beholding as in
a mirror the glory of the Lord, are being changed (present tense) into the
same image from glory to glory, by the Spirit of the Lord." Here we
have the terms for saints in the making, and of holiness in production.

> 'Twas battered and scarred, and the auctioneer
> Thought it scarcely worth his while
> To waste much time on the old violin,
> But he held it up with a smile.
> " What am I bid, good folk ? " he cried,
> "Who'll start the bidding for me ?
> A dollar—one dollar—then two, only two—
> Two dollars, and who'll make it three ?
>
> " Three dollars once, three dollars twice ;
> Going for three ! " . . . But no—
> From the room far back a grey-haired man
> Came forward and picked up the bow ;
> Then wiping the dust from the old violin
> And tight'ning the loosened strings,
> He played a melody pure and sweet
> As a caroling angel sings.
>
> The music ceased, and the auctioneer,
> With a voice that was quiet and low,
> Said, " Now what am I bid for the old violin ? "
> And he held it up with the bow.
> " A thousand dollars—and who'll make it two ?
> Two thousand, and who'll make it three ?
> Three thousand once—three thousand twice—
> And going—and gone " cried he.
>
> The people cheered, but some of them cried,
> " We do not understand :
> What changed its worth ? " Quickly came the reply,
> " The touch of a master's hand."

Melody in the making ; holiness in production ; the image being defined
in the life of the child of God.

In these words we have (*i*) *a principle in operation*. I must forgo a
strong temptation to suggest a Bible study of a rather close order here.

Says the writer, St. Paul, " We . . . beholding as in a mirror with unveiled face the glory of the Lord, are being changed." There is the principle in operation. May I very sketchily give you the historic background. You will remember when Moses came down from the mountain at the top of which, in some mysterious but very real way he had communed with God for many days, he came down with a divine authority that was shining through his face, as later it was to shine through the face of the One whose coming he foreshadowed. He came down with a brilliance of countenance which was fearful, awesome, so that the people cried out that he should veil his face. He veiled his face that morning, and he lost the measure of authority, and consequently the people ceased to be a nation of priests as they were meant to be, and they lost much of their power of witness to the nations. Moses hid the glory of the Eternal God which was shining through his face because the people were afraid, and the veil which was upon the face of Moses fell upon the people, and to this day the veil is upon them and they cannot behold the glory of a greater than Moses. Even when the Scriptures are read they behold not His glory. The veil of Moses has fallen upon the Mosaic people, and the glory of the Lord is hid from their eyes. " There is no beauty that we should desire Him. He was despised and rejected of men ; a man of sorrows and acquainted with grief ; and we hid as it were our faces from Him." The veil has fallen upon poor Israel, and they are blind and will remain so until the time when the fulness of the Gentiles shall come, and then shall all Israel be saved. The blindness will be a thing of the past, vision shall be theirs, and they shall look upon the Lord whom they have pierced.

Says the Apostle, You want to see holiness in the making, you want to experience it, you want to reveal holiness in the making ; here is a principle in operation. Behold with unveiled face the glory of the Lord, and become aware of that which others will note before your awareness, that you are being changed from glory to glory in the might of His glory and grace, as by the Spirit of the Lord.

A principle in operation. The disciples, the few chosen ones, who were led to the Mount of Transfiguration, beheld His glory. What a vision they had on that Mount ! " His face did shine as the sun " ; *out-shining Deity*. " His clothes were white as light " ; *unsullied holiness*, for when He clothed Himself it was not with raiment nor with robes of man's fashioning. Did He not say, " A body hast Thou prepared Me," and in the strange dress of man's humanity, He came a Sovereign in our midst. His dress was as white as the light, for it was unsullied ; an unstained dress He wore until He laid it down in the grave. Outshining Deity, unsullied holiness, *unqualified authority*—" This is my Beloved Son, hear ye Him." The Moses who speaks of religion and ritual and ceremony is caught away ; Elijah, the Prince of prophets, who speaks of ethics and morality, is caught away ; for God will not suffer a rival to stand alongside, or even near, His Beloved Son. His is *unshared efficacy* : He stands in lone, eternal glory. " This is My Beloved Son,

75

hear ye Him." And "They saw no man save Jesus only." Then there is *undoubted sovereignty*, for I overhear, with a pardonable eavesdropping, the conversation of that memorable occasion. Moses and Elijah are speaking with Him. The law and the prophets are bearing witness to atonement, redemption, justification, through the finished work of Christ ; and as I listen I hear Him speak of the decease which He must accomplish at Jerusalem. Men thought when their hands nailed Him to the Cross that they had dealt with the Christ ; men thought they had put Him in the tomb ; some even thought they had taken from Him His life. But He had said that His life was His own to take it up and to lay it down ; He laid it down, no man could take it from Him. And there on the Mount we have the outshining of His Deity, the unsullied character of His essential holiness, of unqualified, unchallengeable authority ; we have an unshared efficacy, and we have undoubted sovereignty—the death which He should accomplish, not a death that man should bring about. Oh, men and women, pray that the Holy Spirit may cause you to see the glory of the Eternal Son. His altogether loving disposition ; He was the most approachable of people. His separation was never isolation, His attachment to His Father's purposes was never spelt in terms of separation. The little children never feared Him, they loved to come to His feet. The sinner was never scared of His presence if penitent ; the broken-hearted women found no consolation like His ; and even the young ruler who was not prepared to pay the price went away in the warmth of the smile of the One who, seeing him, loved him. Incomparable, approachable Lord, if only our eyes might behold Thee in Thy glory even during the days of our earthly sojourn !

With unveiled face we are beholding the glory of the Lord—there is the principle in operation. We are being changed from glory to glory, and ultimately to that glorious sphere and condition to which we have been predestinated when we shall be conformed to the image of His Son. I can understand something of the warmth of the words of John, when he breaks out into a *Te Deum* : " Behold, what manner of love the Father hath bestowed upon us, that we should be called the sons of God : therefore the world knoweth us not, because it knew Him not. Beloved, now are we the sons of God, and it doth not yet appear what we shall be : but we know that, when He shall appear, we shall be like Him ; for we shall see Him as He is" (1 John 3 : 1, 2). The consummation of the change will be due to perfected vision—" We shall be like Him, for we shall see Him as He is," and even now the degree of the change is the revelation which we have of Jesus Christ now. A principle in operation—being changed as we behold His glory.

Now note also (*ii*) *the Person at work*. This thought brings tremendous encouragement. If ever I were tempted to despair, I should yet find great comfort in this second consideration. When the Master takes the violin in His hands and begins to tighten the strings and wipe the dust from the bow—He cannot use an instrument the strings of which are loose ; He will not defile His holy hands in an attempt that His sense of fitness would despise ; He will not make music with a dirty bow—when

76

He has tightened the strings and wiped the bow, and taken the instrument in His hand, he produces the melody ; and the people cry out for some explanation, they do not understand. They have yet to learn the touch of the Master hand. A Person at work. If you think of the Holy Spirit as an influence or an effluence ; if you think of the Holy Spirit as some vague, ill-defined something, just nothing more ; if you think of the Holy Spirit as some evasive something, your whole attitude will be an attitude of one who cries " O God, I do not understand it, but I know I need it. It is somewhere here trying to evade me, but help me to locate it." The moment you realise that in the Trinity of His Being there is a Society of Personalities, and each brings to us the wholeness of Deity, you will realise the Holy Spirit is not merely a Person, He is God. And you will enter into this new conception of things and become possessed of this fresh outlook. It will not be a question of, How can I find it ; and if perchance I find it, how can I hold it ? It will be a question of " Oh God, I give myself to Thee, Blessed Eternal Spirit, take me as I am. I am only an old violin, the strings are loose, all the tunes I have tried to produce have been discordant, but if Thou canst tighten the strings, then graciously do so. If Thou canst produce music from such as I, I will rejoice with others." And our whole thought will be, not " it," but " He " ; not my having more of it, but He having more of me. A Person at work—a principle in operation.

And lastly, and in two or three phrases, (*iii*) *the perfect product*. What is it ? Changed into a spurious imitation ? No. Changed into the same image—not " unto," but " into." It is not the lifting up of the stature of holiness until it approximates to His standard, and as it were two people of similar worth becoming visible : the Eternal Son in His glory, the transformed son raised unto such glory. Oh no ! The believer has been transformed *into* the same image, lost, and made eternally suitable in the eternally suitable One.

The "Geography" of the Heavenlies.

By Dr. DONALD G. BARNHOUSE

A FEW years ago I spoke for several days at one of our Bible Conferences in America, and closed my ministry on a Monday morning. At luncheon just afterwards, I met another Bible teacher who had come to begin his ministry that afternoon. We greeted each other, and then I left to fulfil an engagement in another place. Some time later I met him, and, with a rueful smile, he said to me, " You certainly got me into trouble that last day we met." When I inquired the reason for his remark, he told me that he had risen before his audience with a solemn message. He spoke his first two or three sentences, and noticed smiles throughout his audience. He spoke another sentence, and there was a titter ; and finally an outburst of ill-concealed laughter. As his subject was most serious he was baffled, and turned toward the chairman, who told him to go on, and that he would explain afterwards.

At the morning hour I had made some remarks on the Epistle to the Ephesians. I told the people that they were not to be frightened by Bible teachers who told them that this was the most advanced Epistle in the Scriptures ; that they were not to turn aside from the Epistle because someone told them that it was the deepest truth, the highest truth, the profoundest truth, the Holy of Holies of the Bible, or any such thing. I remarked that Paul had begun to pray that they might know these deep truths as soon as he heard that the Ephesians had come out of darkness and into light. A few weeks before they had been crying, " Great is Diana of the Ephesians." Now they were believers. When Paul began to pray for these Christians of whose faith he had heard, he was praying for yesterday's pagans. They had no background of Bible knowledge. They had never read the Old Testament, never heard a psalm. They had never been to Bible school or to a Bible conference. They were babes in Christ, yet needed no preliminary studies to understand the truth that the Holy Spirit was about to give them in their Epistle.

My friend had stood before his audience that afternoon, and had begun as follows : " During these days we are going to consider the Ephesian Epistle. Here is the deepest truth in all the Word of God. Here, if any place in Scripture, we stand on holy ground. I am bold to speak on this subject here, because I feel that you who attend this Bible conference are the Christian *elite*, and have the proper background to comprehend these infinite mysteries." That was when his audience smiled !

I justified my position before my friend by pointing out that it was the Holy Spirit who moved Paul to write, " I also, after I heard of your faith in the Lord Jesus, and love unto all the saints, cease not to give thanks for you, making mention of you in my prayers ; that the God of our Lord Jesus Christ, the Father of glory, may give unto you the spirit of wisdom and revelation in the knowledge of him ; the eyes of your understanding being enlightened ; that ye may know . . ." three things. These babes in Christ were to know the hope of the Christian calling ; the fact that they themselves became the inheritance of the Father ; and the power that God had wrought when He raised Christ and the Church from the dead and set them both on the throne of heaven.

As we shall consider certain phases of this Epistle in our present study, we shall follow a line of thought that centres in one word in the original Greek, that is to be found five times in the Epistle. Here are five' verses, in the order in which we find them in the Epistle, and all contain the same word :—

" Blessed be the God and Father of our Lord Jesus Christ, who hath blessed us with all spiritual blessings in the Heavenlies, in Christ " (1 : 3).

" That ye may know . . . what is the exceeding greatness of His power toward us who believe, according to the working of His mighty power, which He wrought in Christ when He raised Him from the dead, and set Him at His own right hand in the Heavenlies, far above all principality and power, and might, and dominion, and every name that is named, not only in this world, but also in that which is to come " (1 : 20, 21).

" He . . . hath raised us up together and made us sit together in the Heavenlies in Christ Jesus " (2 : 6).

" To the intent that now, unto the principalities and powers in the Heavenlies might be known by the Church the manifold wisdom of God " (3 : 10).

" For we wrestle not against flesh and blood, but against principalities, against powers, against the rulers of this world's darkness, against the hosts of spiritual wickedness in the Heavenlies " (6 : 12).

After long study of this Epistle we come to realize that these verses form the thread on which all the jewels of the Epistle are strung. If we understand their spiritual continuity we shall understand the revelation that God is giving to us of the warfare of the Christian life, the sphere of that warfare, the means that are at our disposal to wage the warfare through to victory, and the triumph that is already ours, in the Heavenlies.

Let us begin by exploring these Heavenlies, so that we may know our way around, and be able to orient ourselves. Any General Staff, in planning an invasion, must have a complete knowledge of the terrain, of the ways of communication, of the sources of supply, of the strongholds of the enemy. And the Bible teaches us that we are on earth, and that our Lord is in the highest Heaven, and that much of the territory between is possessed by the enemy, Satan, and his powers. If we are to get through to God and the source of our power, and if we are to bring back the complete supplies we need, and if we are to overcome the enemy, we must be aware of the nature of our access to God and of the nature of our warfare. This is the theme of the book of Ephesians.

First of all, we must realise that Heaven is a definite place. Without question we write Heaven with a capital initial letter, just as we should write London, Philadelphia, Keswick, and the other proper names of places, with a capital initial letter. There is no possible chance of interpreting the Scriptures in a spiritual sense on this point. Heaven may not be spiritualised, for if it is, it is a simple matter to destroy all Christian doctrine. For if Heaven is not a physical, material place, then the resurrection body of Christ does not exist, and other Christian doctrines fall down like nine-pins, knocking each other over.

Let us go back to the resurrection of our Lord Jesus Christ, and proceed from that truth to the truth of the reality of Heaven as a place. Our Lord was raised from the dead in the same body in which He died. We do not labour the proof of this proposition here, as it is outside the scope of our present study. We adopt it as a premise accepted by all Evangelical Christianity. Now, if our Lord is raised from the dead, where is the body in which He arose ? He said to His disciples, " Handle Me, and see, for a spirit hath not flesh and bones as ye see Me have " (Luke 24 : 39). Where is that tangible body ? We follow the narrative of the resurrection days and come at last to the story of the Ascension. While the disciples looked steadfastly towards Heaven as He went up, behold two men stood by them in white apparel, which also said, " Ye men of Galilee, why stand ye gazing up into Heaven ? This same Jesus which is taken up from you into Heaven, shall so come in like manner as ye have seen Him go into Heaven " (Acts 1 : 10, 11). The Holy Spirit uses the place name four times in the two verses. Heaven, Heaven, Heaven, Heaven . . . this is now the centre of your thinking and the source of your life and power. The Lord whom you have seen with your eyes and touched with you hands is now gone above, and you are to turn all your thoughts there and live your life in Heaven while you go through the motions of earth.

A soldier in the Burma campaign was forced to live month after month in the rotting jungles. He went from fox-hole to fox-hole, underwent the torments of the tropics, was blinded by the sweat of his labour. He slogged forward with a white cottage in his mind, a garden path running through the flowers, and his love standing at the door. When the turn of the battle called forth some new supreme effort, the etching of his dream was more sharply drawn, and it was from the far source of his life that he drew the sustenance for his morale for his daily fight. " If ye then be risen with Christ, seek those things which are above, where Christ sitteth on the right hand of God. Set your affection on things above, and not on things on the earth, for ye are dead, and your life is hid with Christ in God " (Col. 3 : 1-3).

But this very real place, Heaven, is not all on one plane. When God raised Christ from the dead, He set Him at His own right hand in the

Heavens . . . *far above* all principality, and power, and might, and dominion. Now, it is impossible to have a " far above " without having a " far below." Our Lord Jesus Christ is in the far above Heavens, but Satan and his hosts are entrenched in the far below Heavens, and earth lies still below them. The Epistle to the Ephesians is the chart of the secret track that leads through enemy land into the holiest of all, and it is the revelation of the channels by which blessings from the highest spring and fountain of blessings may be poured down upon us for our daily need.

I know what an etymological *lapsus* it is to speak of the *geography* of Heaven, for the word means " the writing or delineation of the earth." But it is that term which best expresses my thought. The Bible teaches us enough about Heaven so that we may know our way around when, ultimately, we arrive in its glorious scenes. We have a map and a plan of Heaven. Moses was straitly ordered to make all things in the tabernacle according to the pattern that was shown to him on Mt. Sinai (Heb. 8 : 5). And the New Testament declares that the tabernacle was a pattern of things in the Heavens (Heb. 9 : 23). If we study that plan we shall not be a stranger when we walk in Heaven.

Years ago I arrived by an evening train in the city of Florence, accompanied by my bride of a year. Neither of us had ever been in Florence before, and after we had settled our things in the hotel we left to take a walk. There was some astonishment upon the part of my companion because I knew my way. Down this street would be the cathedral, over to the right would be Giotto's bell tower, around the other end of the building there would be the baptistry with Ghiberti's famed bronze doors. How could I know all this, never having been in the city before ? It was that I had prepared for this trip, and had studied the map closely, and knew all that I wanted to see in the short time we would have at our disposal. So, if you look at the map and plan which the tabernacle really is, you will find your way around Heaven quite easily.

Turn the tabernacle up on end, with the altar nearest us, then the laver, the holy place, with the table of shewbread, the candlestick, the altar of incense and finally the holiest of all, with the ark of God, the cherubim and the mercy seat, and you have the general outline of Heaven. The distances when we reach there may be measured in light years— that we do not know—and the glorious details are outside our present comprehension ; but the overall scheme is knowable. We shall enter by outer courts, and come, at last, by the altar, eternal symbol of the Cross of Jesus Christ, to the laver, the sea of cleansing, which then, thank God, will be turned to crystal, as there will be no further need of cleansing from sin, for ever. Then we shall enter into the second Heaven, the tabernacle's holy place, and, finally, into the Holy of Holies, the Heaven of the Heavens, into the third Heaven, the Heaven of the throne of God, far above the outer courts of the lowest Heaven where the principalities and powers, the forces of Satan, still congregate, besetting our path to the throne of grace, and seeking to block the flow of blessings from thence back to us.

There are many more details which could be sketched into this plan, from the picture that the Lord revealed to John in the Apocalypse, from the Epistle to the Hebrews, and from certain Old Testament passages, but it is not our purpose here to study Heaven in detail. We are concerned only with establishing the fact that Jesus Christ is at the right hand of God in the far above Heavens, and that we are on earth, and that between us and our Lord, in the far below Heavens lurks the enemy of our souls.

It is interesting to note that in the last chapter of the Epistle to the Ephesians the translators of the Authorised version have watered down the translation of our key word. In the first four occurrences they have made two words out of it in the English, and rightly put it in the plural, calling it " the Heavenly places " But when they came to the sixth chapter they found Satan's forces mentioned, and (perhaps a little frightened at what they found), hesitated to speak of Satan in Heaven, and so placed his forces in what they call " high places." If we understand these high places as being high above us, but far below the Heaven of the Heavens, where our Lord Jesus Christ is to be found, then the difference in translation may stand.

We must not forget that Lucifer was created in Heaven, that his original fall was in Heaven, and that the sphere of his spiritual activity has always been in Heaven. His rule is over the earth, there are statements that he has a throne upon the earth ; but just as King George may have a throne out in Canada, in India and other parts of the Empire, with delegated authority ruling when he is not there on visit, so Satan rules on earth through his principalities and powers, but his main sphere of activity is in the Heavenlies. That is why the Lord Jesus Christ, our great High Priest, had to pass into the Heavens, with the value of His blood sacrifice, and purify the Heavens themselves where sin had fouled Heaven as it has fouled the earth. And that is why there must some day be a new Heaven as well as a new earth.

Satan even appears at some of the courts of God and brings reports, as in the book of Job, and it is in the sphere of the Heavens that he carries on his main activity as the " accuser of the brethren." We must not be drawn aside from considering the main sphere of our spiritual activity and warfare as being the Heavens, by the statement of our Lord, " I beheld Satan as lightning fall from Heaven " (Luke 10 : 18). This is most certainly a prophecy of something that has not yet taken place. It is put in the past tense, for it is as certain as all of the plan of God, and thereby may be expressed as something done and accomplished. Many future events are thus expressed in the prophetic past tense, even to the thrilling statement about ourselves that we are already glorified and in Heaven. " Whom He did foreknow He also did predestinate to be conformed to the image of His Son (past tense for a past event). Moreover, whom He did predestinate them He also called (past tense for a past event) ; and whom He called them He also justified (past tense for an event that was once future for believers, and is now past for us, but yet future for those who shall be saved in days to come); and whom He justified them He also glorified (past tense for an event that is wholly future) " (Rom. 8 : 29, 30). There are many such usages of the past tense.

When our Lord received the report of the seventy whom He had sent forth to preach, they came with exultation that even the demons were subject to them. The Lord looked up and saw the glorious day when all of the forces of Satan would be swept out of Heaven before the provided might of Michael and all the angels of God. It was then that He said, " I beheld Satan as lightning fall from Heaven." Much later the Lord spoke again of this removal of Satan from the Heavenly spheres, saying, " Now is the judgment of this world, now shall the prince of this world be cast out " (John 12 : 31). But again we must understand this as a prophecy, or a proclamation of a basis of future judgment. He was about to die. He says, Now is the Cross about to come, and this Cross is the basis of the judgment of this present evil world system, and in consequence of the Cross the doom of Satan is sure, and he shall be cast forth.

Many years pass, and Paul is given to write the Epistle to the Ephesians. He is still inspired by the Holy Spirit to describe the forces of Satan, along with his principalities and powers, his delegated rules for earth governments, as still moving in the Heavens, where they had been from the beginning. And on down in the Apocalypse we see the final war in Heaven, with the power of God given to the angels to complete the work that was won by the death of our Lord. And though the dragon shall fight, and his angels, he shall not prevail. Then, in the midst of the great tribulation, the place of Satan and his powers is found no more in Heaven, and they are cast down to earth with great woe to the inhabiters of the earth because the devil is come down to them, having great wrath because he knoweth then that he hath but a short time before he shall be precipitated to his ultimate and eternal dwelling-place (Rev. 12 : 7-12).

I do not think that it is possible for any Christian to know anything about a life of victory, triumph, and resurrection, unless he knows that life through the power of Christ in the Heavenly sphere. To-day, just as the Roman Church rules all her priests, in whatsoever land they may be, from the hill of the Vatican on the Tiber, and as Russia rules all the Communists of the world from the Kremlin in Moscow, so Satan rules all his forces from Heaven, making an occasional sally into the earth, going to and fro and walking up and down in it. If we are to live lives of triumph and blessing we must learn that the sphere of our warfare is in Heaven, and it is there that the Lord expects to give us the victory.

Eisenhower, in ordering the strategy of the advance into Germany, left many a German garrison in slow death because they were totally cut off from their base of supplies. Satan cares nothing how active you are here in work, preaching, praying even, providing you are running around in the earthly sphere without the proper contact in the Heavenlies. God help the poor Christian who lives an earthly life on earth, gasping for spiritual life, as a fish out of water gasps to be back in his own element.

A few years ago I gave some addresses at the Canadian " Keswick," and a friend from Toronto told me of an incident which will bring us to the end of the present address. He moved into a house in Toronto which had been unoccupied for a year or two, and the garden was in very bad condition. The weeds were high and had practically choked the flowers out of existence. On the first morning in his new home he looked down into the expanse of weeds from an upstairs window, and saw one magnificent blossom blooming gloriously from a seeming alien ground. He went down and made his way through the weeds, took hold of the stem and began to follow it down to the ground, to have a long stem for the flower. He found that the stem curved through the weeds, and through curiosity he followed it four or five feet to the edge of his property, and found the flower growing from a beautifully kept garden plot on the other side of the hedge. The flower bloomed in his weeds, but the root was in ground that was watered and cared for. Thus the Christian is in the world but not of it, even as the flower was in the weeds but not of them. We blossom in the world, but we must be rooted in God.

But how can we be rooted in Heaven ? Are we not, like Adam the first man, of the earth earthy ? Yes, we are. But God has made provision for us to live in Heaven, and it is the study of that life we are to consider. The poet has written :—

> We may not climb the heavenly steeps
> To bring the Lord Christ down . . .

but that is just what we may do, and must do if we are to tap the rich resources that are opened for us when we reach Heaven now, in a sense that is far more real than most Christians know, and that is only less real than when we shall touch them with our real hands.

Super-Abundant Blessing.

By the Rev. GORDON M. GUINNESS, M.A.

" Bring ye all the tithes into the storehouse, that there may be meat in Mine house, and prove Me now herewith, saith the Lord of Hosts, if I will not open you the windows of Heaven, and pour you out a blessing, that there shall not be room enough to receive it."—*Mal.* 3 : 10.

MALACHI received this solemn word as a burden from the Lord (1 : 1). It was a burden for Malachi,˙ and it was a burden for the Lord, for this prophecy unfolds tragedy, and in these verses the tragedy reaches its climax. " Will a man rob God ? Yet ye have robbed Me. But ye say, Wherein have we robbed Thee ? In tithes and offerings. Ye are cursed with a curse : for ye have robbed Me. . . Bring ye all the tithes into the storehouse, that there may be meat in Mine house, and prove Me now herewith, saith the Lord of Hosts, if I will not open you the windows of Heaven, and pour you out a blessing that there shall not be room enough to receive it. And I will rebuke the devourer for your sakes, and he shall not destroy the fruits of the ground. . . And all nations shall call you blessed."

Do you doubt that this is the word of God for our nation in this day ? Do you doubt that this is the word of God for this Convention at Keswick ? Do you doubt that this is the word of God for you ? The speaker would not dare to unfold the implications of this word of intolerable burden had he not received it in humble repentance as God's word to himself.

Now, the first thing about this word which is a burden from the Lord, is this :

I. God is Waiting to Give Us a Blessing Far Greater than We Can Ever Receive.

Can we wonder that this is a burden to the Lord ? He looks down upon a largely powerless Church which is neither hot nor cold, conformed very widely to the standards and methods of the world around, and He knows He could transform everything if only we would let Him. God is waiting and longing to open the windows of Heaven and pour out such a blessing that there shall not be room enough to receive it. This is true individually of personal holiness, as well as corporately of our Christian service.

(*i*) *Individually, in personal holiness.* As we look back along the road of our spiritual pilgrimage, most of us find that sin has been our almost constant companion, and the more we ponder the life and teaching of Jesus Christ, the more do we realise that He lived on Alpine heights of

85

moral perfection that we can never reach unaided. And yet this moral perfection is just what He solemnly demands of us : " Be ye therefore perfect, even as your Father which is in Heaven is perfect." Such a standard is so humanly unattainable that men either despair, or evade the whole issue ; or else they must come to realise that God never gives a command without making provision to enable us to meet that command.

Some of us have come up to Keswick almost desperate. Only a few hours ago a Christian worker said to me that she had given up trying to talk about Christ to the people where she lives, because they see, and she knows, that her life is no different from theirs. Despair is really gripping the hearts of many of us. We have tried and failed so often that we begin to doubt whether we can ever live without our hearts constantly condemning us. But God's word is : " Blessed are they that hunger and thirst after righteousness, for they shall be filled," and He is waiting to give us a blessing, far greater than our need, for where sin abounds grace does still much more abound.

The New Testament not only records the demand of the all-holy God, that His people should be holy ; it also demonstrates the practical possibility of holiness. In the Acts of the Apostles we see this as the normal experience of God's people. The disciples were full of faith, full of joy, full of power, full of fire, full of the Holy Ghost. This radiant, overflowing Christlikeness is the personal holiness which God means everyone of His children to have. Of course, there is the possibility of lapsing. God does not want to do anything that is mechanical. Peter compromised, and Paul had to withstand him. They did not reach the place where it was not possible to sin, but rather, through the Holy Ghost, they found that it was possible not to sin. And God is waiting to give this blessing to us to-night. It will have a three-fold expression : toward God—love, joy, peace ; toward others—long-suffering, gentleness, goodness ; and within ourselves—faithfulness, meekness and self-control. This blessing is the fullness of the Holy Ghost ; and because we can no more contain the Holy Ghost than a bucket can contain the ocean, this is something far greater than we can ever receive.

(*ii*) *Corporately, in Christian service.* This blessing will be seen not only individually, in personal holiness, but corporately in our Christian service. The holy union between Christ and His Bride, the Church, is to be a fruitful one. God says to His spiritual creation, " Be fruitful and multiply." But this is just where so many Churches and individuals fail. The New Testament records constantly expanding Churches, " the Lord adding daily to the Church such as were being saved." How many men were added to the Church where you have your membership last year ? The barrenness of a busy life may be a terrible reality. We are too busy to stop still and think. Malachi points out that the evil one, the devourer, is at work, destroying and corrupting the fruits of the ground. Until God's blessing comes, he will make it his business to ruin the harvest. And because we have so rarely seen apostolic results anywhere, we have gradually come to feel that we can never expect them where we live and work. The daily influence of the pagan world all around seems to numb our spiritual faculties, and the incessant demands of the daily routine seem to leave us no time for unhurried communion with God ; special seasons of waiting upon Him, low at His feet, become rarer and rarer, until our early hopes of a harvest worthy of the terrible sowing on Calvary have almost faded away. Sunday after Sunday, season after season, come and go, and we have little to show for our labour. Christian friends tell us that all we are responsible for is the sowing, and we must leave the reaping with God ; but deep down in our hearts we know that God means us to reap as well as sow. We can never forget His promise : " Henceforth thou shalt *catch* men." We remember that Isaiah 53 is followed by Isaiah 54. We are hungry and thirsty, and we will not be put off, and we are longing for God to work in His mighty power. And God says to us to-day, I am waiting to open the windows of Heaven and pour you out a blessing greater than all your hopes and prayers, which are only the shadow of what I am longing to do.

II. THE ABSENCE OF GOD'S FULL BLESSING IS DUE TO THE PRESENCE OF SIN.

Here is the burden of the Lord : " Will a man rob God ? " Will a Christian worker rob God ? Will you, my friends, who hate sin and so long after God that you have come here and got others to come with you ; will you rob God ? " But ye have robbed me, saith the Lord." When Malachi pressed this challenge, they would not admit it until God's accusation was forced home : " Wherein have we robbed Thee ? " " In tithes and offerings." In witholding what is My due, " Ye are cursed with a curse, for ye have robbed Me." So unless our lives and our service are full of overflowing blessing, corresponding to the windows of Heaven being open, somewhere we have robbed God. God holds us responsible for the barrenness we have caused by our lack of passion and fire, by our small faith that has removed so few mountains, by not allowing the waters of the Spirit to surge through our lives. We are cursed because there are men dead in sins who would be living unto God, if we had not robbed God. We are cursed because we have revealed so little of the beauty of Jesus that men have not wanted Him. We have demonstrated so little of the quickening, liberating, infectious fellowship of the Church that men have wanted the fellowship of Masonry, or the fellowship of a political party, or the fellowship of the public-house. We ought to show them that the fellowship of the Church is a warmer, lovelier, greater thing than any other fellowship could ever be.

" Wherein have we robbed Thee ? " Malachi mentions tithes and offerings. They had kept for their own use what was God's alone. They were eating food that should have been given to God, were clothed with wool that belonged to God and was sacred in His service ; they were riding on asses that had no right to be in their stables, that should have been taken to the Temple and given to God. And although we no longer live in a simple agricultural community, our sin is essentially the same as theirs : we keep back for ourselves and our own use what really belongs to God.

There are many things we might think of, but as our whole society is now based upon money, let us consider how easily we may rob God here.

(*i*) *Robbing God of money.* If Christian people really accepted the principle of Christian stewardship, and lived it out, there would be no financial problems in the Church, no hold-up in the mission field, financially, to-day. " Our " money and " our " possessions are no more ours than the money he handles belongs to a Public Trustee. He simply lays it out in accordance with the wishes of the testators. So we are to spend the money God has allowed us according to His instructions ; and it is our business to find out those instructions. There are ways Christians spend money that contribute nothing to God's kingdom, nothing to health, nothing to recreation for service, nothing of any value to mankind ; habits and accepted customs that are frankly self-indulgent and only pander to our pride. But to set free this money for God's service sometimes requires the most bitter struggle, because money is often a symbol of our inner determination to control our own lives. I remember some years ago a great friend of mine came up to this Convention, and he hated it. Meeting after meeting passed and he grew more and more miserable, because at one of the first meetings God put His hand on him and said, " Will a man rob God ? " Then one day he came down radiant, and he has stayed radiant ever since, although he has gone through very deep waters. He told me that that night he could not get to sleep because he knew what God was asking him to do, and he could not face it ; but at last between two and three o'clock in the morning he climbed out of bed on to his knees and said, " All right, I surrender, I will stop robbing God."

This call once came to a member of a Church I served, and every year he gave me £20 for God's work over and above all his other offerings, the £20 being what he had formerly spent, year after year, on a certain habit that was robbing God.

(*ii*) *Robbing God of time.* Another test we must face is : Am I robbing God of time ? How easy to do, and how impossible to repay ! We have lost the sacred art of spending time with God, and nothing else can ever take its place. No repentance however deep, no restitution however costly, no sorrow however complete, can do away with the necessity for a daily time of sacred quiet, alone with God. Our hearts probably condemn us here more than anywhere. When our quiet times have become hurried, how can we expect to give God the adoration that is His due ? How can we receive the guidance that God is waiting to give ? How can our hearts catch the glow of divine fire ? How can we have deep fellowship with those purposes that are really nearest to the heart of God ? I stand before you very humbly as one who has robbed God here, and I believe that when we finish our earthly life we will be overwhelmed as we realise all that God could have done if only we had given Him the time in prevailing prayer. How terrible is the cost of robbing God of time for prayer, because when we rob God of time for quiet, we are robbing Him of ourselves, because it is only in the quiet that we can really know

Him and know ourselves, and be sure that we give ourselves back to Him. Oh, for God's sake, do not risk keeping the windows of Heaven closed by robbing God of time.

We must come on to our last thought.

III. GOD URGES US TO PUT HIM TO THE TEST TO-NIGHT.

" Prove Me now herewith, saith the Lord." The original invitation to Israel through Malachi was never accepted. Israel never proved God by bringing all the tithes into the storehouse, and the curse of God continued to rest on her. There is, therefore, an awful possibility that we may fail to accept God's loving invitation to put Him to the test.

Can we imagine what would happen to the world-wide Church if everybody in this meeting were to prove God now herewith ? There would be such a release of spiritual power and energy that the Christian life of the whole world would be influenced.

You remember D. L. Moody overheard someone say that the world had not yet seen what God could do with a wholly consecrated man and Moody there and then vowed that he would be that man. So the world did see what God could do with a wholly consecrated man. Because God cannot deny Himself, He must fulfil His promise. His promise is supported by His oath, for God has sworn by Himself, " Surely in blessing I will bless thee, and multiplying I will multiply thee." And God is abundantly willing to shew to us the heirs of the promise, the immutability of His counsel.

It is so safe to trust God. If we " prove Him now " by bringing everything into His storehouse, we may not see the windows of Heaven open, we may not hear the windows of Heaven open, but the windows of Heaven *will* open, and God will " pour out such a blessing that there shall not be room enough to receive it." " What things soever ye desire, when ye pray, believe that ye receive them, and ye shall have them."

Purposing and Accomplishing.

By the Rev. W. GRAHAM SCROGGIE, D.D.

" They went forth to go into the land of Canaan ;
and into the land of Canaan they came."—*Gen.* 12 : 5.

THIS striking statement of an event which occurred in the Middle
East, 3,800 years ago, has an unmistakable significance for us
here to-day ; so let us examine it.   The passage speaks of a divine
revelation ; a momentous resolution ; and a joyful realization.

There is first of all,

I. A DIVINE REVELATION.   In these few words, " the land of
Canaan " is spoken of twice, and the " land " is the revelation, both
geographically and spiritually.   God said to Abram : " Get thee out
of thy country *unto a land that I will show thee*," and its spiritual counterpart is also a subject of revelation.

The whole history of the chosen people has its spiritual application.
The people in Egypt tell of men as subjects of Satan's kingdom, oppressed
and wretched.   The deliverance of the people through the Red Sea tells
of that emancipation of men which takes place at the time of their
regeneration.   The passage through the Jordan tells of the regenerated
man's identification with Christ in His death and resurrection.   The
wilderness wandering tells of the experience of those Christians who
get stuck between Calvary and Pentecost.   And " the land of Canaan "
tells of that experience of rest and victory which is entered into, here and
now, by faith.   " We who have believed *do* enter into *that rest*."

As Canaan was the sphere of Israel's life, so " the heavenlies " is the
sphere of the believer's life.   As Canaan was the place of Israel's conflict,
so " the heavenlies " is the place where the Christian wrestles with wicked
spirits.   And as Canaan was the land of Israel's wealth, so the believer
is " blessed with every spiritual blessing in the heavenlies in Christ."
It is a mistake to interpret Jordan as the passage of death, and Canaan
as heaven beyond.   The conflicts in Canaan should have warned us
against this view ; but the whole Book of Joshua, and references in the
Epistle to the Hebrews, make it clear that the spiritual application of this
story relates to the purpose of God for His people in this life ; to an
experience here and now of spiritual rest by victorious conflict.   To such
a life as this we are called.   The word of God to each of us is what it
was to Abram long ago : " Get thee out . . . into . . ." ; and
the promise made to the patriarch is made to us also : " I will bless thee,
and thou shalt be a blessing."

Following on this Divine Revelation comes,

II. A MOMENTOUS RESOLUTION. " They went forth to go into the land of Canaan." Here we see the importance of having *a definite end in view*; and it is such definiteness which makes the difference between a traveller and a tramp, between a pilgrim and a wanderer. The tramp, the wanderer, has no clear objective. It is always sheer accident that at any given time he is here or there. He does not guide his feet, but they guide him. But it is otherwise with the traveller, with the pilgrim, who, although he may not, and indeed cannot, see the path he is to tread, knows, nevertheless, the end for which he is making.

The two things which Abram was sure of were the starting point, and the goal; Chaldea at the one end, and Canaan at the other; but the way between was hidden from his view. When God called him and his company to leave Ur, He said nothing to them of the path between the starting-point and the goal. That was hidden from their view, so that they went out, " not knowing whither they went."

This is always so in the experience of the pilgrim. The main points in every life are its direction and its attainment. They are :—

> Two points in the adventure of the diver,
> One—when, a beggar, he prepares to plunge,
> One—when, a prince, he rises with his pearl.

What matters it if we see not the way, so long as we are sure that we are in the right path, and know with whom we are going.

We are all so anxious to know what the journey will be like, but we are called to " walk by faith; not by sight." The true pilgrim attitude is :—

> So long Thy power has blessed me, sure it still
> Will lead me on ; o'er moor and fen,
> O'er crag and torrent, till the night is gone. . .
>   I do not ask to see
> The distant scene ; one step enough for me.

The Christian life is never represented as a picnic, but as something strenuous ; a race, a contest, a fight, a journey with a cross. The promise of a soft life would appeal to very few, for such a life could not be productive of nobility and heroism ; it would only make invalids, not men and women. To all who long for a true life, Christ is still saying " Get out . . . and go in . . ."

But if this is to be done we shall have to exercise *strong determination*, for much of the journey to the goal will be hard and hazardous, and only the will to continue steadfast will bring us victoriously to the end.

There are certain things of which they should be warned who are contemplating this journey. One of these is *the natural tendency to court delay*. After leaving Ur of the Chaldees, Terah, Abram, and the others, went several hundred miles north-west to Haran, and, we are told, they " dwelt there." One of the chief menaces to the Christian life is this disposition to postpone, to procrastinate, to dawdle on the way ; and we foolishly imagine that the error is largely compensated for by the good

91

intention to go on to the end. But every evil way is paved with good intentions, and by delay risks are run which the Christian cannot afford to take.

No doubt these travellers found Haran an attractive place, surrounded by mountains, watered by rivers, and rich in pasturage. It is the place to which Jacob went when he fled from Esau, and from that story we learn how rich in pasture land it was, besides being a place of commercial importance. Such resting-places are provided for pilgrims, but it is perilous to make them dwelling-places.

Another danger of which we should be aware is, *the constant temptation to shirk difficulties*. Haran was the most northerly point which these travellers could reach, and the time had come for them to turn west toward the promised land. But between them and Canaan was the broad, deep and rapid Euphrates, which would have to be crossed, and such a step would mean an irrevocable cutting loose from the past life. The journey from Ur to Haran was made on the eastern side of the river, and the feeling of entire separation had not been felt; but now a crisis had arisen.

To such crises multitudes are not strangers. There come times in the life of the Christian when he is confronted with problems which are new and startling ; times when momentous choices have to be made ; times when he is conscious of conflicting influences and ideals. One voice says, " Go forward " ; and another voice says, " Stay where you are." Such a time as this is very critical, for the issues are of the utmost importance.

In the story before us, Terah made one choice, and Abram made another. They all set out from Ur to go into the land of Canaan, and they all tarried at Haran, but Terah got no further ; he died there ; and after his death Abram went on into Canaan.

This warns us of *the possible tragedy of losing desire*. The path of the life of multitudes is littered with purposes unfulfilled, with resolutions unredeemed. Everyone at conversion purposes to go into the land of Canaan, that is, to enter into God's best for them ; but, alas, there are plenty of Christians who, when they see the threatening river in front of them, and " realize how completely the other side of it is separated from all that is familiar, take another thought, and conclude that they have come far enough, and that Haran will serve their turn." Of such was Solomon, whose " heart was turned from the Lord God of Israel, who had appeared unto Him twice." and of such was Demas, who forsook Paul, " having loved this present world." And of such are all who are half-hearted and faint-hearted ; who will not step out until they can see the path clearly ; who drop the wider scheme of life when they see that a narrower one will serve their purpose. But let it be clearly understood that Haran must be abandoned if Canaan is to be reached. For earthly gains men make great sacrifices, yet too many Christians think that they can reach high ends without sacrificing lower and rival aims. But if we are to run the race that is set before us, we must lay aside every weight, and the easily besetting sin, and follow at the heels of Christ.

92

This brings us to the third point in our text,

III. A JOYFUL REALISATION. Many begin the journey, but few finish it. This, however, should be known, that " the Christian life is the only one which has no failures, no balked efforts, no frustrated aims, no brave settings out and defeated returnings." Abram and his company set out to go into the land of Canaan, and " into the land of Canaan they came."

For us, as for Abram, the secret of entering in, is *glad submission to the divine will.* This means separation from much to which we naturally cling. For Abram it was from his country, his kindred, and his father's house ; and though it may not mean this for us, yet it will mean submission and separation. Christ still says : " Come out and be separate ; touch not the unclean thing, and I will receive you."

Prompt obedience to the divine word is also a condition of entering in, such obedience as Abram yielded when " he went out, not knowing whither he went." Prompt obedience is an unbending condition of entrance into the land of rest and victory. And this submission and obedience will lead, necessarily, to *complete confidence in the divine wisdom,* to unquestioning trust that what God has provided for us, is absolutely the best thing for us.

One further word. The reward of entering will be threefold. There will be *intimate fellowship with God.* Abram was called " the friend of God." All Christians are God's children, but not all are God's friends. Christ said, " Ye are my friends if ye do whatsoever I command you." All human friendships are based on mutual respect and understanding, but friendship with God is based on obedience. Another part of the reward of entering in, will be *increasing fruitfulness* in one's own soul. Abram's spiritual growth is clearly traceable until his faith is perfected on Mount Moriah ; and everyone who enters into the life of rest and victory in Christ will speedily grow in grace, and in the knowledge of things divine. And another result of this experience will be *inexhaustible fulness for others.* How great a blessing Abraham has been made to the whole world, just because he was " the Hebrew," which means, " the man from the other side." We cannot be made much of a blessing to anyone so long as we are on the wrong side of the river, but if we go over to the other side, if we become true Hebrews, we shall always have an overflow to meet the needs of others.

The revelation is clear, and the resolution may have been made, but have we realized it ; has our purpose been accomplished ; have our aspirations materialized ? If not yet, why not now?

In the quiet of this evening let us say to Him who is nearer to us than our breath—" Lord, I will follow Thee whithersoever Thou goest."

Who ordered Gideon forth
    To storm the invader's camp,
With arms of little worth,
    A pitcher and a lamp ?
The trumpets made his coming known,
And all the host was overthrown.

Oh ! I have seen the day
    When with a single word,
God helping me to say,
    " My trust is in the Lord,"
My soul hath quelled a thousand foes,
Fearless of all that could oppose.

But unbelief, self-will,
    Self-righteousness and pride,
How often do they steal
    My weapon from my side !
Yet David's lord and Gideon's friend
Will help His servant to the end.

WILLIAM COWPER.

TUESDAY,
July 16th, 1946.

10 a.m. **Bible Reading.**

FOUR CHAPTERS OF CHRISTIAN EXPERIENCE.

(*ii*) A CHAPTER OF TRANSFORMATION—EPHESIANS 2.

THE REV. GUY H. KING.

11.45 a.m. **Forenoon Meeting.**

NO MORE JACOB, BUT ISRAEL.

THE REV. RONALD J. PARK.

HONOURING GOD'S HOLY NAME.

THE REV. GORDON M. GUINNESS.

3 p.m. **Afternoon Meeting.**

ACCESS INTO THE HEAVENLIES.

DR. DONALD G. BARNHOUSE.

7.45 p.m. **Evening Meeting.**

THROW DOWN . . . AND BUILD.

THE REV. J. DUNLOP.

STEPS TO HOLINESS.

THE REV. H. W. CRAGG.

Heart Searchings.

MORE kindly weather favoured the Convention on Tuesday than on any other day of the week. The dawn was overcast, but by the time we were wending our way to the prayer meetings there was promise of improvement, which was soon afterwards fulfilled. It was not a brilliant day, but dry—except for an afternoon shower—and with some half-hearted sunshine.

The sun, was, however, smiling its benediction as the tent filled up for the Bible Reading. The Rev. Guy H. King had begun on Monday by likening himself to the Chancellor of the Exchequer on Budget Day, as he opens his despatch box in the House of Commons, with all eyes upon him, and all wondering what surprises he will produce. Well, we knew now the theme of Mr. King's Bible Readings, and the first had created great expectation and zest for the rest. The second of the Four Chapters of Christian Experience was " A Chapter of Transformation—Ephesians 2." Four stages in the transformation of a child of wrath into a child of God, were indicated—from the dead, by the grace, through the peace, into the fellowship. Very graphically, Mr. King depicted the terrible condition of the unsaved—dead in trespasses and sins ; and how deliverance therefrom is possible only through identification with Christ in His death and burial and resurrection. Of God's grace, he spoke with moving eloquence, pointing out that the word has three meanings : God's assistance, His attribute, and His attitude. This wondrous grace is apprehended through faith—which is not a thing of the head but of the heart and of the hand, reaching out and taking hold ; it is also a thing of habit—an habitual attitude following upon the initial act.

At the meeting which followed, the Rev. Ronald J. Park, speaking at Keswick for the first time, re-told the story of Jacob as a parable of resolution, renunciation, and reconsecration ; and the Rev. Gordon M. Guinness, who also was one of this year's new speakers, gave the second address, on holiness in daily life and conduct, through the inworking of the Holy Spirit.

The first sunny afternoon since the beginning of the Convention must have been a great inducement to many to enjoy a walk on the hills or by the lake ; so it was a great tribute to Dr. Barnhouse that the tent was practically full for the second of his studies in the Epistle to the Ephesians, in which he discussed the way of access into " the heavenlies." The Rev. J. T. Carson presided over this meeting. He is one of the members of the recently-formed Keswick Council, and a member of the Committee of the Portstewart Convention—the North of Ireland " Keswick."

Another of the new speakers, the Rev. J. Dunlop—like Mr. Carson, a minister of the Church of Ireland, and Chairman of the Committee of the Portstewart Convention—gave the first address in the evening, on the command of the angel to Gideon, to throw down the altar of Baal, and erect an altar to God. Mr. Dunlop, who had made a very favourable impression with his first address, on Monday morning, spoke movingly of the havoc wrought in lives by the toleration of " idol altars," and he pointed out that the destruction of them is in order to construction—the building of the altar of the Lord. The Rev. H. W. Cragg, also speaking at Keswick for the first time, followed up this address very appropriately, with a message on Rom. 6 : 22, " Being made free from sin, and become servants to God, ye have your fruit unto holiness." It indicates, he said, something to be broken—sin ; something to be bound—the servant ; something to become—holy. He explained in simple terms the great truth of identification with Christ in His Death and resurrection, and went on to point out that when we see to the breaking and the binding, the Lord will see to the becoming : the fruit-bearing will be sure.

Four Chapters of Christian Experience

(*ii*) A Chapter of Transformation—Ephesians 2.

By the Rev. GUY H. KING.

WHAT an amazingly wonderful Epistle this is from which our chapter is taken. It lifts us right up, to consider our relationship with God, *in the Heavenlies*; but it ends by bringing us right down, to consider our relationship with our fellows, *in the earthlies*; nor does it allow us to forget our relationship with our enemy, *in the worldlies*. It is, as an Epistle, at once sublimely spiritual and particularly practical; while the chapter which we are just now to consider is exquisitely beautiful—especially in the great transformation that it portrays as having taken place in the conditions and circumstances of its readers, whether " ye " Gentiles of verse 2, or " we " Jews of verse 3. The passage is so free, so exalted, that there is little evidence that it was penned in imprisonment : verily, it is its own best illustration of the truth it propounds that, whatever the circumstances of our earthly environment, we may, in the words of the ancient Ascension Day prayer, " in heart and mind thither ascend, and with Him continually dwell." Let us, then, carefully and prayerfully, study our portion, and note the four stages of the grand transformation scene : and we begin—

I. From the Dead.

" You . . . were dead in trespasses and sins," are among the opening words, and that dread thought is the theme of the first seven verses ; and as we observe these who " walked " (v. 2) life's way as dead men, we are called, to begin with, to mark (*i*) *The Course* they pursued. Three things characterise it. (*a*) *It is " according to the course of this world.*" They were " in the world"; unlike Christians they were " of " the world (John 17 : 16)—so they naturally followed the course of the world : of *course* they did ! We should expect nothing else. What does surprise us is that so many of us Christians follow the same course—looking at things from no other than the world's point of view, calculating success by no other than the world's standard, regulating conduct by no other than the world's code, seeking satisfaction from no other than the world's sources. There seems to be a woeful lack of the conception and practice of that " separation " which the New Testament so constantly, and, indeed, so urgently emphasises. We may have our own views and opinions about this matter ; but I think there can be no question what is the Bible attitude. The only question is whether we will go the Bible way, or our own way. How much, I wonder, of the Church's sad prevalence of weakness of testimony, ineffectiveness of service, and poorness of experience, is traceable to this widespread absence of " all-out-ness " for God ? " There is no need to stand stiffly aloof from men, or to adopt an irritating air of fancied superiority : that was not the manner of Him who, in Hebrews 7 : 26, is described as " separate from sinners." Paul, I suspect, was no bad " mixer," but he was a " separated " man—" separated unto (for this is a positive quality, and not merely negative) the Gospel of God," as he tells us in Romans 1 : 1. People sometimes call us " narrow "—but, of course, it is they, not we, who are narrow ; their horizon is bounded by the world, they can see no further than now, and here. How dreadfully narrow-minded the so-called broad-minded people are ! But, to return to the worldling, he is naturally restricted in outlook and behaviour, and the Ephesian Christians were once as blind as they, with no hope or scope beyond " this world."

Another point about this manner of life is mentioned, (b) It is " *according to the prince of the power of the air*." It is a most striking *volte-face* in so much of modern theology that, whereas, shall we say, twenty years ago the fashion was to speak and think of a *principle of evil*, we have now returned to the conception of *a personal devil*. That is certainly the view of the Scriptures, from end to end—" when the tempter (not the ' temptation ' merely) came to Him," that phrase of Matthew 4 : 3 represents the teaching of the whole Bible. This sinister personality is a " prince "—here " of the power of the air " ; in John 14 : 30, " of this world." He wields mysteriously acquired, but divinely recognised, authority. He is at the back of all that is sinful, or anti-godly, in " this world " ; he is " the spirit that now worketh "—infinitely subtle, eternally alert, to work his wicked will. Miss Ruth Paxson says, " He is . . . the ruler of the realm of evil, which has two spheres of activity : the air, the abode of evil spirits ; and the earth, the abode of unregenerate men. This prince is the No. 1 public enemy of the whole universe." And to think that, until they were converted, these Ephesians, and we too, were, whether consciously or not, under his control ; if he so wished, at his beck and call. Indeed, he desires also to " have " believers as well, as he did Peter and his fellows, in Luke 22 : 31. It is a dreadful thought that even Christians could be the tools of the devil. Oh, how urgent is the exhortation of Hebrews 12 : 13, " Make straight paths for your feet, lest that which is lame be turned out of the way." Well, you see, both the world and the devil are about the path of the " dead " travellers on life's road ; but, there is more yet—the triumvirate of evil is completed, in this description of his life, (c) It is " *in the lusts of your flesh*." The late Bishop Handley Moule has a note that the " flesh," in St. Paul, means " either the state of the unregenerate being, in which state the sinful principle dominates, or the state of that element of the regenerate being in which the principle, dislodged, as it were, from the centre, still lingers and is felt ; not dominant in the being, but present." Like as in the bowler's " wood," there is in all men a " bias," implanted into man's very make-up at the Fall : however it may want, and aim, to approximate to the white " jack " of holiness, there is always that innate tendency to wander away, unless the bias is counter-acted by the bowler. That old evil nature is not eradicated in the case of the Christian ; but it remains in him till the last—a spy in the castle, in league with the enemy without ; a quality within us which, as in that responsive property of steel that answers to the pull of the magnet, responds to temptation's lure. The only way to deal with it is by the counter-action of a stronger magnet—and we Christians have dwelling within us (I Cor. 6 : 19) that greater power. The secret of victory is, therefore, " walk in the Spirit, and ye shall not fulfil the lusts of the flesh " (Gal. 5 : 16). The unbelievers —among whom we once had our sad place—alas, have no such overcoming strength, and they just have to wage the hopeless battle in their own strength. Unfortunately, we Christians often fail and fall ; but we need not—whereas the others cannot help it.

Here, then, arrayed against us, is the wicked Triple Alliance—the world, the flesh, and the devil. In the old unregenerate days, when we were " even as others," we had no help to conquer ; but since we were born again we have had all the power of God Himself to keep us on the road, " all the attributes of Deity are now upon our side," as Dr. F. B. Meyer used to say. We have the Holy Trinity to oppose and over-master the unholy trinity. How needless it is, then, to be " overcome of evil " (Rom. 12 : 21). How dreadful it is to think of those old days when we had no such help to call upon, when we had to face the onslaught of temptation alone.

Such is how the way is described—the road of the unbeliever, the course he follows. See now how the wayfarer is described—and we " rejoice with trembling " (Psalm 2 : 11) as we recollect what God has delivered us from, for we, Ephesian Christians, or Modern Christians, were once in this dire company. (a) " Children of disobedience " (v. 2)— God has made known His will, has promulgated His law ; but man has preferred his own way (Isa. 53 : 6), has decided to do as he likes. To the divine " Thou shalt not," man, from Adam downward, has said, I will ; to the " Thou shalt," he has replied, I won't. As naughty children disregarding their parents' wishes ; as defaulting soldiers flouting their commander's orders ; as rebel subjects treating with their sovereign's enemies—so is the attitude of the unregenerate toward the Heavenly Father, Commander and King. For all their rebelliousness, Ezekiel 2 : 4 has another name for them, " impudent children ! " Let it never be forgotten that while sin is the depth of folly it is also the height of impudence. They were also, and therefore, (b) " Children of wrath " (v. 3)—of every unbeliever, every " child of disobedience," it is true that " the wrath of God abideth on him " (John 3 : 36). Some people seem to have the notion that Almighty God is just a benevolent and indulgent Father, who takes little notice of sin, and who, though He may *say* all sorts of stern things will not actually *do* anything very much about it. In our stress upon the love-side of God—and we can never emphasise that too much—we have tended latterly to overlook that other side of His Being. This is not a matter of the Old Testament conception of

God versus the New Testament view : no more loving words are spoken in the New than in some parts of the Old, no more stern utterances are found in the Old than in the New. When God incarnate walked this earth, He who spoke such loving and beautiful things, uttered at times such scathing and scorching words as made man wince ; His eyes which ran with pity for individual sorrow, or for a city's sin, could yet look " round about on them with anger," and drive the unholy desecrators from His fane (Mark 3 : 5 ; 11 : 17). The passage says they were children of wrath " by nature "—as Dr. Handley Moule puts it, " by the inward wrongness of our own condition, antecedent to the grace of God." As we look back, with shuddering recollection, to what by His sovereign grace, we have escaped, shall we not look with sacrificial pity upon those who, by their own unbelief, are still in that evil case ? Can anything, *anything*, ANYTHING, excuse a lack of evangelistic zeal, " that I might by all means save some " (I Cor. 9 : 22) ?

And now, having looked a little at the saved sinners' old course, let us give attention for a bit to (*ii*) *The Corner* they come to, for just here begins for them a complete transformation as our chapter gradually and gloriously unfolds. You notice that word " But," in verse 4 : it is, for me, always the corner word of Scripture—we have been traversing a certain road of a specific character, and then we have come to a "but," and we have there turned into a district wholly diverse from that through which we have just been travelling. Take Galatians 5 : 17-23, for instance : a passage which I love to call, " From the Slum to the Orchard." Those first verses form a terrible recital—in terms of house property, we should certainly describe then as a dreadful slum area ; " but "—and now we turn the corner, and are led straight into a list of beautiful virtues—what, in terms of horticulture, we should speak of as a most lovely orchard, with its nine varieties of fruit. How grand to turn that corner ; sometimes the order is reversed, and we move from good to bad, as in 2 Kings 5 : 1, " *but* he was a leper "—from a beautiful avenue to a wretched cul-de-sac.

Here, then, in our present chapter, we have it, and as we turn this corner, we realise what a great difference we are coming to. It will lead us (*a*) *From helplessness to hopefulness.* Those first three verses have been a truly depressing neighbourhood to be walking in, marked as they are by the wickedness of the unregenerate man's conduct, and the weakness of his character. He is in a terrible mess, and he cannot move a finger to help himself ; " but God . . ." : oh, there surely is hope there ? We never forget that " things which are impossible with men are possible with God " (Luke 18 : 27). One thinks instinctively of the salvation we cannot win, the service we cannot render, the sin we cannot conquer, the saint we cannot be—" but God ! " In that remarkable spy story in Numbers 13, ten of them said " we be not able " (v. 31), but two of them said, " we are well able " (v. 30) : the difference between them being that the miserable pessimists left God out, while the glorious optimists put God in—you cannot be a pessimist unless you leave God out ! Things could not possibly have looked blacker for the poor people of our verses here—" but God " ! An artist was once painting a picture of a house ; but the scene was the dead of night. He had put in the doors and windows, and other details, but you could not readily see them, everything was dimmed and blurred by the prevailing darkness—you never saw anything so dismal in all your life. But then the artist dipped his brush in some yellow colour and, with a deft stroke, he put a light into one of the windows. Instantly the whole picture was transformed : the eerie building became a house, warm, snug, cosy and welcoming. Our life was black and dark indeed—our past, black with sin ; our future, dark with judgment. But one happy day we were enabled to let Him in who is " the Light " (John 8 : 12), and that has meant complete transformation. We were helpless of ourselves—" but God." Hallelujah, we turned the corner ! That has meant, further, moving (b) *From His wrath to His wealth.* The Apostle seems to ransack the language to find words that can adequately convey the idea of His illimitable resources. He is (1) " rich in mercy," and Exodus 20 : 5, 6 assures us that while His wrath extends to the third, and even the fourth generation, His mercy runs to " thousands " of generations. Isaiah 28 : 21 tells us that wrath is " His strange work," while we learn from Micah 7 : 18 that " He delighteth in mercy." I have sometimes heard of Americans being dollar-millionaires, worth but a quarter of our own plutocrats ; but here is One who is a multi-millionaire in mercy. Then there is (2) " His great love wherewith He loved us," and it must, indeed, be unfathomably great if such a holy Being could look with anything other than repulsion upon such unholy beings as we, and could be prepared to spend His " precious blood " (I Peter 1 : 18, 19), in order to redeem us. And do not forget (3) " the exceeding riches of His grace " (v. 7), an immense deposit of Heavenly currency more than adequate to meet the tense situation of our moral and spiritual bankruptcy, and to supply the mountainous needs of our everyday life. " Grace there is my every debt to pay," even " Grace fathomless as the sea "—as the old choruses used to remind us. All His wealth, for all our weal. We were poverty-stricken paupers —" but God ! " Praise the Lord that we turned the corner.

So we continue to observe (iii) *The Contrast*—of the Christians' new way of life. We have already noted (a) *The unpromising start*—that they (that we all) were " dead in trespasses and sins " (vv. 1 and 5). Spiritually, they were still-born, " born in sins," born dead, and remaining so until they were " born again "—or inherited the dread alternative of " the second death." Once born, twice die ; twice born, once die—and not even that, if the Lord should return in our life-time, in which case we should be transfigured and translated. We find reference here, next, to (b) *The amazing steps*—of the believer's experience, in identification with his Lord. When the old Israelite placed his hand of trust, confessing his sin, upon the head of his sin-offering, God reckoned the offerer as then identified with his offering, and all that happened to the victim was accounted to the sinner—in it he died. So sings old Isaac Watts :—

> My faith would lay her hand
> On that dear head of Thine,
> While like a penitent I stand,
> And there confess my sin.

When we did that, God reckoned us as one " with Christ " (v. 5), and
" in Christ " (v. 6).   In that saving moment all that happened to Him
is, in God's plan, considered as having happened to us : (1) In His dying
we died—" crucified with Christ," as Galatians 2 : 20 has it.   " Have
been crucified "—so runs the Greek verb : it is a perfect tense, the thing
has taken place, and remains effective.   It is not something I look forward
to in the future ; it has already happened, in the reckoning of God,
consequent upon the identification of faith.   But that is not all, (2) In
His   rising   we   rose—" quickened   . . .   together   with   Christ "
(v. 5).   Let us joyfully accept and act upon God s reckoning : " Likewise reckon ye also yourselves to be dead indeed unto sin, but alive unto
God through Jesus Christ our Lord " (Rom. 6 : 11).   All the pulsating
freshness and energising vigour of the blessed truth should be our common
experience as we tread the road of life—" we should walk in newness of
life," and   " we should serve in newness of spirit " (Rom. 6 : 4 ;
7 : 6).   Oh, that by an early morning touch with Him we might experience
and exhibit that quality of " newness," freshness day by day ; and that
we might " know   . . .   the power of His resurrection " (Phil. 3 : 10).
And, do not forget that (3) In His ascending we ascended—He " hath
raised us up together, and made us sit together in Heavenly places in
Christ Jesus " (v. 6).   He " sat " in token that His work of full salvation
for His believing people was fully and finally accomplished (Heb. 1 : 3).
We, too, are to " sit," as it were, as those who are entering into the
enjoyment of the " finished " work ; we are not meant to busy ourselves
about fighting for daily victory and holiness—as we accepted eternal
salvation from the guilt of sin, so are we to accept daily salvation from its
power.   " This is the victory that overcometh   . . .   even our faith "
(I John 5 : 4)—not our fighting ! The battle is fought and won by Him
with whom we are identified ; He has sat down in the honoured place of
accomplished victory ; we are not to fight that battle all over again, on
our own account.   One Saturday evening many years ago a small boy
went up to a body of athletic looking young men as they emerged from a
railway train—it was the Portsmouth Football Club team returning from
an " away " match.   The youngster was evidently a privileged person,
and going up to his heroes, he asked the all-important question.   Then he
ran out to a group of his pals in the station yard, calling out as he ran,
" We've won ; we've won ! " We ? But, what had he done toward it ?
Nothing ; but, identifying himself with the victors, he felt included in
the victory.   Yes, that's it—in Him we've won : that is why He has
" made us sit together."   *What a distance* we, by faith, have travelled—
from the " in sin " of verse 5, to the " Heavenly places " of verse 6.
What a destination we have reached—" in the Heavenlies."   Five times

the phrase is used in this Epistle—1 : 3, 20 ; 2 : 6 ; 3 : 10 ; and 6 : 12—and we see it to be the sphere of triumph, of conflict, of blessing, of privilege, of vision (an order different from the references given). How changed things look as viewed from the heights of that Heavenly station and session—the way seems clearer, the work seems brighter. That is a great secret which we find in Canticles 4 : 8, " Look from the top." So, in pursuing the thought of the contrast, we see (c) *The wonderful sequel*—that " in the ages to come He might shew " (v. 7) what His " exceeding riches " have procured, in the exercise of His infinite " kindness " : His victory parade, when the war is finally over. How wonderful if, by His " grace," we can have contributed, in however insignificant a measure, to that display of His glory—yes, His glory alone. At that point we finish our study of these opening verses 1-7 of our chapter. From the Dead. From death—and such a death ; to life—and such a life. What a Transformation ! Brought about—

II. BY THE GRACE.

The wondrous transformation of which we have been speaking, and which is the theme of this whole chapter, is called here by that grand word " Saved " (vv. 5 and 8). All too often we have restricted that word within narrow limits which the New Testament does not impose. We have seemed to suppose that salvation is an entirely negative thing, whereas it is gloriously positive, too. We are not merely saved *from* but also saved *to*. The Old Testament has a sentence which puts the matter very truly, where it says, " He brought us out . . . that He might bring us in " (Deut. 6 : 23). It is grandly true that He brings us from our Egypt of sin's guilt and doom and bondage ; but, let us never forget the other side, that He brings us into our Canaan of salvation's multitudinous and multifarious blessings.

Another point that needs to be borne in mind is that the word and thought of salvation are used variously in the New Testament of a past, a present, or a future experience. (a) *Sometimes it refers to the future*—as in Romans 13 : 11, " Now is our salvation nearer than when we believed " ; then we shall be saved even from the very presence of sin. (b) *Sometimes it refers to the present*—as in I Corinthians 1 : 18, " unto us which are (being) saved it is the power of God " : day by day we are being saved from sin's power. (c) *Sometimes it refers to the past*—as here in our verses, " by grace are ye saved " : we have actually been saved from sin's penalty. In this aspect of the matter, we are not left in a state of uncertainty, hoping that one day we shall find that it is all right, the thing is already done. " He that heareth My word, and believeth on Him that sent Me, hath (C. H. Spurgeon used to say H.A.T.H. spells Got it !) everlasting life, and shall not come into judgment ; but is passed from death unto life " (John 5 : 24). Even from such a death, even unto such a life—as we saw a little earlier. We are saved : it is a *fait accompli*. Praise God !

Now we are to see that (i) *The Origin is of God*—it is " by grace." Here again is a word of three meanings. (a) *God's assistance*—Paul uses.

105

it thus in I Corinthians 15 : 10, " By the grace of God I am what I am
. . . I laboured more abundantly than they all : yet not I, but the
grace of God which was with me." Here grace is the great life changer :
what I am ; and the great life charger : what I do. What an inspiriting
reflection it is that the same grace is available, in all its sufficiency, for all
believers. We also, by that same means, can be and do all that God
requires. I mentioned C. H. Spurgeon just now. He tells of one occasion
on which, during his tram journey home to Clapham, he was disturbed
by a certain harassing problem. As he sat there, pondering, the words
of 2 Corinthians 12 : 9, " My grace is sufficient for thee," came into his
mind ; and then he seemed to be transported to the bank of a flowing
river. Presently, he espied a little fish, drinking away ; but all of a sudden
it stopped and said, " I mustn't take too much, or there'll be none left."
The river replied " Drink on, little fish, my waters are sufficient for thee."
Then, said Mr. Spurgeon, I was standing beside one of Joseph's great
granaries in Egypt ; and a little mouse feeding there, stopped his meal,
" I mustn't eat too much now, or there'll not be enough for to-morrow."
But the storehouse answered, " Feed on, little mouse, my grain is sufficient
for thee." Next our famous preacher found himself atop of a great
mountain, where was a man filling his lungs with the refreshing, in-
vigorating air ; but he stayed, " I must be careful not to use up too much
oxygen, or there'll be no supply for future needs." And the vast mountain
amusingly replied, " Breathe on, little man, my winds are sufficient for
thee." Upon this, the great Baptist said that he was brought back with
a bump, to his tram, his trouble, and his text, " My grace is sufficient
for thee." Yes, we know it so well, theoretically ; but oh, that we might
practically act upon the blessed truth of it, and so enjoy God's active
aid. The word also means (b) God's attribute—His quality of graciousness. We see that use in Acts 4 : 33, where " with great power gave
the apostles witness of the resurrection of the Lord Jesus : and great
grace was upon them all." I have known powerful preachers who, alas,
greatly limited their effectiveness because they were strangely lacking in
this gift of graciousness. How greatly we all need it ; and how powerful
an instrument of blessing it is. The third meaning is the one here in
our chapter, (c) God's attitude—instead of assuming toward us an air of
judgment, which He must eventually adopt if people continue to reject
His mercy, He comes to us in loving kindness, and acts toward us in
a manner wholly unmerited by us, a way of undeserved favour. It is
out of that attitude that all our hope of salvation, of transformation,
springs : if we were treated just as we deserve, we should indeed have no
hope. Thank God, " in His kindness toward us through Christ Jesus "
(v. 7) we have every hope—and every blessing ; but, underline it, it is
all of His grace.

Note then, (ii) The One thing asked of us—" through faith." Seeing
how much hangs upon this matter of salvation, both for life here and for
the life hereafter, it is of supreme importance that we know what is our
part of the life-giving transaction. Here it is, then : Faith. Now this
saving faith is (a) Not a thing of the Head—the sort of belief which is no

106

more than a mental acceptance of, or intellectual acquiescence in, a statement. Mere orthodoxy of belief will not secure this mighty boon— " the devils also believe, and tremble " (James 2 : 19), but remain devils still. No, it is no quality of the mind that this " faith " connotes, (b) *But a thing of the Heart*—it is a movement out from the depths of our being, a movement constrained perhaps, by a deep sense of need, because of our sin, or, perchance, by a deep sense of gratitude, because of our Saviour's love. Faith is the outcome of a heart strangely moved thus to act, (c) *And a thing of the Hand*—for it is the soul reaching out, and taking hold. A strong rope is thrown to a drowning man, he stretches out his hand and lays hold, and so is he saved. Not a rope, but a hand, is what is offered to drowners in the sea of sin—a pierced hand, but a hand so strong : " Behold my hands . . ." If we would be saved we must stretch out to grasp it, " . . . and reach hither thy hand " (John 20 : 27). That is saving faith : though it is not faith that saves us, faith is only the link (and the only link) that joins us to Him who does save us. A little party of men were climbing a Swiss mountain with a guide. Presently, they came to a crevasse which they must cross to get to the top. To inexperienced mountaineers it was a fearsome spot : but they did so greatly long to attain the summit. The guide first leapt across, and then, stretching out his hand, he encouraged the men to grasp it and trust him. Somewhat fearfully, they all did—except one, who again and again drew back and hesitated. At last the guide made his appeal to him still more urgent : once more stretching his hand out to him he said, " For thirty years I have been helping men and women across that gap, and I've never let one go yet," at which the timid one risked all and was safely landed. If we are ever to reach the Heaven up there, we must cross that crevasse of sin. Maybe, some even here now have hesitated, fearing to take the step, and the Guide and Saviour reaches out and says, " For many more than thirty years I have been helping men and women across that gap, and I've never let one go yet ! " Faith is our hand going into His—our grip may be feeble : no matter, His is so strong, and His is the one that saves, ours is only the necessary connection. Many years ago it was said by someone at Keswick that the simple meaning of Faith is—Forsaking All I Take Him. Yes, the hand ; and, lastly, it is (d) *Also a thing of the Habit*—a habitual attitude following upon the initial act. As the Christian life begins by faith, so it proceeds by faith, right on to the end—" We walk by faith " (2 Cor. 5 : 7).

Do you think that the words in verse 8, " and that not of yourselves : it is the gift of God " refer to faith ? Personally, with all diffidence, I suggest not—and that on the ground of the grammar of the Greek. The word for " faith " is feminine gender, and the rules surely require that the pronoun " that " shall be of the same gender. But it is neuter ; and this, I think, warrants the conclusion that it is not the " faith " that is here said to be the gift of God, but the whole fact of salvation. Moreover, the phrase, " not of yourselves " seems to be in apposition to " not of works," which latter certainly refers to the salvation, not to the faith. If you still feel that faith is the gift of God, you might perhaps find support for it in, shall we say, Philippians 1 : 29 ; but I venture to submit that it is risky to base it on this verse.

Before we take temporary leave of this " Grace," let us speak of (*iii*) *The Outcome in our lives*—" unto good works " (v. 10). The Apostle has been careful to stress that our salvation is " not of works " (v. 9) : it is not to be secured by any earnest strivings of ours, not to be purchased by any good deeds of ours—" lest any man should boast " that it is our own doings and deserts. But having got that clear, we are next invited to consider that our salvation is " unto good works." What we are is " His workmanship," not our own—" it is He that hath made us and not we ourselves," as Psalm 100 : 3 tells us ; and if that is true physically, it is double true spiritually of all who have been " created in Christ Jesus." This, then, is (*a*) *The expression of our faith*—the outward evidence that it is there. James 2 : 20 says that " faith without works is dead " ; Titus 2 : 14 says that His redeemed people are to be " zealous of good works " ; and Titus 3 : 8, after emphasising again that our salvation is " not by works of righteousness which we have done " (v. 5), says " These things I will that thou affirm constantly, that they which have believed in God might be careful to maintain good works." Such things, such behaviour, are, after all, but the natural outcome of our having faith and having life. And so it is (*b*) *The expectation of our God*—" which God hath before ordained that we should walk in them." If a man create a pick-axe, a cricket-bat, a fountain-pen, you know that before making them, he ordained their certain good works to be performed —that is why he made them. Even so may we be sure that when God made us Christians, He did it with the expectation that we should do Christian things. Grace—faith—salvation—works : that is the natural sequence, and the true order. Let us now proceed to the next step in the progression of this wonderful chapter—

III. THROUGH THE PEACE.

As we turn to verses 11-18 (*i*) *We find a State of War*. We see it first (*a*) *In human antagonism*—between the Jew, the Circumcision, and the, to him, despised Gentiles, all of every such race being lumped together under the one uncomplimentary title, Uncircumcision. Yet, the Jew's was no fancied superiority : it was, by divine providence, a very real thing. He had been most highly privileged—he enjoyed a " commonwealth," a spiritual state, to which the Gentiles were " aliens " ; he was inheritor of " covenants," gracious compacts and glorious promises, to which the Gentiles were " strangers " ; he had a divine " hope " in the world, of which the Gentiles were bereft. These Ephesians were not without gods, as any knowledge of their ways will show, but they were " without God." In that, above all else, lay their inferiority to the Jews. Alas, that in these latter, the true superiority developed into scorn and antagonism—mutually exhibited. But, worse still, we see it (*b*) *In divine estrangement*—if Jew and Gentile were at enmity, they shared at least one thing in common : they were both alike at enmity against the Lord, they were each of them " without Christ." The Master himself

made it plain that " He that is not with Me is against Me " (Matt. 12 : 30) ;
but, thank God, as Romans 5 : 6 -10 tells us, it was not only " when we
were yet without strength," to save or help ourselves, and " while we
were yet sinners," with nothing to commend us to God, but even " when
we were enemies," that He moved to our salvation.

So here, (*ii*) *We see an Act of Peace.* " But now . . ." : there is
that corner again ! And what a transformation it introduces us to—from
the ways of war to the paths of peace ; once, there was animosity " but
now," there is amity. We notice, (*a*) *The Person*—" for He is our
peace." It is fascinating to see how, all the way through, our blessings
are not so much in things, but in a Person. He not only secures our
salvation, but He is it—" I *am* thy Salvation " (Psa. 35 : 3). He not only
shows the way, but He is it—" I *am* the way " (John 14 : 6). He not
only opens the door, but He is it—" I *am* the door " (John 10 : 7). He
not only gives the bread, but He is it—" I *am* the bread of life " (John
6 : 35). So now, He not only wins the peace, but He is it—" He *is* our
peace " ; or, as Micah 5 : 5 has it, " This man shall be the peace." After
all, things cannot satisfy persons. But this Person does satisfy all persons.
Look next, at (*b*) *The Performance*—what is this peace which He, in His
own person, has effected ? Well, it seems to be twofold, looking in two
directions. (1) " *Both one* " (v. 14). The late Dean Armitage Robinson
has said, " Mankind had started as one in the orginal Creation. But in
the course of the world's history . . . a division had come in. Mankind was now two and not one. There was the privileged Jew, and there
was the unprivileged Gentile. It was the glory of grace to bring the two
once more together as one in Christ. A new start was thus made in the
world's history. St. Paul called it a new creation." There in the world
were those two, dwelling apart—the " nigh " and the " far off " (vv. 13,
17). And there was a " middle wall of partition " between them. There
was indeed, symbolising this distinction of race, an actual and literal
wall in the Area of the Temple—it separated off the outer Court of the
Gentiles from all the other Courts of the Jews—the Court of the (Jewish)
Women, the Court of the Sons of Israel, the Court of the Priests. In the
separating wall, leading from the Gentiles' enclosure into the Jews' Courts,
were several openings, through which Jews would pass within ; but at
these entrances were affixed notices warning Gentiles against proceeding
further. They were written in Greek and Latin, one of which languages
would be known by all Gentiles of the period ; not in Hebrew, because
Jews would not need to heed the warning: they were allowed, and expected,
in. One of these very notices was discovered in 1871, during excavations,
and is to-day in the Constantinople Museum. It is written in Greek and
runs : " No man of another nation to enter within the fence and enclosure
round the temple. And whoever is caught will have himself to blame
that his death ensues." Now Christ, by His death for both, has broken
down this dividing wall, and, by embracing in His love each of the two,
has made " in Himself of twain one new man, so making peace " (v. 15).
Peace as between man and man. Henceforth it is neither Jew nor
Gentile, but " all one in Christ Jesus " (Gal. 3 : 28). Real Christians of

all races, all conditions, all sects, all denominations, are " all one " in Him. The other aspect of His peace performance is (2) *"both unto God"* (v. 16). It is not only that man is, in Him, reconciled to man ; but that both (men) are reconciled unto God. And, indeed, this comes first, the other growing out of it. Says Bishop Handley Moule, " The wounds of the crucifixion, for those who have become ' one body ' with the Crucified, have been the death-wounds first of ' the enmity ' of the unpardoned rebel towards his blessed King, and then, and so, of the enmity of the unhumbled and unchanged human heart towards fellow men." But, what of (c) *The Price* of this peace ? Was it a thing easily, and cheaply secured ? Was it effected just by the fiat of Almighty God ? " God said, Let there be light : and there was light " (Gen. 1 : 3). Was it just that way here ? Did He say, " Let there be salvation," and there was salvation ? He could have done so ; but, while there would, in that case, have been power to bring it to pass, there would have been no justice in the transaction—and that would have been to contradict His character, which, of course, He could not do. " He cannot deny Himself," says 2 Timothy 2 : 13. His Word must depend on His work, and that in turn, on His worth. If this blest, saving, reconciliation is to be effected, there is a price to pay ; and what a price ! " By the blood," says our verse 13. " By the Cross," as verse 16 has it. " The precious Blood," says 1 Peter 1 : 19—precious, not merely to us, though it is ever so ; but precious to God, of infinite value in His sight and reckoning. We spoke of it in some detail in our Chapter of Foundation, for it is, in truth, fundamental to all else.

And now, following at once upon this act of peace, in verse 17, (*iii*) *We hear a Message of Love.* To quote again beloved Handley Moule of ever fragrant memory, " When the work of propitiation and peace was effected by the great Peace-maker, He rose up to be the Messenger of His own blessings." " He came and preached peace " (v. 7). Listen to Him on that first Easter evening, having but three days come from the Cross, and but a few hours from the grave, speaking His message, " Peace unto you " (John 20 : 19, 21, 26). Oh, I know that it was the common Hebrew greeting, the formal salutation of the time—but nothing was merely formal when He said it, nothing was ever common when He used it. Many said it ; but no one ever said it as He did : in His lips it took on such meaning, such reality, such fullness. To that little hill He went—to make peace ; to that upper room, then, He came—to announce peace. To us He has granted the amazing privilege of also taking that reconciling message to a distracted, and often distraught, world. He is " the Prince of peace " ; we are " the ambassadors of peace " (Isa. 9 : 6 ; 33 : 7). It is, as He brings it, and gives it, (*a*) *A message for the Whole World*—" to you which were afar off," you Gentiles, at so great a distance, until God spanned the gulf through His love and cross, to reach you, and touch you, and fetch you Home to Himself ; and " to them that were nigh " (v. 17), those Jews who, because of the revelation of God that they already had, were " not far from the kingdom," like the scribe of Mark 12 : 34. Yes, to Jew and Gentile alike, the reconciling Word has gone forth : all the world

110

is embraced within the wide compass of the saving declaration. It is also, if I may put it so, (b) *A message from the Whole Deity*—Each Holy Person of the Blessed Trinity is concerned for our peace, and each involved in the purchase and procuring of it. Jew and Greek, "we both have access" into His very presence ; but that is only because Triune Grace has opened the way. (a) It is "through" Him, the Son—for, as John 10 : 7 reminds us, He is "the door" ; (b) It is "by" Him, the One Spirit—for He is the Usher who leads us in through the door into the Presence Chamber ; (c) It is "unto" Him, the Heavenly Father—for He is the Goal to whom our souls have earnestly aspired.

Oh, wonderful, wonderful transformation : once outside, but now brought in to enjoy all the privileges of the Family ; once at war, like the rebels that we were, but now at peace ; once far off—whether for the Gentile, dispensationally distant from the privileged Jews, or whether for the unbeliever, wasting his substance in the "far country" (Luke 15 : 13) of sin—but now brought near, and allowed habitually to "draw near" (Heb. 10 : 22). There is one further thought, to complete the study of our great chapter, a thought of exceeding importance, yet one which has of late years rather tended to drop out of the consideration of us Evangelical Christians. It is the thought, that, having been rescued from the death of sin, by the grace of love, through the peace with God, we are, as one great issue of all this, introduced—

IV. INTO THE FELLOWSHIP.

That, I suggest, is the theme of the last four verses of this chapter. Salvation is a lone matter ; we are each saved by himself individually ; even in this sense, though it is not the sense of the passage in Isaiah 27 : 12, "ye shall be gathered one by one." But when that has happened, we are not intended to remain alone—we are now brought into a Body, a Church, a Society, a Family. I am persuaded that one of the things which we Christians have to try to recapture in these days is the sense of the fellowship. The men of our Fighting Services have found in the war a great comradeship, and they so greatly miss it when they are demobilised : many of them are somewhat wistfully wondering whether there is any such brotherly friendship to be had in the Church.

> Blest be the tie that binds
> Our hearts in Christian love.

We so often sing it ; but, alas, all too often the love-knot has worked loose, even become untied altogether. That is the outer aspect of the matter ; the inner, deeper, thing is the actual fact, so little translated into practice, that we are, all we Christians, bound together in a new and wonderful way—if only we would realise it, and act upon it in relationship with our fellow believers.

Well now, these Christians, to whom this Epistle is addressed, had been, until the whole utter transformation had taken place, "strangers and foreigners" (v. 19)—but now, they are that "no more" ; now they are in the fellowship. With what a remarkable series of figures is the character and quality of that fellowship here depicted. Let us look into some of the phrases employed—

"*Fellow-citizens with the saints*"—here is the social nature of the fellowship, of which we have already spoken. When we were born we became citizens of our earthly country ; when we were born again we became citizens of the heavenly country and city. When writing to Philippi, which was very proud of being a Roman colony, and which would, as Dr. Plummer has said, be very appreciative of any reference to her citizenship of the Imperial State, Paul speaks of that matter in 1 : 27 and in 3 : 20, R.V. He puts it, in the latter passage, that " Our citizenship is in Heaven " ; and in the former verse he exhorts us to see that our demeanour and behaviour are worthy of such a Fatherland. That implies that ours is not a sole membership, but a social membership : we are not only citizens, but " fellow-citizens "—sharing citizen rights and privileges, as well as citizen duties and responsibilities, with all " the saints." That happy and blessed company comprises Jews and Gentiles alike—all who, from all nationalities, have, by grace, received their supernaturalisation papers of inclusion on the citizen-roll of the Kingdom of Heaven.

" *Of the household of God* "—here is the spiritual nature of the fellowship. The Head of the household is, of course, the Father Himself ; the members of the household derive their life from Him, and gather around His heavenly hearth and home ; theirs are the family interests, and the family resources, and the family duties, and the family pleasures, and the family relationships, and the family meals. How sad it is to see, as, alas, we sometimes do, one member cutting and snubbing, or ignoring, or injuring, or slandering, or quarrelling with another. We are often minded to repeat the counsel of Abram to Lot, " Let there be no strife . . . for we be brethren " (Gen. 13 : 8). We Christians are expected to be kind and helpful to all ; but we have a special call to be considerate to all who are, like ourselves, in the family—" As we have therefore opportunity, let us do good to all men, especially unto them who are of the household of faith " (Gal. 6 : 10).

" *Built upon the foundation* "—here is the stable nature of the fellowship. Many an earthly fellowship falls to the ground because it is flimsily based ; but, thank God, none can allege that of us. As Paul writes to Timothy (2 Tim. 2 : 19), after speaking of those who are " overthrown," " Nevertheless the foundation of God standeth sure." What is this foundation of which the apostle speaks to-day in our chapter ? (*a*) " *The apostles and prophets* "—that is, the teaching that they were divinely inspired and appointed to give. The prophets here are, doubtless, not those of the Old Testament but of the New—as in Ephesians 3 : 5, " it is now revealed unto His holy apostles and prophets," and Ephesians 4 : 11, " He gave some, apostles ; and some, prophets . . ." Such teaching, for example, as that concerning the absolute Deity of Christ, which His apostle and prophet Peter uttered at Cæsarea Philippi, and of which He said " Upon this rock (feminine, indicating the doctrine ; if it had meant the person, Peter, it would have been masculine) I will

Of all ages, of all denominations, and from all parts of the country—and very many from overseas, including several hundred missionaries representing a large number of societies and spheres of missionary activity—Christian people gather to Keswick to hear, in what is probably the largest tent in the world, the message of "full salvation."

[Photo : Abraham

In the Speakers' house-party at the Manor Hotel were, reading from the top left, Prebendary Colin C. Kerr, the well-known Vicar of S. Paul's, Portman-square; Mr. J. Taylor-Thompson, a member of the recently-formed Keswick Council; the Revs. Ronald J. Park, Kenneth Hooker—also a member of the Council, and leader of this year's young people's instructional meetings—G. M. Guinness, and A. T. Houghton and Mr. F. Mitchell. On the left of the middle row is Mr. H. J. Jaeger of the *Sunday School Times* of Philadelphia, who accompanied Dr. Barnhouse on this recent tour through Africa; the Revs. Guy H. King, who gave the Bible Readings, Dr. Donald G. Barnhouse, Dr. W. Graham Scroggie, W. H. Aldis, Chairman of the Council, and W. W. Martin; Mr. C. H. M. Foster and Mr. A. W. Bradley, Hon. Secretary and Hon. Treasurer respectively. In the front are the Revs. H. W. Cragg, J. Dunlop and J. T. Carson—both from Ulster, and the latter a member of the Council, and W. H. Rowdon, who led the open-air meetings nightly in the Market-place.

[Photo, the Authors.

Plate I.]

build My Church " (Matt. 16 : 18). No person (no "religion," or sect) has any right to the name of Christian who does not unequivocally hold this doctrine. To those who have the citizenship, who belong to the fellowship, who are in the family, in the Church, this is foundation truth, (*b*) "*Jesus Christ Himself being the chief corner stone*"—the great stone in the angle of the substructure, where the walls meet, their mighty bond of Unity, as Handley Moule puts it. Isaiah 28 : 16 has " Behold, I lay in Zion for a foundation a . . . corner stone," where the LXX version has " among the foundations," giving the idea not of the apex, but of the basis. Down there, Jew and Gentile are joined together in Him ; deep down, all Christian doctrines converge in Him, and emerge on Him. How firm and sure is the resting-place of the fellowship to which, by His transforming grace, we belong.

"*Fitly framed together*"—here is the symmetrical nature of the fellowship. A place for everybody, and everybody in his place—small stones and great stones ; square stones and round stones ; smooth stones and jagged stones ; seen stones and hidden stones : all of them " living " stones, for they have all come by faith to trust and touch and take Him—" to whom coming, as unto a living stone . . . ye also, as living stones, are built up a spiritual house " (1 Pet. 2 : 4, 5). Each of us, then, in this living Church, has his part to play—not all the same part and function, but all some part and function, as 1 Corinthians 12 so vividly makes clear. Some boys were playing about an area where building operations were taking place, all sorts of cast-off materials were lying about. Standing up against a wall they found a shaped piece of wood which would come in splendidly for the bonfire they had just lit ; but when they went to get it they found a word heavily chalked on it, " Wanted "—so they left it alone. It was meant for some place in the building—to be " fitly framed together " with the other components of that structure ; but it very nearly came to grief, because it had not taken its place. My friends, we may be as insignificant as a mere piece of wood, but we are " wanted," and shaped to play a " fit " part, and only in the fellowship of the other pieces can we play that part—but have we taken our place yet ? Let us ask the Master Builder to shew us our place, to " frame " us in, and to help us to fit smoothly with all our fellows.

" *An holy temple in the Lord* "—here is the sanctified nature of the fellowship. The word used for this temple is the specially holy one of two. In Jerusalem, the whole precinct of the Temple buildings was holy, the lesser word ; but the holy house itself was peculiarly holy, the higher word. It is this latter word that is used here. The whole fellowship of the building is a holy temple, but be it remembered that each brick is also a holy temple. " What ? " says the apostle, and the form of the Greek is so emphatic as to suggest uttermost surprise that any Christian could be unaware of this, " know ye not that your body is the temple of the Holy Ghost who is in you ? " (1 Cor. 6 : 19). They had been sadly desecrating the temple—which, in the very nature of the case, they ought not to have done, and, indeed, need not have done, because the Holy One was there within, their reason for holiness, and their power for holiness, if they would but rely on Him. Is it needful, do you think, for the Lord to cleanse the temple again at this time ? Are there things allowed in the building as a whole, or in any brick in particular, of which He is saying, " Take these things hence " (John 2 : 16). And so we are led on, through this remarkable series of figures to what is the most striking of them all—

" *An habitation of God through the Spirit* "—here is the sublime nature of fellowship. Yes, it is still true, as in the day of Psalm 11 : 4, " The Lord is in His holy temple "—in the whole, in the individual, in you and me. Time was when He dwelt among men in a tabernacle—" Let them make me a sanctuary, that I may dwell among them " (Ex. 25 : 8). Then, in the Person of the " Holy Child Jesus " (Acts 4 : 27, 30) He " was made flesh, and tabernacled (Greek) among us" (John 1 : 14). And now, He tabernacles in His Church, " For ye are the temple of the living God ; as God hath said, I will dwell in them, and walk in them " (2 Cor. 6 : 16). " Through " the Son, in the Person of the Son, He was " God with us " (Matt. 1 : 23) ; and now, here, " through " the Spirit, in the Person of the Spirit, He is God in us. Oh, wondrous truth, with all that it implies—of life, of power, of guidance, of fellowship, and of much else. We say again, what a distance we have travelled since the chapter opened with us " dead in trespasses and sins " ; verily, what a transformation we have seen. Pray God it may not be only theory with any one of us, but also practice—" Be not conformed to this world, but be ye transformed by the renewing of your mind " (Rom. 12 : 1).

"No More Jacob, But Israel"

By the Rev. RONALD J. PARK.

JACOB! His name came to mean supplanter. He was mean, untruthful, selfish, deceitful. And so we are interested in the man. He rings the bell where we are concerned ; there is a responsive chord in our hearts ; Jacob is our name ; the characteristics of Jacob are our characteristics. We shall be as gracious as we can to Jacob, for it is rather ignoble for the pot to call the kettle black : but at the same time we must be absolutely truthful about him if we are going to see the truth about ourselves.

Jacob was a schemer and contriver, and in all his schemings and contrivings his own much-cherished and well-beloved self was the very centre of all his plans. His duplicity aroused the anger of his brother Esau, and at the instigation of a mother who doted on him, he fled from home to become a fugitive and an exile. Then God broke into his life ! At Bethel he had his vision. Are you not glad that God met you on your irresponsible course ? Thank God for Bethel ! Three matters invite our attention in Jacob's experience : First, his resolution at Bethel ; Second, his renunciation at Jabbok : Third, his reconsecration at Bethel.

I. His Resolution at Bethel.

The story is in Genesis 28. From verse 12 we are told how he saw in his dream a stairway set up on earth, reaching into heaven, with angels of God ascending and descending. He discovered that God was present, and God revealed Himself to him. " Jacob vowed a vow, saying, If God will be with me, and will keep me in this way that I go, and will give me bread to eat, and raiment to put on . . . then shall the Lord be my God." That was a grand conversion, a thorough-going conversion ! We would have said, " We must have this man on our platform ; he has a powerful testimony to give, he has a wonderful story to tell ; we must hear all about it ; he has been gloriously converted." And so he had, it was a genuine experience.

That is chapter 28. What is the sequel to that wonderful experience ? What have chapters 29-32 to tell us ? We know what to expect. We expect to see a very different Jacob, a man who is gaining the victory over self, and whose life is glinting the glory of the Lord. We are doomed to disappointment. The bitter fact is that Jacob is Jacob still, the same self-centred schemer. Now, that does not argue that his experience at Bethel was fallacious. It was not, decidedly not. No one could have argued Jacob out of the reality of that experience when God entered

115

his life. But it does argue that you and I may have a thorough-going experience of the Lord, a genuine conversion, and yet go on living with self still predominating ; that we may be truly born again by the Spirit of God, and yet go on living in the energy of the flesh.

What went wrong ? Look carefully at the covenant that Jacob thought he would make with God, in verses 20-22. You cannot fail to see how faulty are its terms. " If God will be with me, and will keep me in the way that I go, and will give me bread to eat, and raiment to put on . . . then shall the Lord be my God ; and this stone that I have set for a pillar shall be God's house : and of all that Thou shalt give me, I will surely give the tenth unto Thee." Do you see what was wrong ? Even in that holy moment, when face to face with God, he was scheming for his own inglorious self. " If God will do this and that, if God will stock the larder and supply all necessities, then I will have God." That was Jacob in very truth. He visualised the balance sheet to make sure he would come out with a balance on the credit side ! He says, If God will subscribe all the capital to the firm of Messrs. Jacob, if God will indeed *donate* the capital, and if He will underwrite all the transactions of the firm, then Messrs. Jacob will be pleased to give God a ten per cent. dividend ! Dear friend, do you remember the day you were converted, the " Happy day that fixed your choice " ? I do not doubt the reality of that experience ; it was absolutely genuine, and none could persuade you to the contrary. But maybe since then you have still been Jacob ; the chapters subsequently written make disappointing reading— no victory, no glory. Why ? Be kind to me in this suggestion. I know my own heart, and therefore I know yours, for it is like mine, and we are all like Jacob. I am going to suggest that SELF was a very important party to that contract you thought you would make with God at Bethel. I am going to suggest—because I know how self intrudes in the holiest of moments—that if the thoughts at the back of your mind could have been clothed with words, they would have been something like this, " If the Lord can give me joy, if He can give me peace and satisfaction, if He can relieve me of an uneasy conscience and of all anxiety, then I will decide for the Lord." Unsuspectingly your eye was upon the blessings rather than upon the Blesser, upon the gifts rather than upon the Giver. God will be no party to selfish bargaining. He would deliver us from the thraldom of self, and as soon as we begin to scheme for personal advantage, He withdraws. Let us not be among the crowd that clamoured to make Christ king because He could give them bread to eat !

Let us understand that the reality of Jacob's experience of God at Bethel is not in question, nor the reality of your conversion and mine. But the regrettable element of self was far from eliminated : it obtruded and, in the case of Jacob, reigned supreme for the next twenty-five years. But God never renounced His claim upon His servant. " For the gifts and calling of God are without repentance." God never changes His mind ; He never will concerning you. You belong to Him, and He will never withdraw His hand.

II. His Renunciation at Jabbok.

After nearly twenty-five years a crisis arose, and poor Jacob faced the greatest trial of his life. He was to meet Esau, the brother he had wronged and whose anger he had fired. He prayed to God in an agony of soul (32 : 9-12), the first recorded prayer for twenty-five years. I do not say it was the first prayer, but the first recorded prayer. I am prepared to believe Jacob prayed every day of those twenty-five years. But that his prayers were powerless is evident from the fact that they made no difference, either to him or to the manner of life he led. But now, for the first time, he is on his face before God in desperate need. Thank God for those crises in life that drive us to our knees ! But this crisis ceases to interest us because it is immediately eclipsed by another and far greater crisis. God confronts Jacob and compels him to a contest. "Jacob was left alone, and there wrestled a Man with him until the breaking of the day. And when He saw that He prevailed not against him, He touched the hollow of his thigh ; and the hollow of Jacob's thigh was out of joint as He wrestled with him. And He said, Let Me go, for the day breaketh. And he said, I will not let Thee go, except Thou bless me. And He said unto him, What is thy name ? and he said Jacob. And He said, Thy name shall be called no more Jacob, but Israel ; for as a prince hast thou power with God and with men, and hast prevailed " (32 : 24-28). God had taken the initiative and was striving with Jacob, and Jacob was striving with God. He had been doing that, perhaps unconsciously, yet hardly so, for twenty-five years, and now came the climax. God has to do something He does not want to do—He cripples Jacob, and Jacob realises that it is as futile as it is foolish to resist God. The initiative passes from God to Jacob, and Jacob clings and says, " I will not let Thee go except Thou bless me." What a glorious experience ! For twenty-five years Jacob had been contesting : now he is clinging. And what did God say ? " No more Jacob, but Israel "—prince with God ! You can imagine the rejoicing in Jacob's heart that morning as he sat in the door of his tent. If only he had had a Keswick Hymn Book he would certainly have turned to the Consecration section and sung :—

> Higher than the highest heavens,
> Deeper than the deepest sea,
> Lord, Thy love at last hath conquered :
> Grant me now my soul's petition,
> None of self, and all of Thee.

After that grand experience of self-renunciation and abandonment to God in chapter 32, we are prepared to see a new epoch in the life of this man in chapters 33 and 34. Let me break the news to you gently ! You are going to be disappointed. These two chapters are as miserable and sordid as any in the biography of Jacob. Now, don't jump to any hasty conclusion ! Let us be patient, and inquire into this unexpected development. Let us hasten to say that his renunciation of self and abandonment to God at Jabbok are not to be questioned. Jabbok, unlike Bethel, finds Jacob wholly surrendered, at an end of himself, and

117

clinging to the Lord. He is now Israel potentially. It is only too bad that he remained Jacob practically. But why ?

There were three enemies that immediately beset Jacob and overcame him—the world, the flesh and the devil. *First, there was the flesh.* Chapter 33 opens by revealing the approach of Esau. And look at Jacob ! He falls to the expedients of the flesh, he schemes and contrives and plots, and when he meets Esau he grovels before him and ingratiates himself with him, tells him a lie and acts a deception. Poor Jacob ! The flesh has completely mastered him. *Secondly, there was the world.* The city of Shalem was not far away. Jacob bought a piece of ground and pitched his tent " before the city." The city, with its fashions and follies, its glamour and gaiety ! Of course, he did not pitch his tent inside the city. He knew he could not consistently do that, because he belonged to God : so he pitched it as near as he could. He did not want to be cut off from the city and its life ; he could not resist its fascination ; he fell a victim to the temptation of the world. *Thirdly, there was the devil.* Jacob's household were carrying gods around with them and he was tolerating, was conniving at, idolatrous practices in his own camp. And behind all false worship is the devil. Jacob appears helpless to interfere with the idolatrous institutions, even of those under his own authority. The slave of the devil !

Why did these enemies prevail against Jacob ? Was he not now Israel ? Should not the mighty experience at Jabbok have ensured victory over all these foul foes ? Had he not clung in self-abandonment to God after a night of wearisome combat ? Listen ! and learn this vital truth : *no past act of surrender, however real, will guarantee victory to-day. The solemn, glad act of surrender must be perpetuated by a day-to-day attitude.* Had Jacob clung to God ? Then ever after he should have been in the attitude of faith, clinging. Did Esau come, arousing his fleshly instincts ? Then he should have been found in the attitude of faith, clinging. Did the world cast its unholy spell about him ? Then he should have been found in the attitude of faith, clinging. Did the devil try to intimidate him ? Then he should have been found in the attitude of faith, clinging to God.

Do you, dear fellow-believer, remember your Jabbok, perhaps in this very tent years ago ? An act of complete self-renunciation, and a clinging to the Lord after contending for years. How good and right it was, and how true. What peace and joy in the Holy Ghost. But . . . ! What a thousand pities it has to be said ! You see, you did not realise that the act was initial to an attitude that ought to have been maintained ever afterwards. Faith should have gone on clinging, and so maintaining the relevance of the act and appropriating its power. In isolation, the act becomes a sad memory, with all its potential arrested. But as initial to a new attitude, it means that Jacob is no more Jacob but Israel. In the New Testament the word for the attitude is " abide " in John 15, and " reckon " in Romans 6, and " keep yourselves " in Jude 21.

III. His Reconsecration at Bethel.

" And God said to Jacob, Arise, go up to Bethel, and dwell there "
(Gen. 35 : 1). Bethel ! He is to go back there, and to dwell there. He
is to return to the place of the first experience. Then, the secret of
victory lay there ? Exactly ! All those years of wearisome failure need
never have been. Away back at Bethel where Jacob " first saw the light "
was the secret of how Jacob could become Israel. What was Bethel ?
It was the place of the stairway reaching from earth to heaven, with the
ascent and descent of the angels, and God standing by Jacob's side (for
such we are to understand in 28 : 13).

What is Bethel to the believer ? Our Lord Himself interprets the
vision for us in His words to Nathanael in John 1 : 51, " Hereafter ye
shall see heaven open, and the angels of God ascending and descending
upon the Son of Man." What, then, is the stairway ? Nathanael had
just said, " Thou art the Son of God." A moment later the Lord said,
" Son of Man." There is the ladder—Son of Man, set up on earth ;
Son of God, reaching into heaven. The Lord Himself is the way. When
then, was heaven opened ? Surely when He ascended up on high. So,
then, Bethel for the believer in the Lord Jesus Christ means " boldness
to enter into the holiest by the Blood of Jesus, by a new and living way,
which He hath consecrated for us through the vail, that is to say, His
flesh." The stairway is set, the heaven is opened. There is a heavenly
sphere, a place of ascendancy, that belongs to us because we are " in
Christ." " In Adam " we dwelt upon earth, we " minded the things of
the flesh." " In Christ " we dwell in the heavenlies, and mind the " things
of the Spirit." That this is the purpose of God, is clearly declared.
He " hath raised us up together, and made us sit together in heavenly
places in Christ Jesus." And that, from Ephesians 2, because of this,
from Ephesians 1—God " raised Him (Christ) from the dead, and set
Him at His own right hand in the heavenly places, far above all principality,
and power, and might, and dominion, and every name that is named."
Back to Bethel this morning, my dear friend ! The Saviour who saved
you is in the heavenlies, the place of ascendancy. And in Him you also
are in the heavenlies, in the ascendancy over the world, the flesh and the
devil. And Jacob could, and should, become Israel.

" Back to Bethel ! " and not only that, but " Abide there ! " " Abide
in Me," was His word. " If ye then be risen with Christ, seek—go on
continuously seeking—those things which are above, where Christ sitteth
at the right hand of God. Set—go on setting—your affection on things
above, not on things on the earth." Here, then, is the attitude of faith
which must follow the act of surrender. " Reckon—go on reckoning—
yourselves to be dead indeed unto sin, but alive unto God through Jesus
Christ our Lord." Morning, noon, and night, enjoy the rest of a faith
that centres in an ascended Lord, and " Thy name shall be called no
more Jacob, but Israel."

119

Honouring God's Holy Name.

By the Rev. GORDON M. GUINNESS, M.A.

EZEKIEL 36 : 22-32 refers primarily to Israel, her past sin and her future restoration, but it is so full of spiritual meaning, and has been so often used by the Holy Spirit, that we apply it personally, to ourselves. First of all, we observe that God solemnly declares to His people that He is going to act. In these verses we find the words " I will " no less than fourteen times—not " I may," but " I will." " I *will* sanctify " ; " I *will* cleanse " ; " a new heart I *will* give " ; " I *will* put My Spirit within you." Here we have the perfect number twice repeated for solemn emphasis—" Verily, verily." God intends to act, to do a mighty spiritual work that we cannot do. There is no sort of doubt about it. This programme is going to be carried out—and that by God Himself. Now, He does that work in regeneration and in sanctification. In regeneration we cannot call for any moral or spiritual resources from within ourselves ; God acts. In sanctification, we cannot by daily watchfulness or by any strength of character enter into the abundant life. God intends to do these great things for us by His Spirit, and His purpose is for every single one of us.

As we look at this passage we find in verses 22-23 that GOD'S HONOUR AND GLORY IS INVOLVED IN DOING THIS GREAT THING. The vindication of God's holy nature demands our sanctification. Anything less than a separated, cleansed and Spirit-controlled people leaves God's name dishonoured. Observe in verses 22-23 that we (for we are the Israel of God) who have professed God's name, have dishonoured it. " O House of Israel, ye have profaned My holy name among the heathen . . . the heathen shall know that I am the Lord when I shall be sanctified in you before their eyes." Here God tells us that we have brought His name low before men ; we have profaned His holy name. Have we who come to Keswick done this horrible thing ? The holiness of the name that is above every name, revealed to Moses in the flaming heights of Sinai, protected by the thrice-holy God more than any jealous husband would protect the name of the wife he honoured and loved ; the all-holy name of God has been dishonoured by His people in the eyes of men. All who are seeking to lead men to Christ can substantiate this. What reason do nine people out of ten give for not joining the fellowship of the Christian Church ? The lives of professing Christians, and the lack of real, warm-hearted love in the Christian Church. Is that true ? It is absolutely true. In the first century it was the lives of

Christians that made people long to find Christ for themselves ; but in the twentieth century all too often it is the lives of Christians that keep people away from Christ. How can we expect a tradesman to be converted when Christians are not paying their bills ?

I know a landlady who is struggling to keep going, but is slowly dying of a painful and distressing disease. In a moment of confidence, sad but uncomplaining, she told me of the unthinking selfishness of some of her Christian, church-going guests. Their demands had never allowed her to ease up, and if she had given way to them all she would never have been able to go to Church. Oh, the lack of tender love that profanes the name of holy love. This unloving spirit also shows itself in a critical and censorious attitude to others ; in a narrow sectarianism ; in stressing differences until secondary matters are magnified into fundamental principles, and the seamless robe is rent to pieces. You remember Christ's command (not suggestion), in Matt. 18 : 15 ? " If thy brother shall trespass against thee, go and tell him his fault between thee and him alone." Do we not profane God's holy name when we deliberately ignore and completely disobey that command? Of Hudson Taylor it was said by one who knew him well, that she had never heard him speak well of himself or ill of anybody else. There are plenty of people who profess to admire Hudson Taylor, but who do not follow that Christ-like example.

How will God sanctify His great name that we have dishonoured ? By doing four great things. First, BY SEPARATING US, DETACHING US, FROM EVERY EVIL THING—" I will take you from among the heathen, and gather you out of all countries, and I will bring you into your own land." " Come ye out from among them and be ye separate, saith the Lord, and touch not the unclean thing " (2 Cor. 6 : 17). Observe that the unclean thing is *anything* that dishonours God's Holy Name. This was dealt with last night by Dr. Scroggie, so I shall not re-iterate, but venture to stress two things. The first is, that the enemy is using infiltration tactics. Small forces of the enemy have been infiltrating all the time into the Christian lines. We think the boundary between us and the enemy is clearly defined. But it is not. He is infiltrating, getting his agents into our lives, setting up his strong points behind positions we have already captured for Christ. God wants to detach us from the enemy. Secondly, it is absolutely necessary for us to confess particularly the sins we commit, as well as to renounce them particularly. A general confession is often a face-saving device. It is too cheap and easy to say, " Lord, *if* I was hasty this morning, please forgive me." We ought to say, " Lord, I lost my temper this morning when Mrs. Smith was so rude to me. I have no excuse. I confess it." When we oversleep and miss our quiet time with God, it is too cheap and easy to say in the evening, " *If* I have not spent enough time to-day with Thee Lord, I am sorry." We need to examine our lives and trace the cause of our sin. If we failed to get to bed in time through our own fault, we must face it and confess it : " Lord, last night I stayed up instead of getting to bed, and so I failed to get up in time to wait on Thee. I am guilty of dishonouring Thy name. I humbly confess this sin. I have no excuse." Let us name our sins before God in confession, for it is when we confess our sins that He is faithful and just to forgive us our sins.

Then secondly, GOD WILL SANCTIFY HIS GREAT NAME BY CLEANSING US FROM ALL OUR SINS (vv. 25, 26)—" Then will I sprinkle clean water upon you, and ye shall be clean : from all your filthiness, and from all your idols, will I cleanse you . . . and I will take away the stony heart (the unresponsive, the unwilling heart) out of your flesh, and I will give you a loving, responsive heart." " I will " and " ye shall "—" I will cleanse you " and " ye shall be clean." If we feel that " filthiness " and " idols " are words too strong to describe what we have done, we do not know our own hearts yet, and we are not ready for the cleansing that He is waiting to give. *It is a full cleansing* : "from *all* your filthiness and from *all* your idols . . ." " He gave Himself for us that He might redeem us from *all* iniquity." And the full cleansing is by *His most precious blood* : " The blood of Jesus Christ cleanseth us from all sin." God could say, " I will sprinkle you " and " ye shall be clean " ; God could say, " I will take away the unloving heart out of your flesh," because He knew the power of the cleansing of the blood. What is it that gives to the precious blood of Christ its cleansing power ? If we can realise that, we can enter into it more fully to-day. Andrew Murray points out that the cleansing blood of the Lamb derives its power from the inner disposition of the Saviour. He came as humbly and meekly as a lamb ; He manifested perfect submission to His Father's will in that meekness and lowliness of heart that man has so completely lost through sin and pride. His meek obedience was so absolute that He chose death rather than the sin of pleasing Himself. He denied Himself and took up the Cross long before Good Friday. This blood is so powerful in its action that it can both cleanse away all our past sin, and actually impart its own nature to our hearts. So part of the cleansing is the taking away of that in us which is our undoing, the taking away of the old heart. This is not only a gracious promise, it is a realised fact to which some of you could get up and testify gratefully and humbly, to-day. One vital fact, however, we must not forget : just as this precious blood could never have been shed without Christ laying down His life, so it could never be received except by one who has a similar disposition, who is prepared to " lose his life " in order to save it. We must receive this precious blood in meek, self-denying humility which is the essence of its love and power. The ever-present danger, however, is the " evil heart of unbelief," which is so slow to be convinced that His precious blood will really cleanse us. We expect to be forgiven, but faith staggers at the promise, " I will take away the stony heart out of your flesh."

Thirdly, GOD WILL SANCTIFY HIS HOLY NAME BY MAKING US OBEDIENT TO HIS INDWELLING SPIRIT. " I will put My Spirit within you, and cause you to walk in My statutes, and ye shall keep My judgments and do them " (v. 27). You remember the old illustration—forgive its repetition and simplicity. You have a glass that has some sour milk left in it, and you want a drink of fresh water. You must empty out the sour milk, you must cleanse the glass, and you must fill it with fresh water. From our lives there must be emptied out the sourness of self, there must be the cleansing of the precious blood of Christ, and then the indwelling of His Spirit. Here again, " I will " and " ye shall." " I will put My Spirit within you, and ye shall keep my commandments." Let us thank Him, let us praise Him, let us breathe in the fulness of His Spirit to the life which He has cleansed ; and then rejoicing in the certainty of " ye shall," go out to walk in the Spirit and not to fulfil the lusts of the flesh.

Lastly, GOD SANCTIFIES HIS GREAT NAME BY MAKING US FRUITFUL— " Ye shall be My people ; I will be your God." " I will call for the corn, and will increase it, and lay no famine upon you. And I will multiply the fruit of the tree, and the increase of the field, and ye shall receive no more reproach of famine among the heathen " (vv. 29, 30). God meant His people to be a successful, fruitful people—not that that will allow us to be easy-going. God makes the garden fruitful, but we have to put in hard, continuous work so that the fruit may come to perfection. With the certainty of harvest to carry us forward, the work is not irksome, but joyful in the Lord. May God give more fire, more passion, more zeal to His people, and give us the faith to know that our labour shall not be in vain in the Lord. So God will reverse the infinite damage of sin (at infinite cost), and the heathen shall know that He is the Lord, when He shall be sanctified in us before their eyes.

" I the Lord have spoken it, and I will do it."

Access into the Heavenlies.

By Dr. DONALD G. BARNHOUSE.

WE know, in our heads, so many things that we do not practice in our hearts and lives. It is true of the unsaved, and it is true of the saved. One evening, several years ago, after one of the meetings in the big tent in Keswick, I walked through the town as the open-air meeting was coming to a close. Some young men were dealing with a man who was drunk, and were not getting very far with him. As I passed by, one of the young men asked me if I would say a word to the needy man. I began to talk with him, and coming to the quotation of John 3 : 16, I was interrupted by the man who spoke to me, drunkenly, " Oh, I know all about it. God sho loved the world that He gave Hish only begotten Shon . . ." I told him that it was possible for a man to be on the road to Hell, with a clear map of the road to Heaven traced in his mind.

It is possible for Christians to fall into a similar pattern of living. They are on the road to Heaven, but are travelling in an overcrowded compartment sitting on their luggage, while, if they would get clean out of the train and walk along to another car, they could find comfortable, first-class accommodation, fully reserved for their use. Too frequently the theme song of the Church has been:—

> Dear Lord, and shall we ever live
> At this poor dying rate ?
> Our love to Thee so faint and cold,
> Thy love to us so great.

Our Lord never meant His Church to live in a defeated way. He provided absolutely all things for us. His blessings are never rationed, and there is always a complete stock in His bountiful store, with absolutely no waiting for service. There would be no brown loaves of rationed bread, and there would be no shortage of roast beef, if you lived in the pampas of the Argentine or the plains of western Canada. There would be no parched days of Christian life without fellowship if you lived at the throne of the Lord Jesus Christ, where God means us to live.

There is one sense in which we should not sing

> Mercy drops round us falling,
> But for the showers we plead . . .

For God has made it possible for us to live in the place where the clouds of mercy are formed, and He has made it possible for us to direct the winds that shall bear these clouds of mercy to the point where they shall break and pour all their blessings upon us, not merely in showers, but in torrents. One of the first things, therefore, that a Christian should learn, is the way into the holiest of all. That way, which he has already learned for salvation, he must re-learn, day by day, for power and victory.

We have pointed out that the tabernacle of Moses was a plan of Heaven. Let us look at it a little more closely, in the light of the second chapter of the Ephesian Epistle. Come with me and stand on the brow of the hill where Balak brought Balaam to overlook the camp of Israel. Had we been there we should have seen certain features that would have struck the eye at once. Rising to the skies in the midst of the camp you would have seen the pillar of fire by night and of cloud by day. This was a symbol of the presence of the glory of the Lord God, Jehovah, who consented in grace to dwell thus among His people for a time. You would make out from you point of vantage that the cloud hung over a building without any outward form or beauty—certainly a building that would be despised and rejected by architects and builders. Out in front of the building you might note two small objects, from one of which you would see a slender wisp of smoke rising. Then a fence, a court, a wall—objects that would be indistinct from your distance.

Now you make your way down the hill and seek to approach this construction in the centre of the camp. As you advance among the tents of the camp of Israel, you would be narrowly looked upon—for you are Gentiles, and the Jews there would have called you "Uncircumcision"— and would have pronounced it with a sneer of contempt. And, if you had continued your wandering toward the centre of the camp you would have been brought up sharply by a wall—the middle wall of partition (Ephes. 2 : 14). If you had attempted to go beyond this wall they would have told you—and they would have been telling you the truth, officially, in the name of the God of the divine revelation—that you could not pass because you had no Messiah, were aliens to the commonwealth of Israel, strangers to the covenants of promise, without hope and without God in the world (2 : 12). You had no access. You were " afar off " from the holy presence that lay beyond.

But had you been a Jew, you could have gone on farther still. After a while, if you had been a Jewish woman, you too, would have been stopped. The court of the women would have been your nearest point of vantage. From thence you could have seen with distant eyes that which you could not approach. Had you been a Jewish man, you could have gone on still farther, and, bringing a lamb with you as the sign of your sin, you could have come to the very gate of the court in front of the building. But here you would have been stopped, unless you had been of the tribe of Levi. They alone could penetrate within the gate. They were divided into four groups, all of them subject unto Aaron and his family, but each having a different service. The sons of Gershon had charge of the tabernacle, the tent, the coverings and the hangings (Num. 3 : 25, 26). The sons of Kohath had to do with all the furnishings of the tabernacle, from the ark to the farther altar (Num. 3 : 31). The sons of Merari were the custodians of the boards, the bars, the sockets, the pillars, the gates and the walls (Num. 3 : 36). If you had belonged to any of these families you could have walked about the tabernacle area at a time when there were no services, and could have seen to the repairs and upkeep of the edifice and all the appurtenances of the worship. But you could not go in at the times of the service of the Lord, lest you die (Num. 4 : 20).

Had you been one of the sons of Aaron, you could have entered the tabernacle. Only the sons of Aaron could approach at a time of service, of sacrifice, or worship. Theirs, too, was the function of putting to death any Gentile who came beyond the wall toward the temple (Num. 3 : 38). It was in line with this that the Jews were ready to kill Paul because they thought he had brought Greeks into the temple (Acts 21 : 28). And it is in line with this that the Christian minister to-day must not hesitate to say that all who deny Christ, and who are Unitarians in any form, have no access to the God and Father of our Lord Jesus Christ, and are doomed to the second death.

But even had you belonged to the sons of Aaron you would have been stopped by the inner veil of the sanctuary, behind the altar of worship, that separated the holy place from the most holy. The priests went always into the first tabernacle, accomplishing the service of God, but into the second went the High Priest alone, once every year, not without blood, which he offered for himself, and for the sins of ignorance of the people (Heb. 9 : 7).

Thus, in a constantly recurring pageant, the Lord taught the children of Israel the doctrine of access. In the time of the object lesson it was more a doctrine of " Stand away " than it was one of access, for there was none of the freedom that is now ours.

We indicated, in our first study, that we may understand our access if we should stand the tabernacle on end and see the Holy of Holies as the highest Heaven, where God and Christ sit enthroned over all the universe. There is the fountain of our blessings, which we now approach.

We walk here in the outer courts, but the first thing we discover is that the middle wall of partition has been broken down (Ephes. 2 : 14). When I was a young preacher I chose the first half of this text as the subject of a discourse, " He is our peace." I took it out of its context and taught from it the truth which has been expressed in the great hymn of peace, " Like a river glorious." Now, Christ is our peace, within the hearts of His yielded own ; but you may not properly teach it from this text. Very frequently certain Bible truths are obscured because a common meaning is given to a text which the Lord meant to convey another shade of meaning. If I had taken the text which speaks of the peace of God which passeth all understanding, or the one that speaks of the peace of God ruling in our hearts, I should have been exegetically correct. But this peace in Ephesians 2 is the peace that may come horizontally between peoples who formerly have had no dealings with one another. The Jews had no dealings with the Samaritans . . . for the Jews knew themselves to be nigh to the priesthood, the altar, the blood, the place of access—while the Samaritans were known to be afar off, on the other side of the wall. Our Lord clearly recognized this when He frankly told the woman at the well that her religion was totally worthless. " Ye worship ye know not what ; we know what we worship ; for salvation is of the Jews " (John 4 : 22). I do not know whether the literal middle wall of partition in Herod's temple fell flat at the moment Christ died. We do know, of course, that the veil in the temple between the Holy place and the Most Holy, was torn in two from top to bottom. Whether or not the literal wall fell down in the earthquake (I believe, by analogy, that it probably did), most certainly the spiritual wall went down. As a result of this, the only place on this earth where there can be an absence of race prejudice is within the true Church of Jesus Christ. Individuals of the Church may still possess the prejudices, but those in the spiritual reality know what it means to be all one in Christ Jesus.

So we read our second chapter thus : But now, in Christ Jesus ye Gentiles who sometimes were far off, on the other side of the wall, away from the altar, are made nigh by the blood of Jesus Christ. For He is our peace, the peace between alien men and races, who hath made both Jew and Gentile one, and hath broken down the middle wall of partition between us ; having abolished in His flesh the enmity, race hatred, expressed in the law of commandments, contained in the Levitical ordinances, in order to make in Himself of the two, Jew and Gentile, one new man, the Church, thus making peace between the races. And that he might reconcile both Jew and Gentile unto God in one body, the Church, by the cross, having slain the enmity thereby ; and came and preached peace to you Gentiles which were afar off from the altar, and to the Jews that were near it. For through Christ we both have access by one Spirit unto the Father.

We have access ! Then let us go in boldly.

We have passed by the middle wall of partition. We have come to the altar. We pause but a moment here, for the ground has been well explored, and the purpose of this study is not evangelisation but progress through to the Holiest of all. At this point we could well think upon salvation by the vicarious, substitutionary atonement made by our Lord Jesus Christ. But we pass over it here and go on toward the sanctuary, where our blessings are found. We soon arrive at the laver. In Moses' tabernacle this was made of the metal which came from the mirrors of the women, then as now, a symbol of human vanity. In Solomon's temple the laver was called the sea. In both instances it contained water, and was the place of the cleansing of the priest. On the occasion when the great High Priest offered the sacrifice for the sins of the people, he first killed one lamb for himself, walked a few steps to the laver, washed his feet, presented the offering before God, returned to the altar, killed a lamb for the sin of the people, returned to the laver, washed his feet, and then took the blood through the outer veil, past the shewbread, the candles, the second altar and the veil, and sprinkled it upon the mercy-seat between the cherubim on top of the ark in the Holy of Holies, beneath the pillar of cloud that hung over the ark of the covenant.

127

This was thoroughly in the minds of all the people of Israel, and the disciples therefore understood perfectly when the Lord Jesus Christ gave the instructions on cleansing to Peter. When our Lord girded Himself with a towel and came to wash the disciples' feet, Peter looked askance at Him as He approached, and announced that the Lord should never wash his feet. It was a failure to comprehend the steps of access. " If I wash thee not, thou hast no part with Me " (John 13 : 8), was the same as saying, After you are saved you will still need daily cleansing. Moment by moment you must come to Me for that cleansing.

There are two types of cleansing in ordinary life, and there are two types of cleansing in the spiritual life. We have special washing and regular washing. You are filling your pen and suddenly you find that it is truly named a fountain pen. It has overflowed upon you. You run to the water and wash away the stain that has come upon you in that moment. But on another occasion you pass a long period of time without any untoward accident of ink or other dirt. Yet when you are coming to the table, or to the end of your day, you go to the water and wash again. This is regular washing. You have lived in the atmosphere of earth, and it is necessary to come for daily cleansing even though you have lived your day in the air of the Cumberland mountains, so much cleaner than that of our great cities.

Thus it is with our cleansing from sin. " If we confess our sins, He is faithful and righteous to forgive us our sins, and to cleanse us from all unrighteousness " (1 John 1 : 9). At times our old nature breaks out, and we need to run to God for special cleansing from special sin. We must not hesitate. We must rush to the fountain. Satan would do everything possible to keep you waiting, for every moment you wait your fellowship is broken. The chink in your armour is displayed, and Satan has his special archers ready to shoot their fiery darts through the opening of your destroyed fellowship. An Abraham leaves Palestine, the place of the promised blessing. A small thing, you say, involving no real iniquity. True, but it was then that Satan was able to get an advantage over him, and soon he found himself in the midst of lying, and came to the dishonourable place of being willing to sacrifice his wife's honour to save his own cowardly skin. Run to God on the least little touch of dirt, and do not hesitate. He who hesitates is vulnerable.

I want to give a personal instance, for it may help me to right a wrong and heal a hurt. On Sunday evening I was preaching in Southey-street Methodist Church. We came to the closing hymn. The church was crowded beyond capacity, with people standing in the doors and seated on the steps. In announcing the closing hymn, I tried to do a good thing in a bad way. Without thinking I rushed forward in the flesh, though I had just been preaching in the Spirit, and said, " As we sing the last hymn, will all the selfish people rush out in order to get one step ahead of the crowd, and will the unselfish people remain till the benediction in a couple of minutes." It was my foolish way of trying to keep everyone in place until we could all go together. We had no more than begun to sing the first verse when a group of people near the front

Mr. and Mrs. J. Taylor Thompson.

Rev. Guy H. King.

Rev. and Mrs. Gordon M. Guinness.

Bishop Maxwell
of
West Szechwan.

—

Rev. A. T.
Houghton.

Mr. F. Mitchell.

Rev. W. H. Aldis, *Chairman.*

Mr. A. W. Bradley, *Treasurer.*

Preb. Colin
C. Kerr.

—

Rev. J. T
Carson.

Rev. J.
Dunlop.

began to make their way out. I realised in a flash that they were not selfish, but were undoubtedly hurrying, unselfishly, to aid a household in its supper plans, that all might go to the evening meeting together; or for some similar reason. Yet in the minds of many people who saw them threading their way through the crowded aisles, they were branded as selfish. I flashed a quick prayer to the Lord for cleansing from the sin of my thoughtless unkindness. And I flashed a quick signal to the organist at the end of the verse, and apologised to the audience. But those I had wronged had already gone out, and I do not know whether they have learned yet of my desire to put things right. We must keep short accounts with God, even as we keep short accounts with dirt that gets on our bodies.

And then there is the regular cleansing; which we must have with the Lord at the close of every day. We come and tell Him that we have a sinful nature, and that it is prone to break forth. We ask Him to reveal to us the things He wishes dealt with.

> Do you think He ne'er reproves me?
> What a false friend He would be.
> If He never, never told me
> Of the sins which He must see!

Thank God for the laver! But there is a sadness at this point, for this is as far as many Christians go. From reading and experience with souls, I would say the majority of believers never get beyond this point. But how are we to bridge the gap between this highest point on earth and the Heavens, the far-above Heavens, where our Lord is enthroned? The answer is in the sixth verse of this second chapter. "He hath raised us up together, and made us sit together in the Heavenlies in Christ Jesus." I read that verse scores if not hundreds of times before I knew what it meant. Raised. . . Did this not mean the life of the resurrection? And then one day I learned that this word raised was something far beyond resurrection. You have heard hundreds of sermons on the Cross, scores of sermons on the resurrection, but how many times have you heard a sermon on the ascension of Christ? This portion is a text on the ascension.

You hath He quickened . . . there is resurrection. Perhaps it is obscured for us because the word has dropped out of modern usage except in a technical sense. You hath He made alive—that is the word. And not only did He make us alive in Christ, but He raised us up together, and made us sit together in the Heavenlies in Christ Jesus. Write this in capital letters in your life. He hath quickened us from death to life. He hath raised us from earth to Heaven. It is in the past tense. In the sight of God it is done. We have been made new creatures in Christ Jesus, and we were created for the throne of Heaven. How are we to bridge the gap? The answer is that we must take it by faith, as we have taken every other step by faith. How do you know that your sins have been forgiven? God says so. Where were they taken from you? At the cross of Jesus Christ. But was not that over 1,900 years ago? Oh, yes! But faith annihilates time, and the Cross is to me a present reality. But was not Calvary many miles from where you are now? Yes, but faith annihilates distance. Those are common questions and well-known answers. We, all of us, if we are believers in Christ as Saviour, have become accustomed to thinking of Him and His death as present realities, present in time and present in space. *In exactly the same way we must become accustomed to annihilating the vertical separation in time and space.* Let us repeat these same questions, applying them to our life and position in Christ. How do you know that you have been raised to Heaven and seated with Christ on His throne? God says so. When does this happen effectually? At the return of the Lord for His people. But is not that at some unknown time in the future? Yes! But faith annihilates time, and the throne is to me a present reality. But is not Heaven very far from us? Yes, but faith annihilates distance.

The following story has meant much to me in my own personal experience with Christ. Ten years ago, while I was spending sixteeen months visiting the mission fields of Asia, my family spent the time in Berlin. The children were learning German, and the home where all stayed was in the west end of the city, not far from what was probably the world's most famous zoo. There was a very fine playground in the zoological gardens, and their mother had purchased annual tickets for them, and the children spent almost all of their play time there. Two years later when I was sent to Germany for the summer by the Carl Shurz Foundation, to make a study of the religious persecutions going on there, the children spent their summer on a farm, and at the end of the season I took them to Berlin, and we spent a week visiting their old haunts. At the zoo there was the famous planetarium, a domed building with a scientific apparatus which enabled astronomers to throw a reproduction of all the visible stars on the inside of the dome, and make the stars move in their courses at will, for the instruction of students. We went to one of these exhibitions, and at the close a scientific cinema film was shown. It began with a scene in the Unter den Linden, and was taken so that we could imagine ourselves in a motor car, driving down the street. The little girl by my side kept telling me where we were as the car moved through the city toward the zoo, by the route that they had most often taken on the bus. When the very building we were in came on the screen the children were caught in the spirit of the thing. They were looking at themselves, as it were.

Then the car took us down the street to the Templehof aerodrome, and we saw the open door of an aeroplane. It was as though we got in, and the plane took off and flew low across the city. It circled around the zoo below us, and then came toward the building in which we were sitting looking at the film. Suddenly, as the plane came directly over the planetarium, it stopped, and began to rise, as though we were in a huge lift, with a glass floor. I was confused for a moment, for I knew that planes could not yet stop still and go upwards. Soon I realised that it was an ingenious photographic trick. At that point the picture of the real city had been cut, and to it was joined a picture made in a studio from a photographic model. We rose and rose. The building grew smaller as the objective covered more and more ground. The whole city came into the picture. The winding Spree, the forests, the countryside. Then more and more of Germany, the jutting peninsula of Denmark, the Dutch coast, and then Britain. Then the world began to turn, and our lift with the glass floor was still rising. All of France came into the picture, then America and the entire world turned before us. The speed of the lift accelerated, and the world grew smaller. Soon the moon came into the scene, and began turning about the earth. Then other planets, then the blazing sun, which put all of the scene out for a moment, before it was turned out by the astronomer. Still we rose, far faster than the speed of light. Our little earth appeared and disappeared around the sun, and became so small that an arrow had to be put in the scene to identify it. Our solar system began to swing among others, and galaxy after galaxy crowded the screen. We were looking at ourselves from the vantage point of a far corner of the milky way.

The illusion was very real. The film had been made with adroit skill and craftsmanship. And from that vast immensity with our world an invisible speck dodging in and out among other specks, I suddenly realised the absurdity of the mad rush to possess a few more acres of it, or to wish to appear to be something or somewhat among those who ruled it.

Oh, that we might come to realise what earth really is, and where God wants us to live in relationship to it. The Word of God tells us that the day will come when we shall never remember the words England, America, London, Philadelphia, Keswick, your corner or mine. " For behold I create new Heavens and a new earth, and the former (that is the one we are living in now) shall not be remembered, nor come into mind " (Isa. 65 : 17). Let us not, then, live our lives in the sphere of earth. As we have reckoned ourselves to be dead unto sin and alive unto God (Rom. 6 : 11), so let us learn to reckon ourselves raised from earth to Heaven, and seated with Christ in the Heavenlies. Then the things of earth will grow strangely dim in the light of His glory and grace. The crown is ours by faith, as much as the Cross is ours by faith. This life of enthroned faith will not make us any the less strong citizens of earth. You will face your tasks better because you are operating from Heaven. You will prepare your sermon better if you lean down from Heaven to do it. You will stand in the queue more patiently when you know that the people around you, who are talking to you, may indeed think you are there when you know down-right well that you are on the throne of Heaven, seated with your Lord.

And now, we shall turn in our next study to the practical step of getting there ; how we shall feel when we arrive there ; what we shall say, right now, to-day, if we come to the real consciousness that we have broken through to our rightful position ; and what we may do after we have accustomed ourselves to Heaven's light.

Throw Down . . . and Build!

By the Rev. J. DUNLOP, M.A.

"The Lord said unto Gideon . . . throw down the altar of Baal that thy father hath . . . and build an altar unto the Lord thy God."—*Judges* 6 : 25, 26.

THE story of Gideon is one of those attractive picturesque narratives with which the Old Testament abounds. He was an unknown man of obscure family, called by God to raise to freedom a nation of spiritless slaves, and to overthrow another nation that was mighty and glorious in the supremacy of its power. The Midianites had at this time conquered the Israelites, and had imposed their heathen religion upon them. In truth Israel had acquiesced without much protest in the worship of their conquerors, and by now the minds of the people were filled with the Baalim instead of with the pure worship of Jehovah. But God did not allow His purpose, and the religious calling of His people, to be forgotten. He never does. From time to time He had raised up persons known as Judges to speak to the people and bring them back to Himself ; and now once again He summons Gideon to such a task.

The call came to him as he was threshing wheat stealthily by the wine-press for fear of the Midianites, lest they might take it. The angel of the Lord appeared unto him with these startling words, " The Lord is with thee, thou mighty man of valour." But poor Gideon was feeling far too weak and dispirited by events to accept that immediately. He refused to recognise himself under that designation, just as we, so conscious of our defeats, strugglings and imperfections in Christian life and witness, fail to recognise ourselves by the designation given to us by our Lord in His Word ; we refuse to believe that we are sanctified in Him, that we are seated in the Heavenlies far above all principalities and powers, that we are more than conquerors. Gideon protested that far from God being with him and with his people, He seemed to have forgotten them entirely, hence their defeats and troubles. As for himself, how could God be with him ; how could he be a mighty man of valour ? He was a nobody, a weakling, the poorest in his father's family. But the divine call may not be evaded. God proceeds to instruct and equip Gideon for his task. He awakens in him a thorough trust in Jehovah, He inspires him with a proper trust in himself as called by Jehovah ; then He commands him : " Go in this thy might, and thou shalt save Israel from the hand of the Midianites ; have not I sent thee ? " As these words fell upon a spirit already exercised with a sense of his country's degradation, and a longing to overthrow the oppressor, Gideon was inspired with a new hope, and was led to a new venture. This thing can be. The time had come to rise, to act, to dare, in the strength of God; and Gideon was prepared to obey.

Gideon's first task was not, however, to rout the Midianites in battle. It was something harder, perhaps, something that would furnish a very stiff test for him, and at the same time give the right emphasis to this new movement he was going to lead, for it was to be primarily a religious movement. Gideon was commanded to throw down the altar erected to Baal by his own father, and to erect an altar to the Lord God in its place. Now, that was no child's play. The Israelites were far from repenting of their idolatry, and a blow struck thus against Baal would infuriate its devotees in Israel and Midian alike. Gideon's work of reformation was to begin at home, hazarding his life by hewing down the idolatrous posts and pillars under which his father and kinsfolk had become accustomed to worship. He would be reproving his own father of sin, and while the older man might in his heart sympathise with his son, it was unlikely from reasons of expediency that he would do other than show his wrath against him. It would not have been so bad if it had simply been a matter of erecting an altar to the Lord alongside the altar of Baal; that would have been an evidence of religious zeal that the worshippers of Baal might have understood or tolerated; but the dangerous thing was first of all to hew down the altar of Baal, and then to erect an altar to the Lord in its place. But that was God's way, and that is the point of the message I bring to you to-night: first throw down the altar; and then build an altar. "And Gideon did as the Lord commanded him"; and we know in the sequel that the Lord did not fail him. He never does. He moved the heart of his father to take his side when the men of the city came seeking his life, and in the end their threatenings and hostility came to naught.

Throw down the altar; then build an altar. God is always thorough. There are things to be thrown down before He will accept the building we erect for Him. He gives His blessing to no divided allegiance, no divided service, to no heart and life that retains sin and disobedience, and that is not cleansed from iniquity. The human tendency is always to go on with good work, so to speak, to make an offer of surrender to God, to enter into consecration, to claim all the blessings of the fullness, and to say, "We will now serve God," and all the time be failing to deal with the evil thing. And God will have none of it. There must be a breaking down before there can be an acceptable building. We have got to go thoroughly and deeply into spiritual things in our dealings with God.

It might be said that this is a true principle in all the deeper issues of life. There must be courage to sacrifice before we can attain to the heights. Death is the way to life: "Except a corn of wheat fall into the ground and die, it abideth alone; but if it die it bringeth forth much fruit." It requires no undue stressing, after our experience of two such wars as most of us have seen in our lifetime, to realise that the way to the heights is so often by the sacrifice of our noblest and best. But that is not specially the thought behind our text. It is that evil things must

133

be put away before lasting good can be built up; they must not be allowed to exist side by side—indeed, ultimately that is an impossibility. Now, that is Christ's way of bringing real joy and peace and victory and fullness of life to men ; and that is God's way of bringing revival to our land and to the world. How we need revival ! The state of our land cries out for it, the state of the Church is desperate for revival, the world is in dire need of new life and movement from the Spirit of God. And God has shown us the way—throw down the altar, then build the altar.

It is a misunderstanding of Christ's Gospel to say He has come to bring blessing and peace to men at any price. He came to bring blessing and peace, yes, and where Christ's will is honestly followed and obeyed there will be blessing and peace. But His peace is designed to be a lasting peace, and therefore is and must be based on righteousness : first righteousness, then peace. So He says in one place, " I came not to send peace on the earth, but a sword." There are things to be rooted up from the constitution of things as we know them, before Christ's peace can be granted ; for the wisdom that is from above is not according to the wisdom of this world, it is " first pure, then peaceable." First throw down the altar erected to unrighteousness, and then build up the altar of righteousness in the name of Christ. There can be no permanent peace among the nations, for example, unless it is based on true righteousness, unless Christ is crowned King in actual fact. And that would mean for every nation a sword cutting out the diseased parts of national life, a putting right of national evils. And in civic life there can only be prosperity and peace if it is based on purity. Let me say that if God's blessing is to come upon us, His laws must be honoured. There is a great altar to godlessness being erected in our fair land, and it has got to be thrown down before God's blessing can come ; it is futile to say " peace, peace when there is no peace"—when the gambling interests are so prosperous and the gambling curse so universal, when there is so much rottenness in life everywhere. If we are to be pleasing to God we need not only the multiplied preaching of the old Gospel, but the sweeping away, in holy reform, of the gambling and drinking and Sabbath breaking, and commercial dishonesty and sin that are on the increase in so many places.

Again, we pray for revival in the Church, and of course that is the only place where revival can come. But as the Church prays she knows where the answer to her prayers will come if she has the courage to face it. God is eager, willing, longing to bless, to pour out new life upon His people and His work ; but He waits for us to fulfil the conditions. First throw down the altar erected to unrighteousness in the Church, the altar of every disobedient thing in the Church, the altar of compromise with the world, the altar of disloyalty to His word and will, of dependence on human strength and wisdom and influence, and the neglect of prayer. Let us apply it to our own parishes and congregations. First throw down the altar, and then build an altar.

What about our homes ? Is not the chief problem of the moral and spiritual situation at the present time just the almost complete collapse of the Christian home ? What real return to God can there be if we do not again have Christian homes ? Well, what about *our* home, *our* family life ? To many of us God is eagerly looking that we might recreate Christian homes. To some of us gathered here God is calling to erect an altar in our homes, the altar of real worship to Him. How long is it since you had family worship in your home ? Did you ever have it ? Do you think it is old-fashioned, or is it that you are afraid or ashamed to be seen by your children and those who know you best in the home, kneeling in acknowledgment to God and honouring Him ? Yet they see you kneeling at many other altars that take up your interest and time, some of them perhaps very doubtful. Maybe that is why you find it hard to erect the altar, because another altar inconsistent with that would have to be thrown down, and your heart rebukes you as you think of praying before your children and your sisters and brothers. Well, let it be thrown down ! Yes, first the sword, and then peace and blessing. Throw down the altar ; it is worth it—it is the only way—then build an altar to God. It was in his family life that Gideon started. It was a specially difficult place, but it was there that God proved and tested and equipped him. He could never have done his task in leading the great movement in his country had he not begun in his own family. It is never easy to throw down altars among those who know us best and love us best, especially if it means the reproving of them, or ourselves, of sin ; but it is where Christ expects our faith to be shown—" Lovest thou Me more than these ? " He says.

That brings us right down to the individual life, where the same principle applies. Indeed, the individual is the key to all the rest ; get the individual right and the other things will come right. So we come to our own lives. If we are really to count for God, if we are to be really right with God, to be filled with all the fullness of God as we should be, there must be repentance from sin. Let us not evade it. Before real Christian living to God's glory can be embarked upon, we must deal with whatever may be interfering with Christ's supreme Lordship in our hearts and lives. We must confess and forsake specific sins, offences and unholiness in our lives. We must humbly then accept cleansing by the Blood of Christ. Yea, we must go deeper. We must go to the whole principle of this thing, we must go to the thing that is causing our defeat and despair. Many of us are anxious and worried, and only too willing to be all-out for God, and we struggle and try, yet we are not knowing the fullness of God as we should. We have to recognise that these sins and failures are just the off-spring of something that is still enthroned in our hearts, that still looms so large with us : Self, the self-life must be thrown down if we are to have victory. Self instead of Christ—self-pity, self-indulgence, self-importance, selfishness. Judgment must be definitely exercised on self; it must be crucified with Christ, if Christ is really to live in us. I know that the tendency is to ignore that or gloss over it. It were so much more comfortable to speak of peaceful things, to urge full consecration ; but if we put up this building without dealing with the root evil, there is still rottenness at the centre. No, we must be crucified, we must pass judgment on sin and self before we can enter into

135

the fullness. I am speaking with all tenderness in my heart. I have been through it, I know the pain of this thing and the struggle, and I am glad people spoke to me like this. And from my experience I must add that the issue of self versus the Lordship of Christ in an individual's life very often does come down to one specific thing, and the battle is decided over that. Is it so with you ? Does the Spirit of God speak about it as I speak ?

In my last year at the University in Dublin, I was asked to go and see a young fellow who had just come up to another college. I had known him some years before as a happy, bright Christian schoolboy. But now his mother was anxious concerning him, and asked that a Christian friend should look him up. I found him at the address given, and I am sorry to say that his mother's worst fears were justified. That lad had gone down a long way from what he was when I knew him. He was not living in the ordinary students' digs, but shared a flat with a much older man than himself, who was anything but a good influence upon him. He was not earnest in his medical studies ; when I asked him about his work, he said he was not going to do any more, he was going to be a free lance and make his fortune in some wonderful way. He was nominally a member of the Church of Ireland, but he said he did not any longer go to Church ; if he did, he rather thought he would go to the Roman Catholic Church. Well, we had a conversation that night, and what we talked about is, of course, private ; but I saw him several times that same term and during the vacation, and for the last time when I came up for my final Degree examinations in October. A great change for the better had by then taken place in him ; he had left the old diggings and was with a Christian landlady who took a motherly interest in him ; he was closely connected with an Evangelical Church of Ireland parish ; and he was carrying on with his medical studies with great enthusiasm. But as I talked with him I knew he had not crowned Christ as Lord yet. He had done many things, but not this, and I felt that the reason was that there was something he had not put right that he knew about. I told him this, though it was not easy. He said, " Dunlop, I don't know how you know it, but that is quite true." I said, " I do not know whether it is something big or little, and I do not ask you to tell me, but if there is something that should go out of your life, it will have to go ; for that will make all the difference between defeat and victory, between self and the Lordship of Christ ; and if you retain it, you will go down, perhaps worse than you did before." He replied with a smile, " Oh, I have learned my lesson ; I will not make a fool of myself again. I am terribly grateful for what you have done for me, and you need not worry about this small thing." I said, " Is it wrong ? " " You would call it wrong." " Would Christ call it wrong ? " " I suppose He would." Then I said, " Put it away, if you want to be out-and-out for Christ ; put Christ on the throne." He said, " It is all right for you, you are going to be a parson, but I cannot be too goody-goody ; Never fear, I shall be all right." I pleaded with him with all my energy over that thing, but we ended there. Three months later that

136

young fellow made complete shipwreck of his life, and broke his mother's heart. And he was a Christian.

Young people, I know what I am talking about on these things. I knew that boy, and I feel very deeply about it as I speak. If you are having a controversy with Christ your Lord on something, small or big, settle it in His favour. Pull down that altar to-night. Self must come down, deal with it. You cannot build an altar of service for Christ if there at the centre is some wrong thing. When the storm comes the structure will fall in ruins, and the enemy will blaspheme and you will have brought discredit upon Christ. I speak to myself as to you. We must throw down the altar and deal with sin, and then build the altar. Remember, it is all for the sake of a building that will really glorify God and bless the world and satisfy you. This destruction is in order to construction ; death is the way to life ; negative work is not Christ's way, but it is the essential step to the positive working of His works in our lives and hearts. Let us face it : first destroy, then build. It is *life* that is at stake, real life ; and for life abundant there must be a surgical operation. " If thine eye offend thee—something that is really part of you—pluck it out. If thy hand offend thee, cut it off." It is better to enter into *life* maimed than to suffer eternal loss. And it is possible to have the soul saved and the life lost. Whatever causes stumbling and hinders life, must be cut away. What sane man would refuse to sacrifice his hand or his eye if it really meant saving his physical life ? We would face it and do it. How much more worth while to crucify the flesh with its affections and lusts in order that we might have the abundant overflowing life of the Spirit !

Let us take God's way, it is the only way. First throw down the altar, then build the altar to His praise and glory.

Steps to Holiness.

By the Rev. H. W. CRAGG, M.A.

*" Now being made free from sin, and become servants of
God, ye have your fruits unto holiness."—Rom.* 6 : 22.

IT has been said that the Old Testament is the best picture book from
which to draw illustrations of New Testament truth, and we have a
very good corroboration of that statement in the fact that we have
seen a picture from Gideon's life which forms one of the best Old Testament illustrations of the doctrinal outlines of this verse from
Romans 6.

" Being made free from sin "—there is the altar literally broken to
the ground ; " and become servants of God "—there is the altar erected
in the life, the altar of consecration and utter abandonment to our Blessed
Lord. And then " ye have your fruit unto holiness "—the third step,
which is going to issue from such a transaction as that which has
been brought before us to-night.

Let us look at these three things. There is something very important
in the fact that this which we have been exhorted to know in our lives
is something which has been revealed to us in the Word of God as the
plan and purpose of God, and for which God in His word has made a
clear provision. Sometimes when men and women speak to me about
their spiritual experiences I have to confess I have not had what they
have had. Sometimes I ask myself : has God a few favourites ? Have
they got something I cannot have ? Then I remember that either God
has provided something I have not yet known, or they have imagined
something which God has never provided. I think it is important
that we should make it clear that every experience in the heart has its
basis in a revelation in the Word. That which is objectively revealed
in Christ in the Scriptures is to be subjectively experienced in the
Christian, and what is not objectively revealed is not to be subjectively
experienced. That is why we were reminded by Mr. Martin that the
truth of which we speak is found in the very heart of our Bibles. We
have no authority on this platform to ask that you should throw down that
altar built to Baal, but God has, and if the Word of God demands that
this shall happen in the life of every believer, and the Word of God reveals
the glorious power to make it possible, then we are under a bounden
obligation to enter into the provision and know the experience. That
which God has revealed in His Word is for the experience of His people,
and I am sure there are many of us who know of these gifts revealed in the
Word and have never yet come to know them in the experience of
daily life.

" Made free from sin and become servants of God, ye have your fruit unto holiness." May I put it like this : first of all, something to be broken, sin ; secondly, something to be bound, the servant ; thirdly, something to become, holy.

I. SOMETHING TO BE BROKEN.

How much we all long that the power of sin in our lives might be utterly shattered ; and that longing is but a poor reflection of Christ's longing for us. God has not placed that longing in our hearts to mock us. God has not placed that longing deep down in our souls to allow us to lose the secret of satisfaction.

Something to be broken. I wonder if I am speaking to somebody here who is saying, " That is exactly where I want to come, but how can I get there ? " I want to review one or two of the things in this chapter which ought to help you to get there, and which, if you will but follow as Christ shall make it clear, will bring you there. For this which is the culmination of a chapter of very clear and important teaching, is meant to be real in your life and mine.

May I remind you that in this sixth chapter of Romans God has laid down the basic facts of spiritual liberty and made them so clear and final that if we will but look at them, God will help us to enter into the experience. God has made it clear that all our cleansing, all our liberty, all our freedom, was purchased for us once for all at the Cross. In this chapter the Apostle reminds us of Calvary : " Knowing this, that our old man—that is the seat of the trouble, the reason for all the problems you are facing—" was crucified with Him, that the body of sin might be destroyed, that henceforth we should not serve sin." We were reminded in our Bible Reading of the great truth as revealed in Ephesians, of the Christian's identification with Christ in His Cross. " I have been crucified with Christ."

The reason why this was done is that the body of sin might be destroyed. The word used for " destroyed " in the Greek is not " to be abolished once and for all," but rather, " rendered inoperative " or " put out of action "—not eradication, which would mean we have no more need of grace, which God has never promised. We are brought to a place where we are utterly dependent on Him. This is not eradication, but the presence of the indwelling Christ by the Spirit so wonderfully enthroned in heart and life that we by faith enter into all that Christ made possible for us on the Cross. Our old man was crucified with Him, that henceforth we should not serve sin. This is a once for all fact of history, and victorious Christian living was made possible at the Cross. You can never forget your indebtedness to Calvary, whatever may be the problem you are facing at the moment. All the breaking down that you have to do can only be done in the power of the victorious sacrifice offered for you once for all on the Cross. That is why, further down in this chapter, we find that this great fact of history has to be met by an act of faith : " Likewise reckon ye also yourselves to have died indeed unto sin, and to be alive unto God through Jesus Christ our Lord " (v. 11). The fact of history must be met by an act of faith. Is it not true in all

Christian experience that God gives in grace and we receive by faith? You received forgiveness in conversion, and you enter into His victory when you take this revealed truth of God and by faith appropriate it to your own experience in your own heart.

But someone may say: Is this breaking down the altar? Yes it is, for it is the whole ground on which you begin to throw down the altar. Of course, just as faith without works is dead in relation to justification, so it is in relation to sanctification. It is no good to claim victory from the sacrifice of Christ on the Cross if we are allowing to remain in the life something which God has put His finger on. The Bible says " mortify your members," " put off the old man," " let all anger and wrath be put away from you." All these things can only be put down in the power of a life of faith. Jesus did the dying, and in Him I died, and everything which is sinful and loathsome and unworthy dies in Him.

I wonder if I can light up what is mystifying all our hearts, with a simple illustration. It used to be said over the wireless during the war when some great campaign had been won, and some great general had withdrawn his advanced forces and sent other subsidiary forces in, that such an army was engaged in " mopping up." That is what you are engaged in when you are breaking down the altar. The great campaign has been won. The great guarantee of personal triumph has been purchased for you with the precious blood of Christ. Christ did the work once for all on the Cross, and as you enter in to possess the land by faith you are left with the little bouts and skirmishes and the " mopping up." Will you, then, do that mopping up? Will you reckon yourself dead unto sin and alive unto God through Jesus Christ our Lord? When we stand by faith at the foot of Calvary's Cross we see not only our sins forgiven, but that wonderful provision for this old sinful nature fully and finally met by Christ's dying for us in which we are identified by faith.

Then we go on from victory, as Capt. Reginald Wallace used to say, not to victory—we stand by faith in a victory purchased for us by Christ on the Cross—but to exploit the gains and to complete the " mopping up." Something to be broken. I do trust some of us are beginning to see why it should be broken. Why should we be living defeated lives and going on with the altar unbroken? Christ has made it possible for that something in our hearts to be smashed.

> He did it for me, He did it for me,
> A sinner as guilty as ever could be,
> Oh, how I love Him now that I see
> He suffered, He died,
> And He did it for me.

Calvary is the place where the altar of Baal is broken down. Will you come afresh tonight for your sanctification, as one night in some Gospel meeting you came for your justification?

140

II. SOMETHING TO BE BOUND.

" Made free from sin, ye become servants of God." In the latter part of this chapter there is a wonderful contrast stated between the old bondage to sin and the new bondage to Christ, and the Apostle Paul gives us two illustrations of the change over. For spiritual freedom is a new form of spiritual slavery, a new form of bondage. Some people think that freedom is doing as they like. That is bondage to self. Real freedom is bondage to Christ, doing what Christ likes, being so tied up with Him in love's fetters that " for me to live is Christ." If the bands of sin have been snapped, and Christ has broken everything that ties us down, there is a new bondage to be wrapped round us, so that we are bound by cords of love to One whose service is perfect freedom.

In the latter part of Romans 6 Paul gives the first of these two illustrations. In effect he says, here is a man who has been a slave to a certain master, then that master has finished with him, and he goes into the slave market and is bought by another master. He goes out of one slavery into another, a new slavery. For the Christian he says—you have come out of the bondage to sin into the bondage to righteousness. You were once the servant of sin, but you have been delivered and are now under a new bondage. Then, lest his readers should think this is an irksome thing he takes his second illustration from wedlock, in the opening verses of chapter 7. He says a woman married to her husband is bound by law to her husband, but once death has intervened and snapped the bond of union, that woman is free to be married again, and when she is married again she is tied up in a new bondage, a happy bondage, a delightful bondage, one in which she rejoices. The point of the two illustrations is that in the case of both the first bondage and the second bondage there was an equal tie, just as severe, just as all-embracing, just as final and complete, but to two different masters.

I wonder if we have sufficiently realised that Jesus Christ is seeking that we should be bound up with Him in just as vital a binding as once enslaved us to sin. When the Apostle Paul was converted he lost a lot of things, but there were a lot of things he did not lose. He is described as one serving with the same zeal, the same enthusiasm, the same mighty demonstration of abilities and power, but all now on the side of Jesus Christ ; out of one kind of life into another, just as vital and all-embracing. The Christian is a man who has not only seen one altar smashed, but the second erected, and with just the same energy and enthusiasm and devotion.

May I ask you a question ? Are you tied to your Lord as much as you were once tied to your sin ? That is why the Apostle says " Reckon yourselves dead indeed unto sin," and then " yield yourselves unto God." This body and its members that once served sin must now serve Jesus Christ. Sin broken, but the servant bound, the first altar down and the second altar up. Are you ready for the experience tonight, reckoning that you are dead unto sin in your union with Christ in His death, and then yielding yourself unreservedly to Him to be His loving slave for ever ? Paul called himself " the bond-slave of Jesus Christ." Are you ready for the binding ?

III. Then There is Something to Become.

"Being made free from sin, and become servants to God, ye have your fruit unto holiness." There are two simple things I want to say about this. First it is a fruit, not a product; holiness is not something we work up, it is something that Christ brings into the life that is utterly dependent on Him. Secondly, not only is it a fruit, it is a sure fruit— "ye have fruit." If we would be more concerned about being broken from sin and being tied up with Jesus Christ in this new bondage, we should have less trouble about our holiness. If you are made free from sin and have become a servant to Christ, you have "fruit unto holiness," for the man who has entered into the blessed experience of the breaking of the bonds at the Cross and has become the loving servant of Christ, that man is going to be a holy man. Watch the breaking of the bond, watch the tying of the new bond, and Christ will watch the holiness. We used to say, "Take care of the pence and the pounds will take care of themselves." If you will take care of both these things which Mr. Dunlop has brought before us, Christ will look after the holiness. Something to be broken, something to be bound, something to become.

I remember the first time I came to Keswick, in 1928. Four of us had cycled from my home town, a distance of about 90 miles. On the final Saturday morning we could not stay for the testimony meeting. As we were leaving the town, climbing the hill which leads out in a southerly direction, and pushing our bicycles, we stopped at the last point from which we could view the tent. We had very little to say to one another, for our hearts were a little heavy as we were wending our way home from our first Keswick, but as we stood and listened there came up from this tent the sound of a chorus we had learnt that year :—

Sin shall not have dominion over you :
What a glorious message, and it's true ;
God has said it, it must stand,
Pass it on, it's simply grand :
Sin shall not have dominion over you.

It seemed as if God had given to us on the top of the hill at the beginning of the journey home a parting benediction, and that is the most outstanding memory of my first Keswick. I would not like to say that the intervening period of eighteen years has always seen that lived out. There are people in this tent who could contradict me if I made such a claim. But I do make this simple claim, that I have discovered in the intervening years that when I have looked away to the Cross and have seen self dealt with once for all, and have re-affirmed the surrender I made that year, when I have seen to the breaking and the binding, Christ has always seen to the becoming. It is when I fail to see myself there, that I fail to be holy. It is when I fail to re-affirm that utter abandonment to Him, that I fail to be fully His. When those two things have been true of me, God has looked after the third, and there has been "fruit unto holiness." "Being made free, and become servants, ye have your fruit unto holiness."

142

WEDNESDAY,
July 17th, 1946.

10 a.m. **Bible Reading.**

FOUR CHAPTERS OF CHRISTIAN EXPERIENCE.

(*iii*) A CHAPTER OF DEMONSTRATION— 1 CORINTHIANS 13.

THE REV. GUY H. KING.

11.45 a.m. **Forenoon Meeting.**

MAINTAINING A HOLY LIFE.

THE REV. A. T. HOUGHTON.

THE PERIL OF WORLDLINESS.

MR. F. MITCHELL.

3 p.m. **Afternoon Meeting.**

HEAVEN NOW.

DR. DONALD G. BARNHOUSE.

7.45 p.m. **Evening Meeting.**

" BY MY SPIRIT."

THE REV. RONALD J. PARK.

THE AGENT OF THE ALMIGHTY.

DR. W. GRAHAM SCROGGIE.

Pressing Home the Message.

HOPES that Tuesday's improvement in the weather had marked a turning-point and the beginning of some fine, sunny days, were disappointed: Wednesday was wet again, and extremely bad weather prevailed throughout the rest of the week. Indeed, the rain at times was torrential. It was a distraction at the prayer meeting in the small tent; but it did not quench the spirit of prayer. In the Pavilion, also, there was a good attendance, and a consciousness of access to the throne of grace.

Before the Rev. Guy H. King's third Bible Reading, the glorious hymn " Ten thousand times ten thousand " was sung, and surely made the hills re-echo the praise of God Most High. Coming to "A Chapter of Demonstration "—1 Corinthians 13—Mr. King said he would not have tackled it but for a profound sense of compulsion. St. Paul's eulogy of love has been the theme of more than one series of Bible Readings at Keswick; it certainly—like all Mr. King's chapters of Christian experience—formed a vast subject for one study: but from its inexhaustible storehouse Mr. King brought treasures new and old. His portrayal of a brilliant life from which love is absent, brought home vividly to all his hearers the fact that " Ichabod " is written across even the most gifted life which lacks the cardinal virtue. From this stern picture it was almost with a sense of relief that Mr. King turned to consider, in glowing words, the beautiful life in which love is apparent; and then to anticipate the blessed life wherein love will be permanent—when " we shall be like Him, for we shall see Him as He is."

Another of this year's new speakers, the Rev. A. T. Houghton, gave the first address at the Convention meeting which followed, and from Psalm 119 : 9-11 he educed several practical lessons concerning holiness and separation from the world. Then, after the singing of Charles Wesley's hymn, " Come, Jesus, Lord, with holy fire," Mr. F. Mitchell— who, although speaking at Keswick for the first time, took a prominent part in the " Keswick in London " Conventions, and has been appointed one of the Trustees—gave one of the most challenging messages of the Convention. Beginning with a reference to some lines of the hymn, he dealt with the problem of worldliness and the lowered standards even of the Evangelical Church to-day. Speaking forcefully and with great earnestness, Mr. Mitchell set before his hearers the New Testament teaching of separation from the world, and gave counsel concerning such practical problems as the Christian's attitude to the cinema, smoking, and other indulgences.

The tent was again full in the afternoon for the third of Dr. Barnhouse's addresses; and in the evening the Rev. Ronald J. Park spoke from the oft-quoted verse in Zechariah 4, " Not by might, nor by power, but by My Spirit . . ." He was followed by the Rev. Guy H. King, who linked together the declaration of God to Moses, " I am come down to deliver " (Ex. 3 : 8) with His command, " Come now therefore, and I will send thee " (v. 10). Showing that God, in fulfilling His purposes, uses *men*, Mr. King invited those to stand who wished to signify their surrender or rededication to the Lord for His service, to be His witnesses ; and a large number, in all parts of the tent, rose, and Mr. King committed them to God in prayer. It was a challenging culmination to a day of heart searching, and one in which the Convention accomplished its truest purpose, in lives newly pledging themselves to His allegiance, or renewing their vows in response to His gracious call.

Come, Jesus, Lord, with holy fire,
Come, and my quickened heart inspire,
Cleansed in Thy precious blood :
Now to my soul Thyself reveal,
Thy mighty working let me feel,
Since I am born of God.

Let nothing now my heart divide,
Since with Thee I am crucified,
And live to God in Thee.
Dead to the world and all its toys,
Its idle pomp and fading joys,
Jesus, my glory be.

Now with a quenchless thirst inspire,
A longing, infinite desire,
And fill my craving heart.
Less than Thyself, oh, do not give,
In might Thyself within me live :
Come, all Thou hast and art.

My will be swallowed up in Thee,
Light in Thy light still may I see
In Thine unclouded face :
Called the full strength of trust to prove
Let all my quickened heart be love,
My spotless life be praise.

Four Chapters of Christian Experience

(*iii*) A Chapter of Demonstration—1 Corinthians 13.

BY THE REV. GUY H. KING.

WHO would not shrink from seeking to expound I Corinthians 13 ? I greatly shrink. One would so carefully handle some exquisitely beautiful object, lest one mark, or mar it ; and here is something which is not only, in Henry Drummond's words, " The greatest thing in the world," but also the loveliest thing in the world. God grant us delicacy of touch—both speaker and hearer alike. And how humbling it is to have to deal with such a chapter—when one realises how dreadfully one comes short of it. Nothing but a sense of inward compulsion would have induced me to take up the study of it.

Well now, we would call it a Chapter of Demonstration, and we have included it in these morning meditations, because it is one of the basic rules of the Christian life that the existence of that life must in some way be demonstrated to others. Let me remind you of the case of Legion. The Lord had cured his poor wracked body, He had given him again his erstwhile equipoise of mind, He had (as I think) brought salvation to his sinful soul. And now, as the Master is about to embark on ship for His journey out from that country, the grateful Legion pleads for a place in the boat—he would go overseas for Jesus, with Jesus. His own fellow-countrymen did not want Christ—they rated swine more valuable than souls ; but he wanted Him. And if any testimony to His saving power would help to gain Him acceptance in the place to which He was sailing, Legion was His man. But the Master had other plans for him. He must first " Go home," and demonstrate there the reality of his conversion and cure. After all, home is always to be the first place, isn't it ? Do you remember that word in I Timothy 5 : 4, " Learn first to shew piety at home." Legion was told to do that—and to do it in two ways. I believe he was given two commands, one of which is recorded by Mark, and the other by Luke—" Go home to thy friends, and *tell* them how great things the Lord hath done for thee " (Mark 5 : 19) ; " Return to thine own house, and *shew* how great things God hath done unto thee." Do you notice : " tell," and " shew " ? The first is not our subject this morning ; but we remind ourselves that the testimony of our lips is required of us all, as well as the testimony of our lives—" Thou shalt confess with thy mouth the Lord Jesus " says Romans 10 : 9 ; and, " Let the redeemed of the Lord say so " (Psalm 107 : 2). No amount of life confession can excuse us the duty of lip confession. My friend, let me say, in all tenderness, that if you have found your Christian life unsatisfactory, one reason might be that you have never openly acknowledged your allegiance to Christ. Do not forget that the experience of what we know as full salvation is, according to that Romans' verse just quoted, dependent, not only upon " belief " in Him, but also upon " confession " of Him. But our particular point just now is that other kind of demonstration—" shew." A boy who had been converted to God was told that, when he got home that evening, he should tell the first person he met what had happened to him. The text had been, " A new heart also will I give you " (Ezekiel 36 : 26) ; so, when his front-door was opened to him by his little sister, he thought he had better tell her. " Marion," he said, " I've got a new heart." Eagerly interested, she answered, " Oh, have you : show it me." Wasn't she right, though not, perhaps, in the way she thought ? If we have the new heart, through the regenerating grace of the Holy Spirit, should we not seek help of God to " shew " it in our demeanour and behaviour ? And so we come to this the greatest of all proofs that we possess Christian life—the demonstration of Christian love. Recall the Master's own words, in John 13 : 35, " By this shall all men know that ye are My disciples, if ye have love one to another." That's it : love, love, love. May the Holy Spirit write the word deep on all our hearts, and the thing be demonstrably present in all our lives. We turn to our chapter ; and in the first three verses we find :—

I. A Brilliant Life Wherein Love is Absent.

How brilliant is this hypothetical man whose portrait is here set before us. I feel that the word " all, " four times repeated, with its suggestion of the perfection of the gifts, is meant to indicate that the Apostle is not thinking of any particular man—least of all of himself ; but suppose, for the sake of argument, that a person could be found who completely filled the bill, yet if love were absent, he would be, in God's sight, of no account.

First you will notice that he is (*i*) *A man of fine speech*—" I speak with the tongues of men and of angels." Here is a linguistic gift of rare excellence. What an accomplishment it is ! I have heard of an English missionary bishop, who, as he started out on his journey to India, began, with the aid of a grammar, a dictionary, and a national, to learn the language of the people to whom he went ; and who was actually able to preach to them, on his landing, in their own tongue. I have heard of another, Senior Classic of his day at Cambridge, who listened to a missionary appeal to go to native tribes of Africa who had never heard the Good News, and who, realising with thankfulness that God had given him this gift, went and dedicated himself to go and learn the languages, and to tell out the message. I wonder if there is someone here in the tent this morning who has this gift, and who, by the love of Christ, will be constrained to come and lay it sacrificially on the altar, to be used, as He directs, by the God who gave the gift and redeemed it (as He has every Christian's every gift) by His precious blood. But the supposititious person of our passage is credited here, I think, with the fabulous facility of speaking all languages. I knew a man once who could read twenty, and speak in most of them ; but—all ! This man also has a divine afflatus —for I imagine that when " the tongues . . . of angels " are mentioned, the reference is to what we usually mean by the gift of tongues, a gift bestowed upon the Early Church for, shall we say, the rapid spread of the Gospel, a gift now normally withheld, since the need for it is no longer so required, a gift that already, in this first Corinthian Church, had shewed signs of getting out of control, and concerning which the Apostle had to write strongly and sternly in the very next chapter of this letter. Well, here he is : if ever there was a man of mighty and moving eloquence, this was he. What a power is speech—to effect reforms, to sway crowds, to propagate causes, to challenge decisions, to win votes, to inspire courageous deeds.

Do some of you feel discouraged because you haven't the gift ? Do you say, like Moses, Exodus 4 : 10, " O my Lord, I am not eloquent " ; then will you hear Him say, " Go, and I will be with thy mouth " (v. 12). Do you say, with Jeremiah, " Ah, Lord God, I cannot speak " ; then will you note how He responded " The Lord . . . touched my mouth " (Jer. 1 : 7, 9). Do you, along the lines of what we were saying earlier, long to speak for your Lord and yet feel tongue-tied ? Listen to the familiar words of Acts 2 : 4—" They were all filled with the Holy Ghost, and began to speak with other tongues." You are not concerned with those other tongues ; it is your own tongue which is your problem. You do not know how to speak, you do not know how to begin ? The Apostles learnt the secret, and " began to speak " to some purpose : and so shall you if " filled with the Holy Ghost."

Yes ; but there is something wrong with the man of our chapter. There's something missing : what can it be ? All his rushing utterance is mere noise—as " sounding brass, or a tinkling cymbal." It may stir emotions, it may rouse excitement ; but it won't do anything for God. Why ? What's the matter ? Oh, that's simple : there's no love in it, that's all. Oh, the tragedy of a loveless pulpit. God forbid that it should be that of Christ Church, Beckenham.

Again, this is (ii) *A man of deep knowledge*—" I have the gift of prophecy, and understand all mysteries, and all knowledge." Once more I remind you that this is merely hypothetical : there never was a man who knew all this. But, just for a moment, suppose there was. You will observe that he not only knows the mystery and knowledge, but he is able, by " the gift of prophecy," to impart it to others : a combination not too frequently found. Often, the most learned are the least successful in passing on their treasures of wisdom. Our phantom friend is expert in both departments.

We shall all agree that such a man is a being of great importance in the community ; but he himself confesses, " I am nothing." This is not just the language of proper modesty, it is the word of not less proper honesty. In his scholars' minds, he is a fine teacher ; in his own heart he is sadly aware that he is a failure—and that because he knows that he

149

has no love. It is all a matter of duty, routine, livelihood ; but there is no love either for the subjects he teaches, or for the students he reaches.

A certain boy used regularly to attend a Sunday school some distance from home, passing several others on his way. On being asked why he went to one that was so far off when there were a number nearer, he replied, with shy hesitation, " Well, you see, they love a feller there." There are Sunday school teachers come up here for the Convention. What a highly privileged person you are, what a strategic task you have. Paul said once, " I magnify mine office " (Rom. 11 : 13). You say it ; not once, but over and over again—say it, and do it. But listen : is there love in your work ? If not, although you may know *what* to teach, and *how* to reach—you won't reach. Your vicar, your pastor, your superintendent may think highly of you ; but in God's eyes, you will be " nothing " without love.

Once more we scrutinise this eminently desirable person, and we discover that he is (*iii*) *A man of high achievement*—" I have all faith, so that I could remove mountains." What a mighty power faith is ! We know about saving faith, which links us on to the Saviour and makes Him our own Saviour. When this faith is ours, there is too, in Christians, a continuance in faith ; but in Mark 4 : 40 the Master said to some Christians, "How is it that ye have *no faith* ? " To a sinking disciple— and this was why he was sinking—He said, in Matthew 14 : 31, "O thou of *little faith*." To a seeking Gentile, He said, " I have not found so *great faith*, no not in Israel." No faith, little faith, great faith : here is a man with " *all* faith." Or perhaps it means, all the faith that is required to remove mountains : a proverbial phrase used at that time, and quoted by our Lord, you remember, in Matthew 17 : 20, for the overcoming of great obstacles, and the overturning of great opposition. This man could do it ; and yet, while outwardly he made a great stir, and a great reputation, inwardly he counted for nothing—was " nothing " ; and, in his heart of hearts, he knew it. There was no love. His wonder-working activities were, perhaps, bold—but cold.

Look again, and see (*iv*) *A man of wide charity*—" I bestow all my goods to feed the poor." My word, there were no half-measures about this fellow ; and it was a right worthy cause that he supported. The feeding of the poor is, surely, incumbent upon all Christian people. In these days of shortage and of threatening famine, in Europe and in the East, I think it is our bounden duty to support any efforts that our Government feels we ought to make to lend a hand, even to the point of sacrifice. But, who will display a like concern for the feeding of the multitude of starving souls, languishing in all the world for the Bread of Life. Say not, as you meditate upon the five loaves of your personality, that you cannot do anything in the face of such vast need : " What are they among so many ? " (John 6 : 9). It is with lives as with loaves, that if surrendered Jesus will take the gift and multiply it to multitude proportions. Tell me, do you think a proper part of your money goes in missionary giving—to distribute the Bread ?

To come back to the material outlook of the matter, it is still true—is it not—that we should take our share in trying " to feed the poor." How kind our chapter man was, to give so much. Zacchæus gave " half of my goods " (Luke 19 : 8) ; this man gives " all my goods." Kind ? No ; I fancy you are giving him credit for virtues that he did not possess. I have an idea that the motive of his munificence was not very high— that his large subscriptions gained him kudos, that his handsome dona- tions were greeted with " loud applause." I am only guessing ; but what I do know is that there was no love there ; and, consequently, while his benefactions certainly profited his beneficiaries, they did not profit him—he admits it himself.

And, then, he was (v) *A man of consuming zeal*—" I give my body to be burned." How grand a quality is real enthusiasm ; but how rarely displayed in Christian things. I have seen a Christian man throw up his hat, a respectable bowler, in the excitement of a rugger international at Twickenham, who, I know, would not throw in more than a bob to the missionary collection next day. When I was a small boy, I listened in church one morning to the curate ! He was a hero in my eyes, because he was a Cambridge double blue—soccer and running—he could not preach, but we boys held him among the orators of our time. That day, he said a simple thing that stuck in my young mind, and that still remains there even now that I am old : he said, " Never mind if we sometimes make mistakes, do let us have enthusiasm." Not perhaps a very profound utterance ; but it made a profound impression upon me. Oh, for a little more burning enthusiasm about God's great cause.

" Burning ? "—Why this man gave his *body* to be burned ; and I am sure his example of supreme self-sacrificing zeal brought big gain to his cause ; but he acknowledges, it " profiteth *me* nothing," for it lacked love. If you ask how anyone could go that length without love, I remind you that pagans have done it, that fanatics have done it, that zealots have done it.

But, look back : what a brilliant life is here described, with its eloquence, knowledge, power, charity, zeal. What a mighty thing must love be if the absence of it reduces such a life to nothingness. But see here :—

II. A Beautiful Life Wherein Love is Evident.

The absence of love is such a deprivation ; the presence of love is such a demonstration. Here, in fourteen lines, is a portrait of what a real loving Christian is meant to be—both in character, and in conduct. It is a lovely presentment ; but, my dear friends, I warn you that the study of it may hurt. Dr. Moffatt, recalling, with approval, that the passage is often spoken of as a lyric, so lovely is its language, but realising how it may cut our convicted conscience to the quick, says, " The lyric is thus a lancet." How greatly some of us are condemned by the sight of this beautiful life wherein love is evident—what ought to be the demonstration of the reality of our profession. Well, let us face it ; the lyric will glorify our Lord Jesus, for He it is of whom it is a perfect

151

likeness ; the lancet may go deep, but it will only aim to cut out the dead tissue, and to clean up the infected area, so that we may, by the secret which shall be our theme tomorrow, ourselves approach more nearly to that likeness here portrayed. Have you sometimes been to a friend's house, and, finding a photograph on the mantlepiece, asked " Who is this ? " to be greeted by the surprised rejoinder, " But surely you know ! " You still maintain that you haven't the slightest idea ; but you are then told, " Why, it's So-and-so." You can only reply, " I should never have known him." In another house, you pick up a photograph in the drawing-room, and exclaim, with a beaming face, " I say, isn't that exactly like him ? " Well, what sort of a portrait are you of Him ? I say " you," because I have already asked the question of myself. Is the likeness so poor that people—shall we say, the people at home—can scarcely recog-nise that you are Christ's ; or, God grant it, is the likeness so good that others can see His reflection in you ? Like the story of the little Indian child who when, at a meeting, she heard the beautiful story of the Lord Jesus, interrupted with, " Please, teacher, that man used to live here." A missionary had lived in those parts, and had been so kind, so gentle, so holy, that when the child heard tell of Jesus, she thought at once that that missionary must have been He. Missionary at home on furlough, I want you to look at this portrait of Him who was Incarnate Love ; worker here at home—you, too ; all of you, each of you in this tent, this morning—you, too. It may hurt ; but, please God, it shall heal. Here, then, are the blessed details of what love does, and is.

" *Suffereth long* "—I think that means : is never hasty, is slow to take offence. Some of us are rather quick that way. Don't we ministers know the member who, from some trivial and imagined slight, threatens to " leave the church " ; and aren't we ministers often only too inclined to resent a bit of criticism ? Man alive ! do you reckon, then, that you are perfect ? Then, suppose what they say is true. If there is love in our hearts, we shall be slow to take offence ; we shall " suffer " it, and love them still.

" *Is kind* "—that is, moved by a heart of benevolence. Sheer good-ness resides in such a heart, fills such a life. Have you ever thought what an effective evangelistic agency kindness is ? I believe that many a soul that has been converted to God, has been predisposed to the acceptance of the Gospel by the simple kindness of a Christian. Do you long to win souls, but feel frustrated because you cannot speak ? Try being just kind ; try it on your neighbours—do not give your game away, but keep on doing acts of kindness. One day you will get your chance, or somebody else will ; and then " he that soweth, and he that reapeth, shall rejoice together." That is a new kind of evangelistic campaign. How enthusiastic about it love would be.

" *Envieth not* "—I think that means, is not jealous of another's success. Maybe, this is one of the special temptations of Christian workers. I do know that it has been the hidden cause of many a failure in service, the subtle stoppage of the flowing of rivers of blessing, the deep-down explanation of much wretched misery in the heart. Love is free from that slow poison.

" *Vaunteth not itself* "—makes no parade of its own success. If such a person as is here photographed has gotten success, whether in business or profession, or Christian service, he will remain humble and unspoiled ; he will recognise that he owes it to God's blessing of him ; he will seek somehow to use it for God's glory ; and he will never dream of parading it as if it were all his own doing. I know many finely successful business men, and many greatly-used Christian workers who, thank God, belong to the non-vaunters.

" *Is not puffed up* "—gives itself no airs. I fancy that one of the chiefest Christian qualities is humility, and I believe it will ultimately prove itself to have been one of the most effective. It is a rare plant ! A certain clergyman announced that he proposed to preach a course of sermons on the Christian virtues, and that the first one would be on humility. A lady of his congregation, meeting him in the street, told him how glad she was, and especially that he was to begin on humility, for, she said, " That's my forte ! " I have a very dear friend, a man greatly beloved of us all, whose sweetest characteristic is a very beautiful humility ; but that dear man hasn't the slightest idea that he has that grace—that is the very hall-mark of its reality. I only know that that humility of his is a frequent rebuke to me. Love is always so truly humble. How God loves humble people.

" *Doth not behave itself unseemly* "—Moffatt translates, " Is never rude." Alas, we Christians can be very rude—in the shops, in the buses, in the homes, in the streets, yea, even in the church. A campaign for good manners is long overdue. Listen to me, my brethren, I am not being just critical—God knows I'm not ; but I am so keenly aware that, in some of these `things, we are greatly harming the cause, and I am so earnestly praying that conviction shall come where it is needed, and that we may all go love's way.

" *Seeketh not her own* "—is not too concerned for her own interests, is not too eager to stand up for her rights. A Christian minister once said to me, " If I don't look after my own interests, nobody else will " ; but why so ? Surely God can take care of the welfare of His own ; surely it is well to leave Him to safeguard our rights—if we, who owe everything to Him, have any. Love is blissfully content to leave its all to His love.

" *Is not easily provoked* "—is not touchy and irritable. Many of us have a very queer temper. Oh, I know we call it righteous indignation. I suggest here is one test : are we ourselves the supposed injured party ? If so, we can be pretty certain that it is just temper—and we had better acknowledge it. We do invent such fancy names for evil, don't we ? A fib, a little weakness, a paddy, a little drop too much. One backslider was confessing, at the prayer meeting, his fall into sin the previous night— " Oh Lord," he said, " Thou knowest I was tempted to take a glass or two—I was a bit too merry—and hazy—and perhaps I had a drop too much," when the gruff voice of the leader of the meeting broke in, " Tell Him you got drunk." Same with temper—call the wretched thing by its right name, and seek pardon, and power to put it right. Love can indeed, be blazingly indignant ; but whoever saw love in a temper ?

" *Thinketh no evil* "—I fancy the meaning here is that love never harbours a grudge. Quarrels, feuds, grudges have arisen between church members ever since Euodius and Syntyche upset the peace among the Philippian brethren. Oh, how the angry, surly spirit bars the way of blessing. If the devil wants to damage a Church, as he not infrequently does, he more often than not does it by getting two members at logger-heads. Such a thing is, of course, the very antithesis of love. If you have a grudge against any, go to that person and try to get it put right. If they will not meet you, you will at least have the satisfaction of knowing that you have done your part. Why not write that letter this very day ? Anyhow, you can't join in Friday night's Communion Service with a grudge in your heart, can you ?

" *Rejoiceth not in iniquity, but rejoiceth (with) the truth* "—the commentators suggest that the first part means that love is never glad at another's fall. It is a horrid thought—but human nature can be horrid—that anybody could rejoice in another person's downfall. But, alas, such is jealousy that it can bring us even to such a wicked pass. Love rejoices only over the true things, the right things.

" *Beareth all things, believeth all things, hopeth all things, endureth all things* "—that is, I believe, that love is ready to cover up the bad things about a man, if there's no need to reveal them ; to be always ready to believe the best about a man until he is bound to accept a contrary verdict ; to be ready never to lose hope of a man, however disappointing he may be ; to be ready to stick to a man ; to be ever content to wait for the happy result whatever the contradictions and difficulties he may have to put up with from him. Such is love's way of trying to win another to the right way.

Does all this disturb you ? I warned you that it might. Do we feel how far off we are from this love's ideal. Well, God will shew us tomorrow, if we are spared, a secret whereby we may personally realise something of the ideal. For the moment, let us consider, lastly :—

III. A BLESSED LIFE WHEREIN LOVE IS PERMANENT.

One of the great reasons for the pre-eminence of love is its permanence. While it is a sad fact that, in the case of some Christians, love is absent ; and while there are others in whom it is evident ; there is coming a time when in all believers, it will be blessedly present, and gloriously permanent. When we may look for that desirable age, and when we may look for the opening of that state, is indicated for us here in our chapter. Look at verse 10, " When that which is perfect is come "—this is not what I may call the " stage perfection," which is expected down here of every Christian, " Be ye therefore perfect . . ." (Matt. 5 : 48). You see a little child smiling and gurgling in his perambulator, and you say, " Isn't he perfect ! " You see a virile young man, with his clean limb, and keen eye, and you say, " A perfect specimen of young manhood." You see an old man, stored with wisdom, out of his ripe experience, and irradiating kindliness, and you say, " What a perfect old dear." The child hasn't the perfection of the young man, not yet ; but he is perfect at his stage. St. John sees all this in the spiritual realm, when he is guided to say, " I write unto you, fathers . . . I write unto you, young men . . . I write unto you, little children " (I John 2 : 13). To be just what we ought to be for our spiritual age, from our second birthday onward : that is stage perfection. But this described here is final perfection—the Greek verb is an aorist tense : " when that which is perfect *shall have* come "—a specific point of time ; the glorious moment of His appearing for His own, when, at long last, after many failures, " we shall be like Him, for we shall see Him as He is " (I John 3 : 2). Or, again, note verse 12, " Now we see through a glass, darkly ; but then face to face." The ancient mirror was, of course, not glass but brass—brightly burnished, which would give but a dim reflection. The word " through " may mean simply, " by means of, through the medium of " ; or it may, more likely, refer to the illusion that the image appears to be there at the back, and we observe it through the reflecting surface. Then we shall see Him not as be-dimmed by any human or earthly instrument, but in all the surpassing wonder of immediate, personal intercourse, face to face. " Now I know in part . . ." Yes, thank God, there is much to be known down here ; but then — ! With what intensity does love look for the coming back of " Jesu, Lover of my soul." That is the moment when love's permanency shall begin—to be no longer fitful, to be for ever stable and true ; then shall it be perfectly seen that " Love never faileth."

Notice here (*i*) *The contrast with the transient three.*—We are taken back to the gifts mentioned at the beginning of the chapter, important and valuable for Christian service here, but which are not lasting. (*a*) " Whether there be prophecies, they shall fail "—or, better, they shall be done away. There will be no further need for them them ; (*b*) " Whether there be tongues, they shall cease "—speaking with tongues was only a temporary gift ; when the place for them ceases, God withdraws the gift. It has already, I am persuaded, almost disappeared. God does not waste miracles. (*c*) " Whether there be knowledge, it shall vanish away "— be done away. Each stage of knowledge shall be superseded by advancing knowledge. " When I was a child, I spake . . . understood . . . thought, as a child "—up to the point of, within the range of, a child's knowledge ; but, " when I became a man . . ." Yes, these things, precious at their time and stage, all disappear ; but love goes on !

Notice then (*ii*) *The climax of the permanent three.*—Not the gifts of Christian service, but the virtues of Christian character : these abide. Yes, all three of them—" now abideth faith, hope, love," not the last only, but " these three." The Greek for this " now " is a different word from the one found twice in the previous verse—they represent the temporal quality, but this, in the main, the logical sense. As to faith— the late learned Dean Alford says, " In the form of holy confidence and trust, faith will abide." As to hope—the same expositor writes, " New glories, new treasures of knowledge and of love will ever raise and nourish

155

blessed hopes of yet more and higher experiences." But " the greatest of these " permanents is love. Why " greatest " ?

Our first section, verses 1-3, gives the first reason—love is the very soul of every other gift of grace. Our second section, verses 4-7, gives the second reason—love is supreme by virtue of its own excellencies. And, what is stressed by Dr. Graham Scroggie, love is itself of the very essence of the Deity—God is not faith, God is not hope, but " God is love." No wonder chapter 14 opens " follow after love ! "

Yes, indeed ; and this is the quality which is the outstanding demonstration of our Christian reality. How high it is, how utterly beyond our *human* attainment—but " the love of God is shed abroad in our hearts by the Holy Ghost, Who is given unto us " (Rom. 5 : 5). And that is the theme of tomorrow's chapter of realisation.

Maintaining a Holy Life.

By the Rev. A. T. HOUGHTON, M.A.

" Wherewithal shall a young man cleanse his way ?"—*Ps.* 119 : 9.

IS not this a question which is being re-echoed in many hearts this week in Keswick, longing for holiness, to live a life of blessing to God, an integrated life, not the half-baked existence that gets stirred up by a meeting and a few hours later loses the effect of it ? There may be some like myself twenty-six years ago, when I came to Keswick for the first time, just out of the Army after four years abroad ; I found the fellowship of young fellow Christians here at Keswick most inspiring. I had been living in isolation, and hardly realised that there were so many like-minded young Christians in the world ! Thank God, I knew I was born again. I had been trying to witness for Christ, without much effect, but it was only at Keswick that I began to realise how much that previous environment in which I had lived had taken its toll of me. Unknowingly influenced by the environment around, I saw other people full of the joy of the Lord with one increasing purpose to serve Him. I wanted to do the same, but how ? My prayer was, " Create in me a clean heart, O God, renew a right spirit within me." " Wherewithal shall a young man cleanse his way ? " I wonder if there are those here who have been in similar circumstances—just out of military service, it may be. You have been living in isolation, cut off from fellowship with other Christians, and you find you have given way to that subtle influence, conforming to the standard around you. It may be that my message is to you, for the Psalmist answers that question, whether spoken or unspoken in our hearts. Yet the emphasis of the answer is not on what the Lord has done for you, though never forget that a holy life is only made possible through the cleansing blood of Christ ; rather the emphasis is on what you must do, by God's grace, to maintain a holy life. There is no magic formula, no short cut to holiness by which you can bring it about and then do nothing further. There is no once-for-all transaction which provides a holy life ready-made to your hand. There *is* a once-for-all transaction that has made it possible—the work of Christ on the Cross, who " bare our sins in His own body on the tree." That is the mainspring of the holy life which provides us with an attitude of mind that longs for holy living.

It is with that essential attitude of mind that the Psalmist gives two divinely appointed means of maintaining a holy life. First, " by taking heed thereto according to Thy word." The life must be guided by the Word of God. There are some who take a short cut to guidance by buying one of those beautiful promise boxes, and every time they want guidance they take out a promise. Of course it is always a winner, and they will always get the guidance they want,

157

but not always the guidance they need. If our lives are to be guided by the Word of God, it must be by systematic study of God's Word. It is so easy to be busy in God's service and take these things for granted, and yet in private to neglect God's Word. There is no substitute for the daily quiet time alone with God, when we pray and enter into communion and fellowship with Him and hear what He has to say to us in His Word. It is thrilling to see those crowds coming to the early morning prayer meetings here, but do not let that be a substitute for your time alone with God. Neglect that, and you lay yourself open to all the temptations of the evil one.

The Psalmist in verse 11 gives a practical tip from his own experience when he says, " Thy word have I hid in mine heart, that I might not sin against Thee." It was by this means that our Lord Himself overcame the evil one. Each time the devil tempted Him he answered, " It is written." We cannot use the sword of the Spirit if we only have a nodding acquaintance with it. Our minds need to be saturated with God's Word. Hide God's Word in your heart.

That Word in both the Old and New Testament makes it abundantly clear that the children of God are called to be a separated people : " Be ye holy, for I am holy." This call is not only a separation *unto* God, but a separation *from* all that constitutes worldliness. A generation or so ago that was clearly understood, and no one needed to have the meaning of worldliness explained, but to-day worldliness has increasingly invaded the ranks not only of the professing Christian Church, but of the Christian Church of living believers. There is a danger of the Church being engulfed by worldliness.

Young people, longing to be used in God's service, are in two minds as to what this separation involves. There are some who say you must do as the world does. The world will never be won for Christ by that means, nor will they respect those who follow that way. There are others who argue that we have been a little mistaken in regard to the meaning of worldliness ; that what it really means is a worldly spirit in regard to money and material wealth, worldly success, social distinction, racial pride, and so forth. These certainly are included, and we must acknowledge that through failure in that respect the witness sometimes has been marred by those who in ordinary ways have taken heed to God's Word. But surely in a world perishing from the lack of spiritual bread, there is a call to separation from those things that are essentially of the world, the artificial pleasures and amusements which the world follows ? They are a form of escapism for the children of this world, an escape from boredom and disillusion. If the Christian resorts to them as a relief from boredom, he is failing to understand that full satisfaction can be found only in Christ. He satisfies the longing soul and filleth the hungry soul with goodness. " Wherewithal shall a young man cleanse his way ? by taking heed thereto according to Thy word." You have got to make up your mind about this. There is no way of holiness along the path of your own choosing. Bring the matter to the touchstone of God's Word, and you will be shown the right way.

Having faced up to these issues, there is a vital step to take in the way of holiness. The Psalmist gives the answer : " With my whole heart have I sought Thee." You may read God's Word with your eyes, but it may never become the living Word to you. When it does, your whole soul will go out in longing, in thirst for God, even for the living God. You will not rest satisfied until you have given yourself to Him. Until you do give yourself to God you never enter into that full enjoyment of the spiritual inheritance that is yours by birthright as a child of God. God's Word will only be a list of precepts instead of a soul-satisfying message to your innermost being, something that controls your life. I think it was this that I realised at my first Keswick twenty-six years ago ; I saw others enjoying the liberty of the children of God, being used to win others to Christ. I realised that there could be no half measures, no standing on one side looking critically on others' enthusiasm ; I must give myself entirely, utterly, wholly, withholding nothing from Him—" with my whole heart have I sought Thee."

It is only when you have begun to do that, that you find how strong is the grip of apparently innocent things which come between your soul and God, which stand in the way of your becoming a channel of blessing to others, because that channel between you and God has been blocked up, often by those little things that seem so trivial. In the experience of God's people it has often been found that God brings to the mind some little thing that is hindering, and then it becomes your part to give up that little thing—or sometimes it may be a big thing ; but whether big or little, we cannot give ourselves wholly to God until we are ready to give up those things that come between. " Thou shalt love the Lord thy God with all thy heart, and with all thy soul, and with all thy mind, and with all thy strength." That means spiritually, intellectually, physically ; all our faculties are to be used. What scorching words these are if we really understand their implication !

It was after that experience when God in His mercy dealt with my soul, and showed those things that stood in the way, and I was able by His grace to yield myself as fully as I knew how and up to the experience of that moment, that I had the great joy of going out from Keswick and for the first time leading a soul to Christ, and experiencing the unutterable joy of being used as a link in the chain of God's providence in bringing a soul into the knowledge of eternal salvation.

I was talking to a young officer a short time ago just back from Burma. He had been through the thick of the campaign during the recapture of the country from the Japanese, and he told me that in the midst of the din of battle he was terribly afraid, so much so that he seized the opportunity of a long overdue leave of getting away for a short time from that campaign back into India. It was rather remarkable that he managed to get the leave, but God was in it, and in India he was brought face to face with the Lord Jesus Christ, and there he learned the joy of sin forgiven. He was full of spiritual joy in the fellowship of other Christians around him, but he felt straight away that he was taking leave on false pretences, and must get back to the front. He applied to return before his leave was finished, but no sooner had he got back to his unit in the front line, and was surrounded again with that old environment of godless officers and no spiritual companionship, than the joy went, and his newly-found faith seemed almost to evaporate. He faced up to the fact that he had accepted God's wonderful gift of forgiveness of sin, but he had never yielded himself to the Lord Jesus Christ. By God's grace he was enabled to do that, and immediately he was filled with a deep and lasting spiritual joy which led him to dedicate his whole life to God's service. " With my whole heart have I sought Thee."

> In full and glad surrender,
> I give myself to Thee,
> Thine utterly and only
> And evermore to be.

But the Psalmist gives another practical tip. He says, as it were, Do not fall into the trap of thinking that, having given yourself to God, you now keep yourself in the way of holiness. Lest anyone should imagine such folly, the Psalmist adds a little prayer, " O let me not wander from Thy commandments." Do not rely on your surrender ; rely on God alone. The recognition of absolute dependence upon the Lord Jesus Christ Himself is important, for St. Paul says, " I can do all things—and I can only do them—through Christ who strengtheneth me." " I know in whom I have believed, and am persuaded that He is able to keep that which I have committed unto Him against that day."

> He will keep you from falling,
> He will keep to the end,
> What a Saviour is Jesus,
> What a wonderful Friend !

Here is the secret of holy living. Do you want it ? Does your whole soul go out in longing for what God is ready to provide for those who give themselves to Him ? Your part is essential ; it arises out of that purifying work of the Holy Spirit in your heart. As the blood of Jesus cleanses from sin, it is His work to go on continuously ; and " He who hath begun a good work in you, will perform it unto the end."

" Wherewithal shall a young man cleanse his way ? by taking heed thereto according to Thy Word. With my whole heart have I sought Thee ; O let me not wander from Thy commandments."

The Peril of Worldliness.

By Mr. F. MITCHELL.

IT always seems to me that when God would preserve to us the blessings of the Evangelical and doctrinal teaching of John Wesley, He encouraged his brother Charles to put the truth into poetry. We might easily have forgotten the doctrine in the sermons, now almost unread, but they are mercifully preserved for us in the grand hymns of Charles Wesley. When I find myself in difficulty in expressing myself to God or man, I often turn to these great Evangelical hymns of Charles Wesley. In the hymn which we have been singing there are three lines of verse 2 which sum up much of what I have laid upon my heart as a burden at this meeting :—

> Dead to the world and all its toys,
> Its idle pomp and fading joys,
> Jesus, my glory be.

" Wherewithal shall a young man cleanse his way ? " What is it that most besmirches the way of the young man or young woman to-day ? What is the most grievous problem facing every Christian worker as he seeks to establish and lead on the young believer ? If I were to ask that question privately of ministers, deaconesses, leaders of Bible classes the answer, in almost every case, would be, " the world." I feel it laid upon me to say some very plain things on this most necessary subject.

The lowering of the moral standards of our day has given materialists who think at all some cause for serious thought. The widespread pilfering—or, to give it its plainer and more wholesome name, theft, stealing—is causing alarm in every quarter of the country. To all those in schools, elementary, secondary and public schools, it is a matter of the most serious concern.

It is a serious matter when moral standards are lowered in the world, but more serious when they are lowered in the Church ; it is pathetic and deadly when they are lowered in Evangelical Christianity. The standards that we have been seeking to maintain in Evangelical Christianity during recent years have been gradually lowering to meet current practice ; now some flags are flying at half mast, and some are not even to be seen. Ten years ago the thought of a Christian going to a cocktail party would have shocked us. I happen to know of some from among Evangelical Christians, from a very conservative section of the Church, and presumably standing for what we stand, actually excusing themselves for going to a cocktail party. The idea of a woman with a cigarette seems so unlike the chaste women of the New Testament that a few years ago we should have rebelled at the idea, and questioned whether she were a Christian at all.

It may be good to get back to some plain speaking on this important matter—" Ye are the salt of the earth, but if the salt hath lost its savour wherewith shall it (this corrupt earth) be salted?" This is not a day for experimenting to see how nearly like the world we can be, but a time rather for being willing to do without some things which we might rightly feel are among the things given us to enjoy.

We cannot help but contrast our Churches today with the Early Church of which it is written, " of the rest durst no man join himself to them " (Acts 5 : 13). Such holy people, such separated people, without any compromise with the standards of the age, that the rest of the people round about dared not join themselves to them. That is very unlike our modern churches with their social attractions, questionable employments, and amusements. A Jew or a heathen in New Testament days knew that if he joined the Church he would be expected to make a clean cut with everything that was sinful and heathenish and doubtful, and the interesting thing is that in the next verse (Acts 5 : 14) we read : " and believers were the more added to the Lord, multitudes both of men and women." May we not see a hindrance to revival just here ? Is it not true that God blesses the separated Church and the holy life, the life that may be doing without some things that ordinarily may be indulged in ?

There are certain preliminary questions which demand an answer before we really plunge into the heart of this burning question. To the young man or woman facing it in his own personal life, this question should be asked first of all : Do we mean to please God ? If we are out to please ourselves, then the matter becomes most complex and will be growingly complex ; but if a man or woman is bent on pleasing God, the problem becomes simpler—that will settle many questions out of hand. We shall ask ourselves : " Would the Heavenly Father and Friend like me to spend my time here or my money there ? " I dismiss the question, having raised it.

The second important question is : Do we want to save men ? John Wesley wrote to his preachers : " Your business is not to arrange so many meetings and attend so many conferences, your business is to save sinners." If our business is to save sinners, then we will bend all our energies to the saving of men, and that will settle many difficult ethical and moral questions.

I shall not forget hearing a friend who greatly influenced my life, tell the following story. He was a minister just taking a living in a large city in this country. Being very musical, the question immediately arose whether he should have, what to him would be the sheer delight of enjoying opera. To him operatic music was beautiful, and he could have enjoyed it to the full. While he was debating the matter in his own mind, an older ministerial brother quite unwittingly told him the story which I now tell you. A young man had left his home in the north and made his way up to London for a new appointment in business. His lodgings were not very comfortable, so having unpacked his bag he made his way out into the streets of the city wondering how he could kill time. He soon passed the inviting entrance of some theatre, and looked in; it seemed comfortable, and his lodgings were very uncomfortable, and he wavered for a moment. He remembered the instruction of the Christian home in the north of England, and was thinking his Sunday-school teacher would not like to know of his being there, when he saw a minister with his ministerial collar walk to the box, pay his money and pass in. Said the young man, "If it is right for him, it is right for me," and he too walked in. That night he found himself in the company of a group of young fellows of his own age, and before many weeks had passed he was in bed suffering with an incurable disease, the result of that night. The landlady was greatly disturbed about his condition, so she said, "Would you like someone to visit you?" "Yes." "I will fetch the vicar of the parish." The vicar of the parish appeared, and was shown in. At his appearance the dying, but angry youth said to him, "Clear out, it is through your influence that I am passing out."

The divine surgeon prefers aseptic instruments, and only uses the other kind when there are no aseptic ones at hand. Do you want to save men? Then in the name of Christ, do not spoil that testimony, or smooth the way to hell for a brother sinner by fooling with the world and toying with its pleasures. A clean cut is called for, in the name of God and for the sake of a generation. World standards are going on every hand—let us make a clean cut, for God's sake and the world's.

Thirdly, what kind of a Christian do you want to be? A half-hearted Christian? Then that will permit the world. But a Christian of the right kind, a victorious Christian, a New Testament Christian, a fruitful Christian, is the kind I read of in the Bible. Half-heartedness may be seen and experienced too frequently, but not much of it in the New Testament. "I am come that they might have life, and that they might have it to the full" (John 10 : 10). That was intended for everybody, but the price of fullness of life is a clean-cut separation to God.

I do not dismiss the matter simply. It is full of pressing problems, and intricate matters arise; but it should be remembered that we have guides to help us in these days, the same guides our forefathers had, if we will heed them. First, there is the guide of the Holy Scriptures; and secondly a guide now too much passed by, namely a Christian conscience. I find as I move about that the whole question is so often met on a purely intellectual ground. The case is argued, Why should not a Christian go here or there; what is the difference between this or that? Is it wise to cut ourselves off from our fellows? So regarded, there is no subject so perplexing, and generally we wander round in a circle, and come back to the place where we started and are still in the same fog. I venture to say a word in passing here, for some things seem to me to be answerable on even an intellectual basis. It seems completely un-Christian for a young man or woman to poison his or her blood stream with alcohol—and there are other poisons, drunk and inhaled, that come into the same category; to use God's money to poison God's body, His temple, seems

163

to me to be un-Christian on purely intellectual grounds ; but I turn rather to the Scriptures. We are told today that the Bible is not a book of prohibitions, it is rather a statement of principles ; which is both true and not true. Of the ten Commandments, eight and a half are prohibitive. You say, We are not under the law, but under grace. We will not enter into a controversy on that matter, but even if that be so, what about the Pauline Epistles ? Say some, Our business is to tell people what wonderful things there are in Christ, and then leave the matter. That may be true in preaching to the world, but not in preaching to young Christians ; at least, that is not how Paul dealt with the young Christians in his day. He gave them the full unfolding of the grace of God in the early chapters of his Epistles, and then proceeded, in the most clear terms, to make both statements of command and definite prohibitions for the guidance of their life in a sinful world. Perhaps some of us are coming to a new appreciation of John Wesley's wisdom in his rules for the Society.

I now turn naturally and read chapters and verses which have been read over and over again—" Love not the world, neither the things that are in the world. If any man love the world, the love of the Father is not in him. For all that is in the world, the lust of the flesh, the lust of the eyes, and the pride of life, is not of the Father, but is of the world. The world passeth away, and the lusts thereof : but he that doeth the will of God abideth for ever " (1 John 2 : 15-17). Here the world is described and condemned and the love of it is stated as the antithesis of the love of God. I wonder if we might put in more modern terms this analysis of the world—the lust of the flesh, the lust of the eye, the pride of life. Could we state it : the lust of the flesh is the desire to indulge ; the lust of the eyes, the desire to possess; the pride of life, the desire to attract.

The lust of the flesh, a strong desire to indulge, or in other words, to take away moral restraint from natural desire ; to take the brake off. That is the opposite of Christian living, for we read in Galatians 5 : 23, " The fruit of the Spirit is self-control." This touches the whole realm of base desire. Man innocent and man redeemed is spirit, soul and body. Man fallen and rebellious is body, soul and spirit. When the body is under control, it is a good servant, but when the body is in control it is a menace. That accounts for a national drink bill of six hundred millions, and a tobacco bill of three hundred millions, and a gambling bill of five hundred millions, while the political parties are talking loudly about economics ! We are not here to criticise the Government, we are here to seek the purification of our own lives and of the Evangelical Church. It is good for us to ask ourselves at this point, Are we free from the lust of the flesh ? Is the hand of God and the hand of our own redeemed will on top and in control ? " But thou O man of God, flee these things " which characterise this age all too much.

Manifestly the lust of the flesh arises from within, but is grievously excited from without. "Take heed what ye see." This raises some of the live questions of the hour in the thought of young Christians—the cinema, the dance, unwholesome reading. I fear that on these matters we have

164

been all too silent, and perhaps guiltily silent. It is only right to say now that for what I have to say I take full personal responsibility, for my brethren on the platform may feel differently. The cinema has come to stay, we are told, therefore we must revise our thinking. Well, so has gambling come to stay, and so has drinking, so that particular argument has little force.

I am under difficulties in criticising the film industry or the cinema, because I do not go. As one who is interested in the Brontes, their life and literature, I might find some personal delight in seeing " Wuthering Heights," but I just do not do it. For twenty years one has been the leader of a Bible class, and I have had that story told me by my vicar friend, and repeated by me earlier in this address, before me for those twenty years. I may be able to discriminate and choose a good film, but my Sunday-school scholar may not, and the wise course is to deny oneself. " It is good neither to eat meat nor drink wine, nor anything whereby thy brother stumbleth." Is your brother stumbling through the cinema, is he being offended ? Is that fellow man working beside you in the office being polluted by the abominable sex film of to-day ? Then " it is good neither to eat meat nor drink wine, nor anything whereby thy brother stumbleth or is offended." There is nothing marring the testimony of young believers to-day like the cinema. I am not saying every film is unclean, it is not ; but in God's name let us be safe.

I understand, though I may be misinformed, that in Soviet Russia no child under fourteen is allowed to see the films, which is a terrible condemnation of films, expecially in a land where everything is controlled. One of our headmasters writing recently, said, " After fifty years experience in schools I should say the increase in juvenile crime dates from the introduction of the gangster film, glorifying to the child's mind ideas which have always been held repulsive. The children of these days are the parents of tomorrow, and there is ample evidence that social ethics now supplant those of Christianity in many homes." A well-known film critic writes : " Talking pictures have stripped woman not only of her clothing, but of her moral decency, truth, vitality and every civilised quality of virtue." I will leave it at that.

We are engaged in total warfare. It is an inadequate view of the state of the Church and of the progress of the Kingdom of God which lightly allows us to face these questions in such an unsatisfactory way.

The desire to indulge arises from within, but the desire to possess arises from without ; the lust of the eye. Beelzebub and Legion are still in business in Vanity Fair. They may have changed a little, but the world is always appealing to us in this way, so that the Christian becomes consumed with a desire to get. But the Lord Jesus said, " It is more blessed to give than to receive."

Thirdly, the pride of life, the swagger of life, the desire to attract. That covers very wide interests in life, affecting our dress, cosmetics, our home, our car, our pose, and perhaps even our style of preaching. Our business is to attract to Jesus, the altogether lovely one. It has been wisely said by Dr. Denny, " No man can leave his congregation under the

165

impression that he is a great preacher and that he has preached a great Saviour at the same time."

So the Bible sums up and analyses the constituent principles of the world. How far are we yielding to and being governed by them ? They are all symptoms of one desire—the love of the world, which is an antithesis to the love of the Father, and is quenching to the love of the Son, and almost always withers love for the sinner.

So as we face these problems to-day, problems at which I have only just hinted, hear the word of the Apostle to Timothy, " From such " people and practices " withdraw thyself " (1 Tim. 6 : 5). And to the same young man, " From such turn away." And again, " Let everyone that nameth the name of Christ depart from iniquity." And the old text on which I was brought up, which is not mentioned very often to-day : " Come ye out from among them, and be ye separate, and touch not the unclean thing, and I will receive you and be a Father unto you."

So I venture to send out a very needed warning in a needy day, in calling attention to one of the supreme perils of the Christian life : worldliness.

Heaven Now.

By Dr. DONALD G. BARNHOUSE.

AT times there are scoffers who say, " All the Hell we ever have is on this earth." I always answer them, " That is absolutely true for me, but absolutely false for you." When they inquire my meaning, I tell them that the Lord Jesus Christ took my Hell, and the Hell of every one who puts full trust in His atoning work. God can never demand payment twice, and having received it from the hand of my Saviour, He cannot, in righteousness, demand it from me. All of Christianity can be summarised in three sentences. I deserved Hell. Jesus Christ took my Hell. There's nothing left for me but His Heaven. But in faithfulness I always tell the unbeliever that while all my Hell is past and gone for ever, it is his Heaven that is fast slipping from him, for all the Heaven he will ever have is here upon this earth. This world of wars and atom bombs, this world of horror camps and exploitations, this world of utility goods and short rations, is all the Heaven that the unsaved man will ever know. He may reply that he finds his Heaven in the misty clouds rising from the lake at dawn to caress the green brow of the mountain, in the laughter of his child, in a good book and an easy chair beside the logs of the library fire, and in a thousand other like things. But the clouds shall disappear before the great darkness, and the elements shall melt with fervent heat ; the child shall grow old, wither and die ; the easy chair shall be empty, and the book shall lie on the floor where it has fallen from the reader's hand as he falls into his last earthly sleep, and all of his Heaven will be gone for ever.

But though the Heaven of the believer is the future, and all the Hell the true child of God knows is here upon this earth, yet there is Heaven here and now for us. We enjoy the things of earth far more than any unsaved man can ever enjoy them, comparing natural capacity with natural capacity.

> Heaven above is softer blue,
>   Earth around is sweeter green ;
> Something lives in every hue
>   Christless eyes have never seen :
> Birds with gladder songs o'erflow,
>   Flowers with deeper beauties shine,
> Since I know, as now I know,
>   I am His and He is mine.

But our present Heaven is something far more real and rich than this. We have access to the highest Heaven. We have been made accepted in the Beloved. When God the Father raised Him to His own right hand in the Heavenlies, far above all principalities and power and might and dominion, He raised us up together with Him.

There is a point at the close of Ephesians 1 and the opening of chapter 2 that must be understood in order to illustrate the full truth of our union with Christ. Almost every commentator who has approached Ephesians has noted the fact that there is no verb in the opening sentence of the second chapter. The phrase hangs loosely, " And you . . . who were dead in trespasses and sins . . ." and seems to trail off inconclusively. It may be that some missionary has found a language that can get along without verbs, but the Greek and the English cannot. The A.V. translators added, as we can see from the words in italic type, the subject and the predicate for the sentence, *hath He quickened.* Thus it reads, " And you hath He quickened who were dead in trespasses and sins." This is surely a truth, and a great truth ; but I believe that very much is lost by the addition of these words. There is a way of reading the sentence with the words struck out, that will bring a wonderful light upon the truth that is before us.

In order to understand what I am about to bring out it is necessary to remind ourselves that Paul was very fond of using long parentheses in his epistles. The translators have been correct when they put between parentheses five different long passages in the epistle to the Romans, three of them a full verse, one of three verses, one of five verses (Rom. 1 : 2 ; 2 : 13-15 ; 5 : 13-17 ; 9 : 11 ; 11 : 8), and though no parentheses are used by the translators, it is well known that three entire chapters of Romans, the ninth to eleventh, must be read as a parenthesis. In our brief epistle to the Ephesians, five verses are printed between parentheses (3 : 3, 4 ; 4 : 9, 10 ; 5 : 9). Let us apply that principle here, remembering that the chapter divisions are not put in by the Holy Spirit, but are a technical device to aid us in finding our way through the Scriptures.

In the close of the first chapter we read of the tremendous power which God manifested in raising the Lord Jesus Christ from the dead. The vocabulary of the original language is ransacked to find terms to express the exceeding greatness of His power toward us who believe, according to the working of His mighty power which He wrought in Christ when He raised Him from the dead (1 : 19, 20). Then the apostle digresses and describes what happened to Christ when the Father raised Him from the dead, and completes the chapter in three and a half verses describing Christ in the highest Heaven, enthroned with the Father and Head of the Church. Reading it this way, half the force of verse nineteen is lost, for here is the declaration of a manifestation of power *toward us,* without any description of a power that is directly related to us. And half the force of the opening verse of chapter two is lost because it speaks of the quickening of the believer without relating it, directly, to the resurrection of Christ. But let us cast a parenthesis around the last three and a half verses of the chapter, and see what we have. Paul prayed that the Church might know " what is the exceeding greatness of His power toward us who believe, according to the working of His mighty power, which He wrought in Christ when He raised Him from the dead . . . and you who were dead in trespasses and sins. . ." Wonderful! Easter day was my resurrection day also. When Christ died, I died; when Christ was raised, I was raised. And we can continue into this chapter, and find that when Christ ascended into Heaven by the power of the Father, I was raised from earth to Heaven with Him; when the Father enthroned His Son far above all, there was also a seat prepared there for the Bride. Then keep me not back from my rightful place! Make not of the Church an exiled Bride! Hold me not at walls of partition which Christ has cast down! Stop me not at gates which Christ has unlocked! Stay not my steps at a sea which He turns to crystal before me! Forbid me not to enter within the veil, where my Bridegroom has gone before me! Christ has died! Christ has risen! Christ has gone on high! Christ has taken us with Him!

Believe it! Accept the boldness which He gives, and enter into the Holiest of all and take our rightful place. Heaven wants a triumphant Bride now! And while it does not yet appear what we shall be, yet even now, we are far short of that which God wants us to be. Let us now be where we would be; let us now be what we should be; so many things which are not now, really could be, if we would take our seat upon the throne of Heaven.

I remember so well the day I first went to Heaven! I was on shipboard, travelling alone. I had set myself to read the Book of Ephesians a hundred times on the Atlantic crossing. I had known it by heart, of course, since the days of my youth. I had my Testament in my hand, but was lying in my deck chair with my eyes closed, seeing every line, and poring over its meaning. Suddenly I saw the great truth I have been expounding to you during these days. My heart leaped in a joy that is totally inexpressible. I saw the whole new and living way, from myself all the way to the throne of God, with the Lord Jesus Christ seated there, desiring me to join Him. It was like looking at a castle through a long lane of trees. Fortunately, I was almost alone on my section of the deck. I lifted my Testament in a sharp gesture, as though it had been the hilt of the sword which it really is, and with the whole of the Ephesian truth aflame before me, I shouted, I shouted in utter silence so far as human ears were concerned, " Lord, I'm coming through." I believe that shout roused all the forces of Hell. I felt their angry, hateful stares. But I knew then that they were absolutely defeated. They had been overcome by the Lamb, and were about to be overcome by the word of my testimony that I was completely joined to the risen, ascended Lord. Back, you slavering dogs of Hell! Lie down in your kennels! Your fangs have been drawn, for those who identify themselves with the ascended Lord. And I cried, " Lord, I am not sufficient for these things, and if he brings out forces that are beyond my power, deal Thou with them. Even Michael, the archangel, called Thee to deal directly with Satan. I must be nothing in myself, but everything in Christ." And suddenly, I saw, far below me (a passer-by would have said that there was a passenger, half asleep, leaning over one knee) I saw, far below me a ship, a tiny dot on a blue sea. And I knew that I was one of the specks on that ship, but I knew that henceforth that ship and that ocean and that world were for evermore unimportant. I was in the Heavenlies, joined by faith to my Lord. He was nearer than when I had seen Him at the Cross. The eternal life which He gave me when I was saved was now realised to be the life of eternity which I was privileged to live in time. I was to spend the rest of my life seated in the Heavenlies with Christ.

Someone may fear that, as I turn to describe the believer's privilege, Heavenward, that I am about to tell of some vision. This was not a vision. This was no experience such as Paul knew when he was caught up into Heaven. Every once in a while some one will come to me after a meeting—generally a person who seems quite neurotic—to tell me of some vision or revelation which he has had. I always stop him and say, " Wait one moment. Let us be scriptural. This is not the age of visions. But if the Lord has done something that would seem to be quite out of the scope of His present plan, and if you have had a vision that will stand the tests of Scripture, I am sure that you have heard unspeakable words which it is not lawful for a man to utter (2 Cor. 12 : 4), so please don't try to utter them to me ! "

No ! Not a vision, but faith entering into Heavenly life, enthroned life ; faith entering into all of the triumphs of the risen Saviour, joined to the risen Lord.

The universal experience in Scripture and in Church history is that every man who approaches the Heavenly places is immediately conscious of a great sense of his own sin and a great sense of the holiness of God.

> Eternal Light ! Eternal Light !
> How pure the soul must be
> When, placed within Thy seaching sight,
> It shrinks not, but with calm delight
> Can live, and look on Thee.

If ever we rise, in any sense, into the presence of God, this fact is borne in upon us. We are, indeed, sons of ignorance and night. If we were forced to come in our own purity of soul we could never find entrance. We should then be like a slum dweller who approached the reservations desk of the Savoy or the Waldorf Astoria. We should most certainly be told that there were no rooms available. But, upon arriving in Heaven, our one great and overwhelming thought is that Christ is our availability. We are accepted in the Beloved.

I shall transgress no further with my own thoughts upon the day when I first arrived in Heaven. I shall take you to an illustration of another sinner who reached there before me. We read of a lesser-known Joshua, high priest in the days of Zechariah, who reached Heaven, while still alive, I believe. We read in the third chapter of that prophecy, " And he showed me Joshua the high priest, standing before the messenger of the Lord, and Satan standing at his right hand to resist him." Note that Satan was in Heaven, and seems to have been able to come very high into Heaven. " And the Lord said unto Satan, The Lord rebuke thee,

170

O Satan : even the Lord that hath chosen Jerusalem rebuke thee : is not this a brand plucked out of the fire ? Now Joshua was clothed with filthy garments, and stood before the angel " (Zech. 3 : 1-3).

You must pass through this consciousness of the filthiness of your garments. Job defended himself against the visiting deacons for thirty-odd chapters, but when he got a vision of the Lord he said, " I abhor myself, and repent in dust and ashes " (Job 42 : 6). One has translated it, " I shrink with terror." It was to Christians that Paul spoke the same word, " Knowing the terror of the Lord . . ."—toward Christians in His judgment of the believer—"we persuade men " (2 Cor. 5 : 10)—Christian men who must face this terror when they arrive in Heaven ultimately if they are not willing to face it now, and learn a new abomination of sin. There must be no slackness in our attitute toward sin, above all toward our own sin. I have no place in my ministry for the attitude and teaching of those who think that because they have been justified through Christ they can relax their vigilance. We can believe in eternal security, but we must never believe in eternal presumption.

Isaiah knew his sinfulness as soon as he caught the vision of the Lord Jehovah of Hosts. " Woe is me ! for I am undone : because I am a man of unclean lips, and I dwell in the midst of a people of unclean lips : for mine eyes have seen the King, the Lord of Hosts " (Isa. 6 : 5). And there must come the coal of fire to touch our lips. This was fire from the altar. It had been kindled, originally, by God Himself, on the first day of tabernacle worship, and it had consumed the body of the lamb. Blood had dripped on that live coal before it ever came to the lips of Isaiah. It was God's fire ; the same fire that consumed Christ. That is the fire into which we must fall.

This is what the Lord caused Joshua to see as soon as he came into Heaven. For the Lord answered, " and spake unto those that stood before Him. And unto (Joshua) he said, Behold I have caused thine iniquity to pass from thee, and I will clothe thee with change of raiment. And I said, Let them set a fair mitre upon his head. So they set a fair mitre upon his head, and clothed him with garments. And the angel of the Lord stood by." This is not the cleansing of the laver. This is the cleansing of the throne. And it is a cleansing that is far deeper than anything that is experienced in any ordinary confession of sin. This is in reality, the realization of our crucifixion.

At the Portstewart Convention in Northern Ireland I used an illustration that brought me into conversation and discussion with one of my ministerial brethren. I spoke of being crucified with Christ. I said that it was not a thing a man could do to himself, that it had to be done to him. I used as an example the fact that of the thousand ways that might be known to put a man to death, all of them could be used by the man himself to commit suicide, except the one method of death by crucifixion. A man may hang himself, drown himself, shoot himself, stab himself, throw himself down from a high place—but he cannot crucify himself. Nail one hand to the cross, and the other is free. Crucifixion must be done by someone else. And our crucifixion and

171

death must be done to us by Christ. My friend came to me in perplexity. Were there not statements in the Scripture which made it possible to hold that we must mortify—put to death—our members on the earth ? Yes. Are there not several such passages in the New Testament ? Yes. Then was I right ? I maintained that I was, and told him this story.

A minister in America had trouble with his throat, and was told by his physician that he would have to have an operation. But he had a heavy programme and kept putting it off. A year passed, and his throat gave him more and more trouble. Finally he went to a famed specialist, and told him the story. The surgeon looked at the man's throat an instant and said, " Programme or no programme, if you don't operate on your throat you are going to stop preaching altogether." Did that statement mean that the minister was to perform his own operation ? Of course not. It was a manner of stating that he must submit himself to a surgeon who would do the work for him.

But does this life of crucifixion mean that you become utterly other-worldly, mystical, pietistic ? To me it does not. In fact, as I grow older I find that my desire for active work increases. " So much to be done ; so little time." And as the fires of sense and sentiment are banked for the evening, the keen desires for work and service and love and life abundant, do not diminish.

I had in my church one of America's most famous surgeons, whose skill had brought him fame, and whose fame had made him a member of most of the orthopaedic societies of the world and brought him highest honours everywhere. I once was admitted to the operating theatre where he performed an amazing operation, taking a long piece of bone from the shin of a man and sewing it to his spinal column, to prevent the advance of tuberculosis of the bone. That great surgeon stood there with iron nerve and unquivering eye and surveyed the great wound in the back, talking calmly with his assistant who was handling the wound in the leg. He seemed utterly cold and dispassionate. Later he told me that when he was a youth seeing operations for the first time, he fainted in pity at the sight of blood and trembled at the thought of taking the scalpel himself. Has he lost his pity because he is more helpful now ? Has he ceased to love humanity because he no longer faints ?

George Matheson uses a similar illustration in one of his messages and says, " Is the heart less tender because it has less nerve ? Is it a callous thing to be calm, ministrant, equal to the hour ? The bird that at morning perched upon a tree may light in the afternoon on the ledge of a warehouse wall. Is its plumage thereby less beautiful ? Nay : neither is my love less fair because its song is less free. . . Can I read without tears that story of Calvary which once made me weep ? I can. Be it so ; that is no proof of declining love. But have I gained facility in doing a mean thing, a heartless thing, an ignoble thing ? Can I malign my brother to-day more easily than yesterday ? Can I leap more nimbly the fence of forbidden things ? Can I tread more airily the labyrinth of the crooked way ? Can I repeat the *path* without the *pain* of wrong ? Has the poison ceased to sicken me ? Has the sting ceased to wound me ? Has the arrow ceased

172

to gall me ? Has the sword ceased to smite me ? Has the cloud ceased to blind me ? Has the conscience ceased to upbraid me ? Then, my soul, thou hast wandered ; let thy Father lead thee home. Come out from the cold that benumbs thee. Come out from the painlessness that deceives thee. Come out from the sin whose penalty is that it smarts not. Come out into the scorching sun of God's judgment-day ; and its heat shall make thee troubled, and by love's stripes thou shalt be healed."

When we sit upon the throne of Heaven we shall discover that it is not a throne of reigning over others. It is a throne of reigning over self. And for that it must first be the judgment throne. We shall one day sit upon the throne of reigning over the angels and over the world (1 Cor. 6 : 1-4). Christ Himself is not reigning to-day in the sense that He shall one day reign. He is interceding. He has told us, " To him that overcometh will I grant to sit with Me in My throne, even as I also overcame and am set down in My Father's throne " (Rev. 3 : 21). There will be reigning, but now in Heaven it is learning to reign over self.

When we reach the throne we hear our Lord say unto us, " Paul, we have a very interesting case up for judgment to-day. It is a fellow by the name of Saul of Tarsus." And Paul replies, " Lord, in the light of this place, I concur with Thy judgment. I abhor myself. Woe is me. I acknowledge that the heart is incurable. I consent unto the law that it is good. . . I join in the sentence of death." And our Lord puts Saul to death, and then accompanies Paul to survey the riches of the deposit that is there to his account. He hath blessed us with all spiritual blessing in the Heavens. It is when we live from these supplies that our life is rich.

Someone asked me if the freshness of the entrance into life in Heaven did not fade. Certainly there is a change in our emotional attitude toward the life that is the life of Heaven, but I do not think that it is any the less real because it is not exactly the same as on the first day. A man does not love his wife the less because he picks up her letter after twenty years of married life with less tremble in his hand than when he was courting her. The straight unblown flame that burns quietly may have more true warmth than the smoky flame that first ignites the brush heap.

And it is further true, that, once the way into the holiest is known, it is not hard to find again. Sense and circumstance distract us for a moment, but when we know the way we are back again in an instant. A few weeks ago we were travelling to Addis Ababa from Khartoum. Our plane came down for the night at Asmara in Eritrea, and we got in touch with a missionary couple of the Sudan Interior Mission who were there for a few days on their honeymoon. We went to the mission house for dinner, and the young American bride and her Australian husband received us and we had a good time of fellowship. The subject of their wedding came up, and they brought out some pictures that a friend had taken. There was some good-natured chaffing on our part, and he said, " I had always said that the last thing I would do is marry an American." We laughed, and he continued, " You know, she never let me kiss her even once until the wedding ceremony." We all laughed ;

173

she blushed and started for the kitchen. He called after her, " But after I got the first one, the rest come easy." She turned as she went through the door and cast him a blushing look, and it did not take much perspicacity to know that he had found the way to her heart and that he might come instantly. It may have taken him a year to find the way, but once it was found it was for ever open.

And this is our Lord's way with us. We do not have to repeat the slow processes of Christian growth. The steps, once taken, are taken for ever. As we awaken in the morning it may be that the first object that swims into our consciousness is something as mundane as the crack in the ceiling plaster. But the very next second we may cry in our hearts, " Good morning, dear Lord ! It is wonderful to begin another day in Heaven." And there we are, seated on high, and the problems of home and office and school and market, yea even the problems of pain and emotion, become so very secondary and unimportant.

"By My Spirit."

By the Rev. RONALD J. PARK.

" Not by might, not by power, but by My Spirit, saith the
Lord of Hosts "—*Zech.* 4 : 6.

IN Ezra 4 : 24, we read, " Then ceased the work of the house of God
which is at Jerusalem." Was that right ? Can it be right in any set
of circumstances that the work of God should cease ? " But," you
say, " the previous verse declares that the enemies ' made them to cease
by force and power,' so what alternative had they ? " Then the work of
God was thwarted ! The divine enterprise in the earth was doomed !
The portion of the people of God was one of failure and defeat ! It was
the end ! But was it ? Was there no alternative ? Was it possible for the
people of God to mobilise more might, to amass greater force and power ?
Even if it was, that was no guarantee of success. The Lord had a word
to say through Zechariah, His prophet : " Not by might, nor by power,
but by My Spirit," saith the Lord (4 : 6). With the declaration, God
gave His servant a remarkable vision—a golden candlestick, or lampstand,
with seven branches, each branch surmounted with its own lamp of
gleaming light ; above the structure a golden bowl serving as a reservoir
for the oil : by means of pipes running from the bowl the oil was fed to
each of the seven lamps. Two evergreen trees, rich with olive oil, were
standing on either side, pouring their golden oil into the bowl which fed
the lamps. To the Jewish people the meaning of the vision was clear.
The lampstand was a familiar piece of furniture in their Tabernacle and
Temple, symbolising the function of God's people on earth. Symboli-
cally it summarised God's purpose for the nation of Israel among all the
nations of the earth. They were to be light-bearers, the light of God
among the nations. Through them God was to shine forth, His truth
was to be diffused, His excellency to be known to the uttermost parts of
the earth. The flowing oil is interpreted by the words, " Not by might,
nor by power, but by My Spirit." That is to say, there was an abundant
supply to maintain the seven-fold flame, and the supply was from God.
There was no reason why Israel should cease to function, why the Jews
should be compelled, whatever the force and power of the enemy, to
abandon the work of the house of the Lord which was at Jerusalem.
The supply was plentiful, and it was of God, to maintain the flame. The
two olive trees are interpreted as the two anointed ones that stand before
the Lord of the whole earth—Joshua the high priest, and Zerubbabel
the governor.

Now let us see what application this vision and message have to us,
for indeed we have here a message most relevant to ourselves in these

175

dark and desperate days in which we live. We are acutely conscious of the force and power of the enemy. We have come together into this glad convocation this week ; our faces are radiant, our hearts aglow, but, I ask you, is this true or is it not ?—everyone of us at heart entertains a grave anxiety, and because of that anxiety, perhaps, we felt impelled to come to Keswick. We know that there is opposition, vigorous and determined, from three sources—the world, the flesh and the devil ; and that from any of those sources the opposition can manifest itself in ten thousand subtle forms. It would be the height of folly to belittle the force and power of the enemy, and we have no disposition to do so. Well then, let us look into chapter 4, and here are four pegs upon which to hang our thoughts : First, the function of the saints ; second, the flow of the supply ; third, the fulness of the source ; fourth, the fulfilment of the service.

I. THE FUNCTION OF THE SAINTS.

This is suggested to us by the lampstand, a very comprehensive symbol of the function that we should exercise in the world. The lampstand was to bear light : we are to be light-bearers, not only in the earthly sphere, but also in the heavenly. So far as the earthly sphere is concerned, we are told, " Ye are the light of the world." The Lord Jesus did not say that to a brains trust or a fellowship of philosophers ; He said it to very humble folk who had believed on Him to the saving of their souls. He says it to you and me, " Ye are the light of the world." " Let your light so shine before men that they may see your good works, and glorify your Father which is in Heaven." The Apostle Paul spoke of " this wicked and perverse generation, among whom ye shine as lights in the world. John the Baptist was a " burning and a shining light." Said the Lord to Paul, "I have set thee to be a light of the Gentiles," and Peter says to us that we are to show forth, to diffuse as light, the excellencies of Him who hath called us out of darkness into His marvellous light. In the heavenly sphere, also, this is our function. We read that, by the Church, the principalities and powers in heavenly places are to come to know the manifold widsom of God. By the Church, too, the ages to come are to see and wonder at the exceeding riches of God's grace. We have a function to fulfil, therefore, which is comprehensively symbolised in the lampstand—we are to pour forth light, and that, in the earthly and Heavenly spheres. The symbol is so rich that one is tempted to elaborate, but we must forbear. Note only this, the lampstand uplifted and diffused the light, but could produce no light of itself.

II. THE FLOW OF THE SUPPLY.

The flame could be kept aglow only by the oil, and there was the bowl with its supply to each lamp. The oil was indispensable ; without it the lampstand was useless and an encumbrance. But it received oil in order to consume it. Note that ! It received and consumed : it functioned only by absorbing the oil and transmitting it as light in the darkness   Then God has a ministry to do *toward us* and *in us* before there can be a ministry *out from* us. The lamp received the oil from with-

176

out, something happened within, and the light went out from it. You will remember how the Lord, in John's Gospel, spoke of the living water, first, as a gift from without, " Thou wouldst have asked of Him, and He would have given Thee living water; " second, as a movement within, " The water that I shall give him shall be in him a well of water springing up." And then, and not until then, " Out of him shall flow rivers of living water." There must be, therefore, a work of God toward us and in us : the full supplies of the grace of His Spirit must inflow and inwork, before there can be any outflow ; or, reverting to the vision before us, before there can be any gleaming of the light. We must be blessed if we would be a blessing. " I will bless thee, and thou shalt be a blessing."

Notice two things about this flow. (*i*) *It was continuous.* Through the pipes to each of the lamps the oil flowed, and went on flowing. Remember that ! " It is God which worketh (goes on working) within you both to will and to do of His good pleasure." " Working (going on working) that which is well-pleasing in His sight." " I also labour, striving according to His working which worketh in me mightily." God's work toward and in us is unceasing. (*ii*) *It was abundant.* An interesting point arises in verse 2, for the Hebrew there would seem to require us to understand that there were seven pipes to each of the seven lamps, that is forty-nine in all—seven to the first, seven to the second, and so on. This suggests to us the perfection of the supply—how full, how abundant ! On God's side there can be nothing lacking. The riches of His grace by His Spirit for His people are never in short supply. " His divine power hath given unto us all things that pertain unto life and godliness." God continuously working, and an abundant supply ! Then what is this talk about " the force and power of the enemy " ? Can such opposition be effective against the people of God, when such a God as our God is working continuously and abundantly on our behalf ? God is thus working, I say. But is He ? Really now, *is He* ? The question pulls us up rather sharply. If the flow of the oil is continuous and abundant, why are our lamps nearly out ? There must be a blockage, and since it cannot be on His side, it must be on ours !

III. THE FULNESS OF THE SOURCE.

This is suggested to us by the two olive trees, one on either side of the bowl, into which they pour their rich, golden oil. In the local application of the vision, the trees represented Joshua the high priest, whose ministry was Godward, and Zerubbabel the governor, whose ministry was manward. There are two who jointly exercise a ministry toward the believer, the one is in Heaven, and exercises a Godward ministry ; the other is in the heart, and exercises a manward ministry. There is eternal efficacy in their ministry on behalf of the believer ; there are unlimited resources behind their ministry on behalf of the believer. The same word is used to describe the ministry of each—the word Paraclete. Of the first it is translated " Advocate," of the second it is translated by a less adequate word, " Comforter." Of the first we read, " We have an Advocate with the Father, Jesus Christ the righteous." Of the second we read, " He (the Father) shall give you another Advocate, that He may abide with you for ever, even the Spirit of Truth." Notice, the first is " with the Father," the second is " with you." The one is in Heaven, now appearing in the presence of God for us, ever living to make intercession for us ; by His present life with the Father, He is saving those whom He reconciled by His death. The other is in the believer's heart, there to apply the ministry of the first in Heaven. All that the first Advocate is, and is doing, for His people, while in the presence of God above, the Second Advocate is, and is doing for His people, in their hearts on earth.

Here are three instances briefly, to illustrate the joint ministry of the two Advocates. Take first our spiritual life. Christ lives in the presence of His Father. He says, " Because I live, ye shall live also." " Christ who is our life," we read. He, our life, is there, but we are here. Therefore we read of the Holy Spirit, " The Spirit is life because of righteousness." He, who is with us, is the life of Christ to us. Take secondly our sonship. Our Advocate there is the Son of God, the first-born among many brethren. Through Him God is going to bring many sons to glory. Christ, there, is not ashamed to call us brethren. This matter of Sonship is represented by Christ now in the presence of God. But what about us here ? We have the Spirit, and " The Spirit Himself beareth witness with our spirit that we are the children of God." A supplementary ministry ! A third illustration, our resurrection. Our Advocate in Heaven in there in bodily fashion. He is the firstfruits of the resurrection, the first-begotten of the dead. He is there in a body, the body that rose from the tomb, and upon which the incredulous Thomas gazed, the body that ascended to Heaven. We read, then, of the Holy Spirit who dwells within us that " God shall raise our mortal body by His Spirit that dwells within us."

Look, two olive trees, one either side of the lampstand, and each is there in the interest of the lampstand, and both to minister to the maintenance of the glow of the seven-fold lamp ! And here are the two olive trees, the two anointed ones, one in Heaven and one in the heart ! These two, the Lord Jesus Christ and the Holy Spirit, are ministering in the interests of every true believer. You say you cannot understand this ? No matter for the moment. But do you know, and rejoicingly believe, that the Holy Spirit indwells you, and waits to minister the fulness of the risen, glorified Christ to your soul ? If you and I respond by faith to that revelation of truth, with what a mighty enrichment of grace our life would be continually endowed !

IV. The Fulfilment of the Service.

The light is to shine ; the purpose of God is to be realised ; whether Israel, the Church, individual believer, each is fully to exercise the function assigned by God. The light must be kept burning. The force and power of the enemy cannot thwart the divine purpose for the people of God, if it be remembered that it is " not by might, nor by power, but by My Spirit, saith the Lord."

Our chapter indicates four happy results from the service of those people of God whose lives are open to the supply of the fulness of the

ascended Christ through the Spirit. (*i*) *Opposition will be overcome*:
" Who art thou, O great mountain ? before Zerubbabel thou shalt become
a plain " (v. 7). The unscalable mountain, the impassable obstacle
the force and power of the enemy, are to melt away ! Dear child of God,
what is the mountain that blocks the path of God's will for you ? What
about next Monday morning at nine o'clock ? There is going to be a
mountain in that home of yours, or at that office. It is grand here at
Keswick : here we feel so strong in the Lord : we are surrounded by
Christian love, prayer, sympathy and helpfulness. But next Monday
there will be a mountain. Look again at this verse, and read it as it
should be read, " Who art thou, O great mountain, before Zerubbabel ?
Be a plain ! " It is a command. Yes, faith " as a grain of mustard
seed " shall say to the mountain, " Be thou removed, and be thou cast
into the sea." Such faith will be yours " through the supply of the Spirit
of Christ Jesus." (*ii*) *Glory will be given* : " He shall bring forth the
headstone thereof with shoutings, crying, Grace, grace unto it " (v. 7).
Glory will be given where it belongs—to the Headstone, and we know
who that is. Christ is the Headstone of the corner. I will give all the
glory to the Lord. That is rather difficult, isn't it ? Self is always claiming
appreciation and applause. But when His Spirit is having His own way
in our hearts, self is out, and Christ is all. You give the glory where it
belongs : you bring forth the Headstone, and cry " Grace, grace unto
it." (*iii*) *The construction will be completed* : " The hands of Zerubbabel
have laid the foundation of this house ; his hands shall also finish it "
(v. 9). Nothing can hinder its completion. God's plan will be carried
through right to fulfilment. Our Lord said, " I have finished the work
which Thou gavest Me to do." He purposes that we should be able to
say the same. His plan for you need not fail : it will not fail of fulfilment
with the continuous and abundant supply of His grace by the Spirit.
(*iv*) *Righteousness will be revealed* : They " shall see the plummet in the
hand of Zerubbabel " (v. 10). The construction is going to answer to
the plumbline. All God's movements have exalted righteousness ;
and your life and labours for your Lord will be marked by a rectitude,
an uprightness, that will satisfy the plumbline of Heaven. David sang
with glee, " He leadeth me in the paths of righteousness, for His Name's
sake." Paul declared, " I am not ashamed of the Gospel of Christ,
for it is the power of God unto salvation to everyone that believeth . . .
for therein is the righteousness of God revealed." So shall we answer
to the plumbline, as does everything begun, continued and ended in God.

We are up against opposition ; the force and power of the enemy
are formidable. But let us be more conscious of the mighty Spirit
of God, for it is " not by might, nor by power, but by my Spirit, saith
the Lord." Do remember this—there are two who minister on your
behalf continually, the Advocate in Heaven and the Advocate in the
heart. Say, " Lord, all that Thou hast for me, I will so eagerly have.
Help me, O Lord, to keep the channel clear and clean. Lord, I must
be efficient for Thee : the light must not flicker or grow dim ; it must
be a glowing flame, so that others may come into the light."

179

The Agent of the Almighty.

By the Rev. GUY H. KING.

YOU will, I am sure, realise that the purpose of our Convention is not only that we ourselves should be blessed. It is a grand thing to be blessed of the Lord, and it may well be that a great number of us during this week have entered into a very real blessing. But what do you think is the reason why God so graciously blesses us ? What is the ultimate purpose of our gathering together like this ? Do you not think that it is with a view to others ? There is a multitude far and wide throughout this land and across the seas in dire and desperate need ; and we have come to this place, not just that we might be blessed, but that we might be adjusted to go out to those others. This Convention will assuredly fail if it ends with ourselves. That " oil " we have just been hearing about is for the showing to others. So I want to say another word to you, and I am going to give you two texts, both in Exodus 3 ; one of them is in v. 8, where the living Lord says "*I am come down to deliver*" ; and the second is in v. 10, "*Come now therefore, and I will send thee.*"

I. The Method of God.

Will you notice the method God has adopted. You remember the situation. The people of Israel are under cruel bondage to Pharaoh. They have had a desperate time, they are in sore straits, in bitter bondage, longing for deliverance. Well, does God care ? Oh yes, He cares. Do you remember how the disciples once said, " Master, carest Thou not that we perish ? " Oh, that you and I could get just a sight of the broken heart of God over the wandering, desperately needy multitudes ! God cared.

When He was come down to deliver, what did He do ? He came to a man and chose him for the purpose. I read a helpful little book on the subject of prayer many years ago, and I recall one sentence that came on the first page : " Man is God's method." We see it here. God came to a man, that that man might be His agent and instrument in carrying out this glorious purpose of deliverance. But the amazing thing was that this man began to make excuses. It seemed he did not want to go. That tremendous privilege offered to Moses—and offered to you and me ; humble and insignificant and erring though we may very well be, yet to the very least believer in this place to-night there is offered the enormous privilege of being God's instrument in the deliverance of sinful men and women. Yet here is this man hanging back, as perchance some of us

180

have been hanging back. God is calling for those who will go and do His work ; but we have been making our excuses.

II. THE MAN OF GOD.

The first excuse Moses made was a very strange one on his lips. He said, " Who am I that I should go ? " Moses would not have said that forty years before. In the earlier part of his life he was quite persuaded that he should deliver his people—indeed, he struck the first blow for freedom ; but he found it was useless, and had to fly the country. He was not ready. The life of Moses is divided into three clear periods, each lasting for forty years. During the first forty years he was learning to be somebody. When he was " learned in all the wisdom of the Egyptians," brought up in the Egyptian Court, he became somebody of considerable importance ; I imagine he felt himself somebody at the end of that time. See him as he struck that blow for freedom ; he is somebody—a Prince of the Royal Court. Then the tragedy happened. He had to go, and for the next forty years he had to learn to be nobody ; and at the end of the period he comes before God and says, " Who am I ? " Of course, for those forty years he had been principally engaged in looking after sheep, and if that does not teach a man to be nobody, I do not know what will ! Do you know anything about sheep—lovely little things, on Christmas cards, and as you see them gambolling in the fields as your train rushes by ; beautiful little creatures, but do you know anything about them ? It is no compliment that we are so often in Scripture likened to sheep ! Moses was engaged for forty years in looking after sheep. No wonder that at the end he had learnt to be nobody ! That is when God went to him. That is where God spoke to him, in the place where he was nobody. That is God's chance. And for his final forty years Moses was learning to help everybody, God's man.

My dear friends, it might well be that there are those in this assembly to-night who are feeling that, although they are longing to be of service for God, it is no use their contemplating it, because they are just nobody. " I cannot do anything, I am insignificant, I am ungifted, I cannot speak, I am just nobody." I want to tell you in all seriousness that I believe if you have got to that point where you feel you are nobody, that is just the very condition God wants to get you into. I verily believe that Almighty God, purposing to deliver sin-bound souls, looks around this tent even now for the nobodies.

That was Moses' first excuse, but it was no reason. God says " I will be with thee."

III. THE MESSAGE OF GOD.

Then Moses makes another excuse ; he says, " When the people of Israel ask who it is that has sent me, what shall I say unto them ? " Are you troubled because, though you want to undertake Christian service, you would not know what to say ? God says, in effect, to Moses, " Go and tell them about Me." You will recall that in Acts 1 : 8 the Master, as He is going up to Heaven, says as one of His final words to the disciples, "Ye shall be witnesses." " Yes, Lord, but what am I to say ? " " Ye shall be witness *unto Me.*" That is the message ; and God says to Moses, " This is the message I entrust to you ; go and tell them, ' I AM hath sent me unto you,' the God of your fathers." What a message to take— to go and tell of God, the great I AM. Have you ever studied that signature ? Some people profess to be able to tell your character from your signature (I hope not !). Have you ever studied this autograph of God, I AM ? I can see at once that it means that God is real : I *am.* I can see that it means that God is personal : *I* am. I can see that it means that God is inexhaustible : I am—what ? Well, anything you need. It is as if God puts into the hands of Moses a signed, blank cheque that might be filled in to any amount. How the Lord Jesus loved to take that name and to use it as one of the marks of His Deity, and He so often filled in the blank cheque. He said, I am the good Shepherd ; I am the door ; I am the bread of life ; I am the resurrection and the life ; I am the first and the last. I am anything you need.

You and I are entrusted with that message about God. He says to the sin-bound people to whom we go, " God is able to meet you in all your need, to save you from all your sin, to satisfy every aspect of your being, and to use you to be an instrument in His hand."

But the signature tells me also that God is unchangeable. I AM. The God who lived in Abraham's time, Jacob's time, Moses' time, is just the same to-day ; and you and I may look back upon this old record, and all the records in this beloved Book, and tell ourselves as we turn its pages, This wonder-working God is just the same to-day. We turn over into the New Testament and see our loving Saviour, and we say, " He is just the same—I AM—the God of your fathers hath sent Me unto you." What a message to take, to speak, of a Person who is a Deliverer, a Saviour who died to save ! Do not hesitate to take up with alacrity, though with becoming humility, this chance to be God's messenger to this needy world.

IV. THE MIGHT OF GOD.

But Moses still has excuses to offer. " But, Lord, they will not believe me." And that introduces us to the might that God provided. He says, " What is that in thine hand ? " And Moses throws down his rod at God's command, and it becomes a serpent ; then another miracle follows—the leper's hand is made clean. God wants Moses to understand that as he goes upon his errand, he goes with all the mighty power of God at his disposal. Don't you worry, my friend, about not being able to do this service, for all God's power is available to you.

When Mr. R. T. Archibald was sailing for India to begin that wonderful work of his among the children of India, he went to say good-bye to that wonderful man, the Vicar of Christ Church, Gipsy Hill, to which we both belonged, Canon Robert Charles Joynt—a man to whom I owe, as does a multitude of people, more than can ever be described. He said to Mr. Archibald just as he went out, " Roddie, remember whenever you stand up to speak that God is at your side." I am trying to remember that fact tonight. All the might of God is at our disposal as we go about His service.

V. THE MOUTHPIECE OF GOD.

Then, will Moses go now ? No. He has one further excuse to offer ; he says, " O Lord, I am not eloquent." But let it be said that God can take any mouth to act as His mouthpiece. He used a very uneloquent mouth once to proclaim His message—you remember His humble messenger to Balaam ? You say, " I am not eloquent." Some people are, but most of us are not. And then God says a wonderful thing to Moses : " I will be with thy mouth." And He assures us that, if we are willing to go for Him, to busy ourselves by His grace in His service, He will give us words to say. Open your mouth and begin, and you will find the words are there. They may not be swiftly flowing words, they may not be poetic words, but they will be words whereby men shall be saved. God can use your mouth, my friend.

Think of the glorious message, " I am come down to deliver." Here is this bound multitude of people outside, these sinners heading straight for Hell, going to a Christless grave, burdened and depressed beyond measure, looking for satisfaction and finding none, casting about for someone who will bring to them a message of salvation, though they would not put it like that. And God in His mercy says, " I am come down to deliver. . . Come, and I will send thee." Well, may He ? He can read hearts ; He can see the response of your soul, but I think it would be a lovely thing if some of us, after all the teaching and help we have gotten in this Convention, and the gracious influences we have received as we have heard the voice of our Beloved Saviour, if He were to see some of us standing to our feet in token that we are willing to go. It may be here or there, it may be this or that, it matters not ; He will appoint the place and the message, just as He will supply all the power. He wants you for this " light " which Mr. Park spoke of ; the oil is assured, may He have you as the lampstand ?

The Lord came alongside Moses alone there in the wilderness. No less really does He stand at your side now, alone here in the crowd—to commission you for His service. Would you like to stand as an intimation of surrender to the glorious service of your infinitely glorious Lord ? Young man, young woman, you are wanting to tell the Lord, " I do not know what it is going to mean, but I want the privilege, the joy, and if you will see me through, I am your man, I am your woman."

" I am come down to deliver. . . Come now."

Will you stand if you want to re-dedicate yourself to His mighty service ? [At this point many rose to their feet.]

" I am come down to deliver. . . Come now, I will send thee."

183

Holiness on the head,
  Light and perfections on the breast,
Harmonious bells below, raising the dead
  To lead them unto life and rest.
Thus are true Aarons drest.

Only another head !
  I have, another heart and breast,
Another music, making live, not dead,
  Without Whom I could have no rest ;
In Him I am well drest.

Profaneness in my head,
  Defects and darkness in my breast,
A noise of passions ringing me for dead
  Unto a place where is no rest ;
Poor priest ! thus am I drest.

Christ is my only head,
  My only heart and breast,
My only music, striking me e'en dead ;
  That to the old man I may rest,
  And be in Him new drest.

So holy in my head,
  Perfect and light in my dear breast,
My doctrine tuned by Christ (who is not dead ;
  But lives in me while I do rest) :
Come, people ; Aaron's drest.

—George Herbert.

THURSDAY,
July 18th, 1946.

10 a.m. **Bible Reading.**

FOUR CHAPTERS OF CHRISTIAN
EXPERIENCE.

(*iv*) A CHAPTER OF REALISATION—ROMANS 8.

THE REV. GUY H. KING.

11.45 a.m. **Forenoon Meeting.**

ASKING FOR THE HOLY SPIRIT.

THE REV. H. W. CRAGG.

THREE ASPECTS AND ACTIVITIES OF FAITH.

DR. W. GRAHAM SCROGGIE.

3 p.m. **Afternoon Meeting.**

SPENDING OUR INHERITANCE.

DR. DONALD G. BARNHOUSE.

7.45 p.m. **Evening Meeting.**

THE ALL-SUFFICIENT ANSWER TO ALL
OUR NEED.

PREBENDARY COLIN C. KERR.

The Secret of Victory.

ON Thursday lowering skies and heavy rain once more began the day ; but fitful sun had taken the place of the rain by the time of the Bible Reading, when the Rev. Guy H. King came to the last of his chapters of Christian experience, " A Chapter of Realisation "— Romans 8. Here he had to deal with a " key " chapter of the Keswick message, and he did it in characteristic fashion—with headings and sub-headings, and much alliteration, helping to make the profound depths of the Apostle's reasoning clear and plain to the ordinary listener. The " life more abundant " in Christ Jesus was presented in all its attractive-ness and power. The Bible Readings certainly accomplished their purpose of instruction in the Word, of exalting the Lord Jesus, and commending the life of true submission to Him.

Mr. F. Mitchell presided over the meeting which followed, at which the Rev. H. W. Cragg spoke on the secret of victorious living, and Dr. W. Graham Scroggie, having read Hebrews 11 : 4-7 suggested that the record there of Abel, Enoch and Noah, reveals three aspects and activities of faith—Abel stands for the truth of salvation by blood-shedding ; Enoch, of fellowship ; and Noah, of testimony. From the lives of these three patriarchs Dr. Scroggie educed lessons which were both practical and thought-provoking.

Mr. J. Taylor Thompson, another member of the Keswick Council, who had presided on Wednesday afternoon, did so again on Thursday, when Dr. Donald G. Barnhouse spoke on " Spending our Inheritance."

In the evening, Preb. Colin C. Kerr, who gave the address, began with Mary's question to the angel, " How shall this be ? " and his reply, " The Holy Ghost." In the Third Person of the Trinity, the Prebendary emphasised, is the answer to all our need. He who justifies also sanctifies.

> *Jesus, mighty Saviour,*
> *Lover of the soul,*
> *Who but Thee can quicken,*
> *Who but Thee make whole ?*
> *This that I have brought Thee*
> *Is too hard for me,*
> *But is anything too hard, my Lord, for Thee ?*
> *By Thy Cross and Passion,*
> *Precious Blood outpoured,*
> *Plead I now, command deliverance, Blessed Lord.*
>
> AMY WILSON CARMICHAEL.

Thou to us, O Christ, art given
Force and freedom still to be ;
Let us ante-date our Heaven
Evermore by trusting Thee ;
      Thee opposing
Always to our Enemy.

Teach us thus to live believing,
Using Thee for all our need ;
To Thy care our spirits giving,
By Thy Spirit fill'd and freed ;
      Thus made ready
For the Master's use indeed.

H. C. G. MOULE.

Four Chapters of Christian Experience

(*iv*) A Chapter of Realisation—Romans 8.

BY THE REV. GUY H. KING.

I ALWAYS quarrel with one word in one of our Convention hymns— "Lord, I hear of showers of blessing." It was written by Mrs. Codner, who lived in Croydon when I was a curate there. One day, when visiting her, I asked if she would allow me to criticise this one word of her hymn. By her gracious permission, I asked why, if " *showers* of blessing " were being scattered, she allowed us to be content to ask " Let some *droppings* fall on me." After a moment, she said " Young man, you're right." And she gave me leave to alter it, whenever I liked, to " Let some *showers* fall on me." If showers are going, I'm not going to be content with droppings !

One very hard winter, the Lady Bountiful of a certain village published a notice that on a certain day, if the inhabitants would bring their own jugs up to the Big House, they should have them filled with nourishing soup. When the morning arrived, the housewives took down their jugs from the kitchen dresser, and went eagerly for the promised gift— a long line of them. Presently was to be seen an old dear, who had got her bedroom water-jug ; and when folk laughed at her she replied, " They only said *jugs* ; they didn't say what size." They were very amused at the house when the bedroom jug came through the hatch ; but her faith was honoured ; it was filled with soup, which she bore triumphantly homewards. What sort of a jug have you brought to the Convention ? Don't be satisfied with drops : " Open thy mouth wide, and I will fill it." According to your expectation will be your realisation. But how big *is* your expectation—your jug ? As you have listened to the messages and teachings of this week, has your heart been drawn out in desire to have all this fulness of blessing—up to the limit of your capacity ; and then what ? Well, a simple old Christian prayed at the prayer meeting, " Oh, Lord, Thou knowest that I can't hold much ; but I can overflow lots." Yes that's it. You shall have, for yourself, " a well of water " (John 4 : 14) ; and, for others, " out of (you) shall flow rivers of living water " (John 7 : 38). Says Malachi 3 : 10, " I will pour you out a blessing that there shall not be room enough to receive "—the overflow is for others.

Something of the vast stores of blessing has been presented to us ; and a great longing has been awakened in our hearts. But this is Keswick, with all its lovely landscapes, and all its beautiful fellowship : what about next week, way back home ? How can we have all these blessings in daily, continual, perpetual realisation ? The answer is in three words, the Holy Spirit. He is the secret of the making all this real and actual in ordinary every-day living—let us turn to think upon Him, and His ministry for the believer, remembering always that it is His passion to " glorify " the Lord Jesus in it all (John 16 : 14). Note that this work is done for the real Christian, one for whom there is " now no condemnation," because of the Foundation Chapter on the Cross ; one who is " in Christ Jesus," in pursuance of the Transformation Chapter of the glorious new position ; one who is desirous to " walk " aright, in the light of the Demonstration Chapter, in love. This one seeks to discover, in this last Realisation Chapter—Romans 8—how it can all be done. We think of the Spirit, then, in :—

I. The Making of the Holy Life.

In the previous chapter, Romans 7, such a life has seemed quite impossible. The constant, unsatisfactory, up and down contest has ended in utter failure, until at last the poor defeated believer is compelled to cry out, " O wretched man that I am ! Who shall deliver me ? " Thank God, there is an answer, as the closing verse, foreshadowing chapter 8, declares. In chapter 7 there is failure : of course there is, for the characteristic word of the chapter is " I "—it comes no less than thirty times. In chapter 8 there is success : of course there is, for the characteristic word of the chapter is " Spirit "—it comes no less than twenty times. There are three principles here which make for a holy life.

The first is (i) *The Principle of Counter-action.*—Throughout the chapter there is a succession of contrasts. (a) In verses 1 and 4 there are *two walks*—" Walk not after the flesh but after the Spirit." The unbeliever is a one-natured man, the flesh ; the believer is two-natured—the old sinful flesh, and the new Spirit-nature, which came to him when, at his new birth, the Holy Spirit came to take up His residence in his heart and life. Galatians 5 : 19 explains the contrariness of these two—" The flesh lusteth against the Spirit, but (not ' and ') the Spirit against the flesh . . . in order that you need not do the (wrong) things that ye (otherwise) would." The old nature does not vacate the premises when the new Tenant takes up His residence. Take an old illustration. Here is a dark room at night—it has a darkness nature, in common with the night outside. Now you switch on the light, and at once a new nature is manifest—a light nature, at variance with the night outside. Now that the new nature is present, has the old darkness nature gone ? Turn out the light and see ! No, the old is still there ; but the new counteracts it. So when we admit Him who is " the Light," the new does not eradicate the old, but counteracts it—" till the day dawn, and the shadows flee away." The old darkness nature of that room we spoke of will disappear when the morning breaks. For the complete riddance of " the flesh," we await the morning. In the meanwhile, it is not only that the " flesh " lusts, " but "—and in that " but," in turning that corner, lies all our hope of constant daily victory and holiness—the Spirit wars, too.

190

The secret is to let the Spirit do the fighting. You say, but where do I come in ? You don't, if you're wise. We are to walk, that is, to live, not flesh-wise, but Spirit-wise.

Next : (*b*) In verse 2 there are *two laws*—" the law of the Spirit of life in Christ Jesus hath made me free from the law of sin and death." The late Mr. George Goodman used to tell the story of a boy standing with his father in their garden. Presently he asked, " Dad, what's the law of gravitation ? " " It is the fact, my boy, that all material objects fall to the ground. It is a law of nature that they all do so." " Well, Dad, would you say that a tulip is a material object ? " " Certainly." " Well, then, why don't those tulips in that bed there fall to the ground, instead of standing up like that ? " " Because there's another law, a law of life which counteracts the law of gravitation. Look : I'll cut one down. See, the life is no longer there to operate ; and now it can only fall to the ground." Need I apply the simple illustration further than just to say : We are all, by nature, subject to a law of gravitation—a downward tendency ; a " law of sin and death." But when, at our new birth, the Holy Spirit enters our heart and life, a new counteracting law becomes operative—" the law of the Spirit of life in Christ Jesus."

Then (*c*) in verse 5 there are *two minds*—" do mind the things of the flesh . . . (do mind) the things of the Spirit." I wonder what is in our mind about things ? By what standard do we judge things : by the worldly standard, the fleshly standard ? Do we occupy our minds with carnal things, or with spiritual things ? If our minds are disturbed and distressed by " the things of the flesh," let us counter that move of the enemy by filling our minds with " the things of the Spirit " ; the latter will counteract the former. We do not forget verse 6, that " to be carnally minded is death, but to be spiritually minded is life and peace."

And (*d*) in verse 9 there are *two spheres*—" ye are not in the flesh, but in the Spirit, if so be that the Spirit of God dwell in you." The Christian's environment is the Spirit. Do you notice that while the Spirit is in you, you are in the Spirit. If the sponge is in the water, the water is in the sponge ; if the poker is in the fire, the fire is in the poker. If the Christian is in Christ, Christ is in the Christian ; if the believer is in the Spirit, the Spirit is in the believer. What a lovely sphere to live in ! Have you learnt yet that you cannot be in two places at once ? If you want to be quite assured of not living *in* the flesh, you should experimentally occupy your dwelling-place *in* the Spirit. The one will most certainly counteract the other. And by virtue of His dwelling-place in us, " we are debtors " (v. 13)—we owe it to God, not to live the " flesh " life.

You will notice the place of the Spirit in all this. It is He who is the divine instrument in the making of the holy life—by the principle of counteraction. But you will observe here also (*ii*) *The Principle of Vivification*. Take up that verse 11. (*a*) *What a Person we have in us*—" His Spirit. . . dwelleth in you." Do you not think that one of the things we Christians need to grip, until it grips us, is the blessed fact that the Holy Spirit actually is there within us. " Now if any man have not

191

the Spirit of Christ, he is none of His " (v. 9). This tremendous thing is true of every Christian, even the most unsatisfactory. Look at that passage in I Corinthians 6 : 19, " What ? know ye not that your body is the temple of the Holy Ghost who is in you ? " The form of the Greek conveys the sense of Paul's uttermost surprise that these people were unaware of this truth. They were Christians, but they were living at a very unholy level. We won't judge them ; they had only just come out of heathenism, and that of a terribly unclean character ; they were still dwelling in that fœtid atmosphere. All the same, they had *no business* to be acting thus : the Holy Ghost was in them. Did they not realise that ? Moreover, they had *no need* to be acting thus : the Holy Ghost was in them. Did they not realise that ? With such a Presence within, every Christian *should* be holy, and *could* be holy ; for (*b*) *What a Power we have in us*—" the Spirit of Him that raised up Jesus from the dead." The pull of the world around is ever mighty, as with those Corinthians. " I pray not that Thou shouldest take them out of the world, but that Thou shouldest keep them from the evil," says the Master to the Father. Here we are perforce ; but here is He, with force, enough to meet and master the power of the world. The lure of the devil is ever fascinating and seductive ; but we have the very same power to overcome as the Master Himself. As God, He " cannot be tempted with evil," says James 1 : 13 ; but as Man, He was—and as Man He lived and served in the power of the Eternal Spirit. It was in the urge of the Spirit that He went to His wilderness meeting with the evil one. Immediately after He had been anointed by the Spirit for His ministry, He was " driven " by Him to that dread encounter, Mark 1 : 12 tells us ; and it was, I surmise, in the power of that same Spirit that He conquered. You and I can have daily, hourly, momentary victory by the same means. The " flesh," too, is strong ; but how infinitely stronger is He that dwells within. So, (*c*) *What a Prospect we have in us*—" shall also quicken *your* mortal bodies by His Spirit that dwelleth in you." And this, not only at the *Parousia*, but also, in a certain sense, at the present. There may be a veritable vivification of these members of ours that they may be delivered from evil service and devoted to His. Paul had written, in 6 : 13, " Neither yield ye your members as instruments of unrighteousness unto sin : but yield yourselves unto God, as those that are alive from the dead, and your members as instruments of righteousness unto God." Paul would write later, in 12 : 1, " I beseech you therefore, brethren, by the mercies of God, that ye present your bodies a living sacrifice." Elijah, on Carmel, " cut the bullock in pieces," when he presented that body a dead sacrifice. Should not we place our offering thus piece and piece, that our " living sacrifice " may be an intelligent detailed thing. Our hands—for Him ; our feet—for Him ; our lips—for Him ; our knees—for Him ; our shoulders—for Him ; our eyes—for Him ; and our hearts—for Him. How many problems would be solved for us if only we realised that the offering is not merely a general one, but a particular one—piece by piece. So " yielded," the Spirit will vivify the whole, and make, indeed, a living sacrifice.

We must not forget (*iii*) *The Principle of Mortification* that is here. Just as in a grafted rose tree the gardener will be alert to observe any shoot of the old life, and to lop it off at once, so are we to be ever watchful of any appearing of a bit of the old life, and to nip it in the bud. Thus, " if ye through the Spirit do mortify the deeds of the body, ye shall live," indeed. Observe, once more, that it is all of the Spirit—He is the Christian's secret of a holy life. There is no realisation without Him. We go further, and see Him in :—

II. THE MANIFESTATION OF THE FAMILY LIFE.

Let us never, never forget that when we were " born of the Spirit " (John 3 : 6), we were, indeed, born into a family—and not left as " waifs and strays," to get on as best we can by ourselves. And be it ever remembered that we cannot properly develop our Christian life in isolation, but only in taking our place in the family. Our corporate Church life is of enormous importance, if we would grow apace, and walk aright. It is part of the Holy Spirit's office to make the family Head real to us ; to make the family members loving to each other ; to make the family likeness seen in us ; to make the family business important and urgent to us ; to make the family resources available to us ; above all, to make the family's unique Son infinitely adorable in our eyes. In that family atmosphere we see, in our chapter, the believer growing up.

(*i*) *Here is the lisping babe*—" ye have received the Spirit of adoption, whereby we cry, Abba, Father " (v. 15). The same thing is in Galatians 4 : 6. There is something rather fascinating about that Aramaic word— pronounce it for yourself, *Ab-ba* : do you notice that it needs no teeth to say it ? It is the spiritual infant's first attempt at speech ; and what more appropriate than to lisp the Father's name. How good to know that from the very beginning the Holy Spirit is ready to take in hand the little child in the faith, and to teach him step by step. Do you remember those remarkable words in I John 2 : 20, " Ye have an unction from the Holy One, and ye know all things." What is even more remarkable is the fact that they were addressed, not to " you fathers," nor to " you young men," but to the " little children " in Christ. They are in a position to know " *all* things " that are needful to their early stage of growth, because the Holy Teacher is ever at their disposal. And so :—

(*ii*) *Here is the instructed child*—" the Spirit Himself beareth witness with our spirit, that we are the children of God " (v. 16). Note, please, that the " itself " of A.V. is only there on grammar grounds—the actual Greek word for " Spirit " being neuter ; but the New Grammar of our New School calls for the personal " Himself." The Holy Spirit is no " It," but a glorious " He " : see how careful the Master is about this in such a passage as John 16 : 7-15, where He and Him are used of the Spirit no less than twelve times. Among the " all things " of His curriculum, the one subject of our *assurance* is here singled out for mention, as it is one of the most important lessons we have to learn—a lesson that some scholars in His school seem to find very hard to grasp. " We are "— there is no doubt about it ; there is no delay, as if we cannot know till hereafter ; there is no difference, for it applies to every believer alike : we are, all of us, most certainly, here and now, His children. You see, our assurance rests upon a threefold basis—(*a*) *The work of Christ*—what He did, on the Cross ; not what we did, or didn't do. (*b*) *The word of God*—concerning His " finished " work, and those who trust on Him, not on themselves, not on any rites and ceremonies. (*c*) *The witness of the Spirit*—which comes to us as we do in very truth rely only and solely on the work of the Word. Being, then, by Him, made certain of our place in the family, we discover that :—

(*iii*) *Here is the fortunate heir*—" if children, then heirs ; heirs of God, and joint-heirs with Christ " (v. 17). Sanday and Headlam remind us that our Lord had described Himself as " the Heir," in Matthew 21 : 38. How happy are the children to have such a rich inheritance—the interest is our portion here ; the capital is our possession hereafter. It would be impossible to live beyond our means, for those means are so vast— " according to His riches in glory by Christ Jesus " (Phil. 4 : 19). Seeing, then, that we have such infinite resources to draw on, let us live, not as paupers, but as princes. We do not forget that our inherited fortune will likely contain " suffering " as well as " glory " ; but whatever we may be called to undergo will be as nothing compared with the glory that shall overtake us. Let us not be surprised, or saddened, if we have to put up with something because of our being Christians. And now :—

(*iv*) *Here is the developing adolescent*—" as many as are led by the Spirit of God, they are the sons of God " (v. 14). Babe—child—son : such is the natural, as well as the spiritual, progression. A son is a child grown-up : the father would not introduce him as " This is my child," but " This is my son." You will observe that the chosen mark of this stage of the believer's growth is, that he is " led of the Spirit." That leading is sometimes given to us in the unfolding of circumstances—the door opens, or closes, and so on ; sometimes it comes through the advice of a wise and experienced friend ; but the Spirit's main method is the Word. That is one of the many reasons why it is so important for us to study the Bible, so that we may become gradually steeped in it, and may thus often know instinctively what is the will and way of God about things, even if we do not find " proof " texts. Let the child be happily content with " the sincere (unadulterated) *milk* of the Word, that ye may grow thereby " (I Pet. 2 : 2) ; but, as he grows, let the developing adolescent become increasingly desirous of the " *meat* " of the Word (I Cor. 3 : 2), masticating, and digesting, and assimilating the heavenly food that makes for moral muscle and spiritual sinew. The same Spirit who inspired the record will, thereby, inspire the reader, guiding him to the right decision. And then :—

(*v*) *Here is the perfected man*—" the manifestation of the sons of God " (v. 19)—God knows now who they are, we know that we are, then shall all, both men and angels, know, for we shall be manifested as such ; " the redemption of our body " (v. 23)—the body, now the subject of weakness, the target of temptation, the heir of limitation, will then be glorified, and redeemed entirely from all weakness and wickedness, and be the perfectly fit and unwearying instrument wherein " His servants shall serve Him " spirits and bodies being utterly saved ; " for we are saved by hope " (v. 24)—it is to such a hope of perfected redemption that we have been saved ; it is in that sense that this Apostle writes subsequently, " Now is our salvation nearer than when we believed " (Rom. 13 : 11). There is so much more here in this passage that we might profitably have touched on, but the exigencies of time forbid. We must content ourselves now by re-iterating that all this growth from spiritual childhood to manhood is to be healthily effected only in association with our fellow-believers, as members of the family, as in what the " Grace " of 2 Corinthians 13 : 14 calls "the communion (or, fellowship) of the Holy Ghost." Let us go on now to another ministry of the Holy Spirit on our behalf, and see Him as—

III. THE MAINSPRING OF THE PRAYER LIFE.

Nothing is more important in the life of the Christian—prayer is his very life's breath, prayer is his most exalted privilege, prayer is his most powerful employ, prayer is his most exacting test. In an African village there were a number of Christians, who used in the early morning to go to a certain spot in the forest for their daily prayer. It was interesting to observe, in course of time, how the grass was worn down into a track leading from each Christian hut to the place of prayer. Sometimes it would happen that one of them would grow slack, and his track would begin to shew signs of disuse. One of the others would then say to the backsliding member, " Brother, there is grass on your track." May I ask you if there is any grass on *your* track ? How much we lose, how much the cause loses, if we lose the prayer habit, and the prayer spirit. Says Archbishop Trench, in very familiar words :—

> We kneel, how weak ; we rise, how full of strength.
> Why, therefore, do we do ourselves this wrong
> And others—that we are not always strong ?

I can well imagine that if all of us were to give ourselves seriously to get our prayer-life into a right and proper condition, we should find so many other things falling into their right place, and we should—as in no other way—really " pull our weight " in the mighty endeavours of the kingdom. And this, whether in private or in public prayer.

Now our chapter tells us that, as in all else that pertains to Christian life and experience, and service, and witness, so in this, the Holy Spirit is the predominant secret of prevailing prayer. You will notice (*i*) *that word " infirmities,"* in verse 26—" our infirmities . . . we know not what to pray for as we ought." Sometimes it is the matter of our prayers that is the difficulty—the " what " : after all, it is more than half the battle if we ask for the right things. Sometimes it is the manner of our prayers that is the difficulty—the " as " : it is possible to ask for the right things in the wrong way—" ye ask amiss " (James 4 : 3). What with the one thing, and with the other, we have plenty of infirmities. Have you noticed that, on the two occasions when the Master taught what is generally called " the Lord's Prayer," but which is, more accurately, the disciples' prayer, or the children's prayer, or even the family prayer, He introduced it differently, saying, in Luke 11 : 2, " When ye pray, say . . . ," while in Matthew 6 : 9 it is, " After this manner therefore pray ye." The first was the matter—" what to pray for," and the second, the manner—" as we ought " : both are illustrated in that pattern prayer.

Look next at (ii) *that word* " *helpeth*," in this same verse 26—" Likewise the Spirit also helpeth . . ." I think we might seek His help in all sorts of things connected with our intercession time. (a) *What about sleepiness?* This is a real trouble to quite a number of Christians. If it is one of your " infirmities," may I commend to your attention again the words of verse 11, " He . . . shall . . . quicken your mortal bodies." Is this not one of the ways of " vivification," that we spoke of earlier, that we can ask Him to do for us even now ? and (b) *What about wandering thoughts* ? Is this a distress to any of you, I wonder ? Many have told me how greatly disturbed they are even in their most solemn moments. Indeed, probably none of us is entirely free from this unwelcome interruption. Well now, turn to 2 Corinthians 10 : 3— " we do not war after the flesh " : no, our Romans chapter would shew the blest alternative, " after the Spirit " (v. 1). It is the Spirit, then, that is to bring about the victory of verse 5 of the Corinthians passage, " . . . bringing into captivity every thought to the obedience of Christ." The very moment a wandering thought steals into our mind, let us at once ask the Holy Spirit to do His police work for us and to arrest it !

Yes, He helps in every way ; but here, a particular way is mentioned in that rather difficult part, verses 26b-27—the " groanings that cannot be uttered " : desires too deep for words, longings that language cannot adequately express, wishes that baffle words. Alexander Maclaren says, " Inarticulate utterance is the most self-revealing. Grief can say more in a sob and a tear than in many weak words ; love finds its tongue in the light of an eye and the clasp of a hand." So in our Godward life there are sometimes deepmost desires that are, in reality, motions of the Spirit— they are His intercessions, not only " for " us, but " in " us, forasmuch as He is Himself in us. Nowhere, so far as my own study has gone, is the gist of this passage more admirably put than in these words of the late Dean Vaughan, " The Holy Spirit makes entreaty to God for us in those unuttered yearnings which the Searcher of hearts recognises as the breathing of His own Spirit, and therefore the expression of His own will." Half-a-dozen of you are grouped around a perambulator in baby-worship, when suddenly the little person sets up a yelling and a squealing. Five of you have no idea what it is saying : it knows its distress, but it cannot describe it. The sixth member of the group is mother, and she " knoweth " this strange language means, " Please mummie, I've got a pin sticking in me ; will you hurry up and take it away." Yes ; He " knoweth " what you cannot tell Him in words.

So is He intimately concerned with the believer's prayer-life ; for He knows, if we don't, how great is the power of prayer. Revivals have begun in prayer ; lives have been changed by prayer ; distance has been annihilated by prayer ; miracles have been wrought by prayer. Do you remember Acts 12 : 5, " Peter therefore was kept in prison, but prayer was made . . ."—what was the good of that ; why didn't they do something ; why not get a monster petition signed for his release ; or organise an attack on the prison ? " But prayer was made." Do something ? Why, that was the greatest thing they could have done ; as the event proved. May the Spirit continually help our infirmities, and teach us what " praying in the Holy Ghost " (Jude 20) means.

It will readily be seen that we are not attempting a complete exposition of this wonderful chapter, We are obliged to omit much that is here, and to select for treatment a few of the great matters wherein the Holy Spirit is seen to be the realisation of our high hopes for the life to which we move forward as we go down from this mountain of rich blessing. How can we realise it all, had been our question : the Holy Spirit has been our answer. And we proceed to one final consideration as we think upon :—

IV. THE MINISTRY OF THE EXULTANT LIFE.

What a tone of exaltation creeps into the Apostle's dictation as he draws his chapter to a close. Whoever was his amanuensis must have been conscious of a certain thrill as the vital words and throbbing sentences gushed forth from this man, strangely moved by his own previous, and preparatory, utterance. Paul would have us all understand, the One who inspired him would have us all understand, that a life utterly yielded to the great and gracious influences of the Holy Spirit is bound to be an exultant life—to respond to that influence is to receive an insight into things, which none other has. For instance, (i) *We rejoice in the Providence of God*—" all things work together for good to them that love God, to them who are the called according to His purpose " (v. 28). Some, relying on a certain variant reading, would make God the subject of the sentence ; but we must be on our guard, for so learned and exact a scholar as Dr. A. T. Robertson, in his Grammar of the Greek New Testament, says that the validity of that reading is " more than doubtful." Anyway, it is certainly true in fact that " all things " do not of themselves work for our good : that result is only brought about because God does Himself take them in hand, and mould them to our good ; and in that sense our A.V. translation may be allowed to stand. Do you " love God ? " Then, you are one of His " called " people, with the truly blessed result that everything that happens in your life comes to you only by way of the moulding hands of God. Poor old Jacob, not knowing what he said, exclaimed, " All these things are *against* me " (Gen. 42 : 36) ; you may say, " All these things are *for* me." Yes ; but I have left out two most important words in my quotation from our verse 28. I have omitted them only that I may now emphasise them the more : don't you ever omit them ! They are the words, " We know "—we do not always think it, nor feel it, nor appreciate it, nor understand it ; but " we know " it. Dr. David Brown says this was as a " household word " with the early Church. What peace, and rest, and even joy come to our hearts when we look at our " all things " in this way ; when we accept them, not grumblingly, but trustingly, as from the loving hand of God, shaping them all for our ultimate blessing. Don't you think that one of the many happy surprises of the Life hereafter will be to see the way in which our " all things " have worked out. How we shall rejoice then in the wisdom, and power, and love of our God. The Holy Spirit would have us rejoice now in unswerving faith.

A second cause for our exaltation is that (ii) *We rejoice in the Programme of God*—" foreknow . . . predestinate . . . called . . . justified . . . glorified " (vv. 29-30). What a tale of divine grace ; what a story of Christian gladness—no wonder he exults ! It all runs back to a time long before we were born, and to (a) God's *foreknowledge* of us. We recall with interest that another statement of the believer's election, in I Peter 1 : 2, also runs back to this same point—" elect according to the fore-knowledge of God." I am myself persuaded that this implies that God's election of people to eternal life is applicable to all those who, as He well knew, would come to believe on the Son of God. Anyhow, we believers know that we are " elect "—and the comfort is that this doctrine is not something to keep us out, but something to keep us in ! Great tomes have been written, great minds have been exercised, on the apparent contra-diction between predestination and free-will. I know it sounds arrant presumption for such as I to rush in here where angels fear to tread ; but one can only speak, though with becoming humility and diffidence, what one feels. I believe that there is no contradiction ; but that those have been predestinated who were foreknown to come to use their free-will aright in trusting the Saviour.

So we consider (b) His *predestination* of us. Let me remind you that we are " the called according to His purpose " : what was that purpose ? Here it is : " to be conformed to the image of His Son." When we were saved, we were not removed from the world, but left here to serve and honour Him : we are to be careful, however, not to be worldly-minded— " be not conformed to this world," says the Apostle, in Romans 12 : 2, but, as here, " be conformed " to His image. That is true sanctification, real sainthood. The Holy Spirit has, in this, one of His great aims : to bring to pass in us what we were predestined for. Look at 2 Corin-thians 3 : 18—" We (Christians) all, with open face (nothing between us and Him ; no controversy with Him) beholding as in a glass (the mirror of the Word) the glory of the Lord, are changed (as we obey that Word) into the same image from glory to glory (a gradual likeness) even as by the Lord the Spirit." As we yield ourselves to His touch, the likeness goes on, until the Great Day when the portrait shall be finished, and " we shall be like Him, for we shall see Him as He is " (I John 3 : 2). Another Apostle, I Peter 2 : 9, has the same thought of the reason for our being chosen in Christ—" that ye should shew forth the praises (the excellencies) of Him who hath called you." This is the family likeness we spoke of earlier. He " the Firstborn " has got Home first ; we, the " many brethren " shall follow Him, bearing " the same image," in due course.

And now, moving out from eternity into time, we come to (c) His

198

calling of us. In how many, and how diverse, ways He does it—and how intensely fascinating the stories. From the first disciples, and the way " He called them " (Matt. 4 : 21), from the great Apostle who writes our chapter, and the way He called him, on that Damascus road ; right on down through the years each call has been different—sometimes quiet and even gradual, sometimes cataclysmic and quite sudden. During this age, it is the Holy Spirit who is the " calling " Agent of the Godhead ; and we believers are the " called-out " ones, which is the meaning of the word *ecclesia*, the Church.

Which leads on to (*d*) His *justifying* of us. We have not room here to go into that amazing transaction whereby, in a phrase, we are made right with God—all our unrighteousness being laid upon Him, as our first chapter taught us, and all His righteousness being reckoned to us. Sufficient, for the moment, to know that, not just by an act of mercy, but by an act of justice, we leave the court, without a stain on our character, to go and live a reformed—" conformed " (8 : 29) ; " transformed " (12 : 2)—life. And even as we emerge from the court, the Holy Spirit meets us, and undertakes from the outset the " reformation " that our acquittal demands.

So we arrive at (*e*) His *glorifying* of us. This is the end of the wonderful journey, the last step : and be it noted that it is here envisaged as having already taken place—it is a spiritually automatic certainty that " whom He justified them He also glorified." We shall have occasion presently to return to the theme ; but, meanwhile, let us stand in wonder at the sovereign grace of God that pre-determined for us believers such a marvellous programme of joy and blessing.

And now we hurry on to the last spring of our Christian exultation, (*iii*) *We rejoice in the Perseverance of God*—C. H. Spurgeon was once asked if he believed in the perseverance of the saints. He answered, " No ; but I do believe in the perseverance of the Saviour." This is the theme of the remainder of our chapter of realisation. The Holy Spirit is at pains, by a series of questions, to direct Paul to stablish the believer's confidence and security upon God. (*a*) Upon His power—" If God be for us, who can (with any success) be against us ? " He can deal victoriously with any sort, or size, of opposition and difficulty. (*b*) Upon His gift—" He that spared not His own Son, but delivered Him up for us all, how shall He not with Him also freely give us all things ? " He has *given* all things needful *in* Christ who saves me ; therefore " I can *do* all things *through* Christ which strengtheneth me " (Phil. 4 : 13). So we turn to consider how He so wondrously perseveres " for us " in the face of all that is " against us."

Opposition is mentioned as likely to come from three directions. (*a*) *The demands of judgment* (vv. 33-34). The " it is " in the second part of each verse should be omitted ; the words are italicised because they are not in the Greek, but are employed by the translators to give what they conceived to be the sense of the passage. Most scholars now, however, agree that the sense is obscured by their insertion, rather than clarified. In each verse, the one question is answered by another,

(1) " Who shall lay anything to the charge of God's elect ? God, that justifieth ? " At infinite cost, and in infinite love, He has already justified us ; completely acquitted as we are, no further charge will be preferred against us in the divine justiciary. (2) " Who is he that condemneth ? Christ that died, yea rather, that is risen again ? " His vicarious sacrifice was offered for the very purpose of setting us free from condemnation ; and lest it should be for one moment supposed that His claim for His death was unwarranted and unsubstantiated, God raised Him from the dead, in token that the sacrifice was accepted. Thank God, " He that heareth . . . and believeth . . . shall not come into condemnation, but is passed from death unto life " (John 5 : 24). The case is all over ; the charge is dismissed. There is nothing to fear from that direction.

(b) *The blows of circumstance* (vv. 35-37). Not even the cruellest blows that life can inflict can make any rift in His love—whatever else goes, that abides, because He abides. We in our comfortable conditions can scarcely appreciate the distressful surroundings of those early believers. I wonder if we should be as faithful as they in the face of "tribulation, distress, persecution, famine, nakedness, peril, sword ? " Verily, for some of them life was, circumstantially, a living death—" killed all the day long." Yet Paul is able triumphantly to say, " in all these things we are more than conquerors." Super-conquerors, we may say, for the Greek of " more than " is *huper*. What *does* that last phrase mean ? I know what " conquerors " would imply, but what is this " more than " intended to signify ? I cannot be sure ; but perhaps the first has to do just with the overcome, while the second deals with the outcome—the results of the victory. Maybe, it is not only " subduing " the enemy, but " spoiling " him of his goods. Applying the point here, shall we say that they not only refused to be defeated by their untoward circumstances, but that they actually got positive good out of them—thus was the promise of verse 28 abundantly fulfilled to their trustful souls. Circumstances : be they what they may—these cannot cause the Lord's hand to relax its hold on us. There is nothing to be feared from that direction.

(c) *The forces of the Universe* (vv. 38-39). The Holy Spirit has brought our writer to such a pitch of certainty that he is prepared to assert, without fear of contradiction, that there is absolutely nothing in all God's universe that can sever the believer's union with his Lord. Writing in 2 Timothy 1 : 12, he says, " I am persuaded (the same word of conviction as here) that He is able to keep that which I have committed unto Him against that day " ; writing in our chapter, he says that he is " persuaded " that nothing can interfere with His keeping, " *Neither death, nor life* "—nothing, as we have seen, in the often mysterious happenings of life here ; nothing in the even more mysterious passage through the door into life hereafter. " *Nor angels, nor principalities, nor powers* "—the formidable forces of evil would do anything, give anything, to effect a separation ; but they will never succeed. The Master Himself assures us, in John 10 : 28, " they shall never perish, neither shall any (man, or devil, or

200

self) pluck them out of My hand." How safe we are ! " *Nor things present, nor things to come* "—we cannot prophesy the future, but we may be quite certain of one thing, that it will produce nothing that will be able to tear us apart from Him. " *Nor height, nor depth, nor any other creature* "—no created thing in the seven heavens above, no created thing in the nethermost regions below, can do it. The Spirit has caused Paul to ransack every spot and circumstance to try to discover anything that could be used to drive a wedge between the believer and his God ; here and there he searches, and finds nothing ; hither and thither he travels, and returns empty-handed—there is nothing, nothing, nothing, that is " able to separate." What blest security we have. No wonder ours is an exultant life.

I once saw a small girl standing on the edge of a pavement, obviously wanting to cross the busy, dangerous street, but fearing to step off the curb. Before I could reach her, a policeman came along. She put her little hand in his, and together they ventured forth. A great lorry came lumbering along, so close that it seemed to her almost on top of them ; and I am sure I saw her little hand tremble and slip. But it was all right, for her safety depended, not upon her hold of the policeman, but upon his hold of her. Our hand—yes, that was essential, to make the connection of faith ; but, thereafter, His hand—that will never, never let us go. George Matheson, the blind poet and preacher, knew what the cruel blows of circumstance could be, but he could sing triumphantly :—

> O Love, that wilt not let me go.

The following words were handed to me at the close of this Bible Reading :—

> Let me no more my comfort draw
> From my frail grasp of Thee.
> Let me henceforth rejoice with awe
> In Thy strong grasp of me.

Well, there it is : all the blessing that has been set before us during this week, awaking in us a longing to possess it all, and to experience it all in the coming days. The Master said, in John 16 : 14, " He (the Spirit) shall receive of Mine, and shall shew it unto you "—He reveals it all, and makes it all real. He is there with us to be, and to give, the realisation of all that is ours in Christ.

Ah, that reminds me of something. Away back in the beginning of our consideration of this sublime chapter, I said that it is the Holy Spirit's passion to " glorify " the Master. Sure enough, He caused Paul to conclude the study, not with Himself and His work, but with " Christ Jesus our Lord."

Asking for the Holy Spirit.

By the Rev. H. W. CRAGG, M.A.

"If ye then, being evil, know how to give good gifts unto your children, how much more shall your Heavenly Father give the Holy Spirit to them that ask Him?"—*Luke* 11 : 13.

IF you were to ask me to summarise in one brief phrase the secret of holiness and of victorious Christian living, I would reply that you have it in this one—" God the Holy Ghost." May I mention two reasons why I think God the Holy Ghost is the answer to all our needs. First, because He has already been the answer to our need in all the days that have passed. We should not be here this morning, we should not sing the Lord's praise and worship with the Lord's people, if we had not already been recipients of the gracious ministry of the Holy Ghost. Every converted man and woman in this tent is a product of God's grace. We have been born of the Spirit. Romans 8 : 9 reminds us that, " If any man have not the Spirit of Christ, he is none of His," and we need a continuation, a deepening assurance of that which we already have. The Third Person of the Trinity, who brought us to Christ the day we were converted, will be absolutely sufficient for all our need in the days that lie ahead. How wonderful it is to know that the one who brought us the new birth maintains the new life! It is all the work of the Holy Ghost.

The second reason why we have the answer to our question in the Holy Spirit, is that the Third Person of the Trinity is concerned with magnifying the Second. We must always keep clearly in our minds the fact that Christianity is Christ ; that the whole of our experience from start to finish is an experience of Christ. It is what Christ is able to be to the heart, and can do in the heart in which He is enthroned, that is the secret of our victory as Christians, and of our holiness of life. I would remind you that the Holy Ghost is given not only to lead us to Christ, but to make Christ more beautiful, more real and wonderful to the Christian. If we study our Lord's discourse to His disciples at the end of His earthly ministry, we find Him mentioning the approaching advent of the Holy Spirit. In John 14 : 26, He says : " He shall . . . bring all things to your remembrance, whatsoever I have said unto you." John 15 : 26, " He shall testify of Me." John 16 : 14, " He shall glorify Me." When we come to the day of Pentecost, we find that Peter stands up to expound that which has become a fact of history. He says that this is the fulfilling of the old promise to which they had so long looked, and goes on to preach, in the power of the newly given Spirit, the Christ of the Resurrection. You will not find in the whole of your New Testament, or in the whole of your Christian history, a single event which has been marked by the fulness of the Holy Ghost that has not brought glory to our Blessed Lord. His ministry is the ministry of magnifying Christ, and Christ Himself is the answer to every need of the human heart. How important it is, then, that this Blessed Holy Spirit of God should infill His children in order to make them more like Christ, more conscious of the presence of Christ, and more fully aware of the claims of Christ, and to enable them to face those claims and live them out.

It is precisely because the Holy Spirit is given to us to make our Blessed Lord more real and more wonderful, and to lead us into all that He has provided for us, that we seek to-day the fulness of the Spirit ; the Holy Spirit in His complete control of the heart and life, so that He may minister Christ to my need and display Christ in my daily life.

In this eleventh chapter of Luke our Lord is speaking to His disciples ; they have come to Him with the simple request, " Lord, teach us to pray," and having answered their request by giving them the Lord's Prayer, He says, " Ask, and it shall be given you ; seek, and ye shall find ; knock, and it shall be opened." Then He goes on to instance the possibility of a son coming to a father, and " If he shall ask bread, will he give him a stone ? or if he ask a fish, will he give him a serpent ? or if he shall ask an egg, will he give him a scorpion ? " Seeing that is how a father treats his child, by giving him the thing for which he asks if it is within the circle of the father's will, do you think you will ask for the Holy Spirit's power, and not receive that for which you ask ? " If ye then, being evil, know how to give good gifts unto your children, how much more shall your Heavenly Father give the Holy Spirit to them that ask Him." Are you ready to ask, and ready to receive ?

This must refer to something beyond the work of conversion, which is the Holy Spirit's ministry. It is clear that we have many references in our New Testament which show that there is something more than regeneration in the ministry of the Holy Ghost. We may each one of us receive that something more, and that is why God has gathered us here. Paul says in Ephesians 5 : 18, " Be filled with the Spirit." It is one thing for the Holy Spirit to be resident, and quite another thing for Him to be president. It is one thing to have Him indwelling, and quite a different thing to have Him infilling. The Holy Spirit indwells every one of us if we are converted, but it is the purpose of God that He should infill. Every part of us should be not only yielded to Christ, but filled with the Holy Ghost, that the whole life might be the outworking of the infilling of the Spirit of God—" Be filled with the Spirit."

May I suggest four simple conditions of this filling, and as we are ready and willing to fulfil these four conditions, God in His mercy will grant us that for which we seek. Do we want the fulness of the Holy Ghost ? Are we content to live as we are ? Are we content merely to be Christ's, and not to be altogether His ? Are we content merely to have the Holy Ghost, or are we prepared to let the Holy Ghost have us ?

I see in this verse that the first condition of this great blessing of God which is the right of every child of God if he will but have it, is *asking*

" to them that *ask*." " I will yet for this be enquired of," says God. " Ask, and it shall be given you." God will not give you that for which you do not ask. God does not waste His blessings ; He is not going to pour out His Spirit into a life that does not want Him, or is not prepared to fulfil the conditions. "Ask, and it shall be given." Does not James say, " Ye have not because ye ask not." Asking is the expression of a deep, earnest desire, of a great longing, which has proved repeatedly that life without the sufficiency of the Spirit is a barren thing, even in the Christian Church. Are you conscious of your need, so that you are ready to come before God with this simple prayer, " O God, fill me with the Holy Ghost " ?

Then the second simple step is *taking*. Taking is the other side of our asking, for our Lord said : " Whatsoever things ye desire, when ye pray, believe that ye receive them and ye shall have them." One of the things lacking in the lives of some who do not enter into blessing is just the simple faith to believe that what God has promised He is able also to perform. There is so much introspective inquiry which makes us look into ourselves instead of away to Christ. Faith is simply taking what God has promised. If you humbly and simply ask for the Holy Ghost in all His fulness, then you may take by faith. Someone said to me in my early days as a Christian, "For every one look at yourself, take ten looks at Jesus Christ." Instead of searching your heart to see if you have the fulness of the Spirit, look up into the face of your Lord and take Him at His word. You will never find what you are seeking within yourself, but you will find it if you seek from your Blessed Lord and by faith appropriate all that He offers you.

Dr. F. B. Meyer, speaking in this tent several years ago on the filling of the Spirit, said that he often used to go out on the mountain-side and throw open his whole being to the lovely fresh air, and as he breathed in the fresh air, he made his own what God had provided. So as a simple act of taking by faith, we throw open every avenue of our being and personality to the incoming of the Holy Ghost, and we believe that God is not only able to do, but by His loving grace he does exactly what we ask—

I take the promised Holy Ghost,
I take the power of Pentecost,
To fill me to the uttermost,
I take—He undertakes.

The third step seems to me to be *honouring*. You remember how James also says : " Ye ask and receive not, because ye ask amiss, that ye may consume it upon your lusts." God never gives to His people unless those gifts will magnify Christ ; God will not magnify you or me by His gifts; all that God has to give will magnify Christ. You can apply that to any spiritual grace or blessing you may be seeking, but pre-eminently is this true of the filling of the Spirit : " The journey that thou takest shall not be for thine honour," not for your own blessing, credit, or magnifying, but for the magnifying of Jesus Christ. How often those of

204

us who have to speak ask for power; and all of us going about our daily duties ask for grace. Do we want power in order that we ourselves might be effective? Do we want grace in order that it might be known that we are so wonderfully like Christ? God has nothing to give in answer to that motive. If we are to know the fulness of the Holy Ghost, it is for the honouring of Jesus Christ and for the glory of His name in every relationship of life and in every aspect of service; God will not give the fulness of the Spirit for selfish aims or ends.

Asking, taking, honouring, and then *obeying*. Acts 5 : 32 speaks about the Holy Ghost " whom God hath given to them that obey Him." Are you ready to obey your Lord? Have you brought into this tent some disobedience, and yet claim to be seeking the fulness of the Holy Ghost? That is such a contradiction; it means you will go out without that which you are seeking, for disobedience was never blessed of God with the fulness of the Spirit . . . " to them that obey Him." Are you ready to obey your Lord in everything, to do exactly what He says, to render immediate obedience in every little detail, to the very last jot? Are you ready to be absolutely faithful and obedient to your Lord? No man was ever filled with the Holy Ghost who set up any disobedience.

This fulness of the Spirit is a moment-by-moment matter. We talk about the once-for-all transaction when we hand over our lives to Jesus Christ. That transaction is demanded of us (Rom. 6 and 12). But this is not a once-for-all transaction, it is a moment-by-moment experience, as we fulfil the conditions. Therefore it is possible for us to be filled with the Holy Spirit to-day, and not to be filled tomorrow. How important it is that we should see that moment by moment we are fulfilling the conditions—asking and taking by faith. As I rise from my bed morning by morning, this should be my prayer—" O God, fill me with the Holy Ghost." " If ye then, being evil, know how to give good gifts unto your children, how much more shall your Heavenly Father give the Holy Spirit to them that ask Him." Let us ask in faith, nothing wavering. Ask, take, honour, obey.

205

Three Aspects and Activities of Faith.

By the Rev. W. GRAHAM SCROGGIE, D.D.

I WANT to speak to you about three aspects and activities of faith. In Hebrews eleven, the God-fearing celebrities of the Old Testament are made to pass before us. There are several things in the record as a whole that we should mention in passing. One is that faith is made the test and standard of the worth of these people. Another is that the facts here set before us are in their historical sequence. First our attention is called to the primeval period, in vv. 4-7; then to the patriarchal period, in vv. 8-22; and then to the national period, in vv. 23-38. It is therefore a historical survey. Another thing that we must not overlook is that the selection of the names in this chapter is of considerable significance. There are names that we naturally look for, but do not find. Adam is not mentioned, Aaron is not mentioned, Saul is not mentioned, and others who have prominence in the Old Testament records. But as we read again we find the names of people that we would not have expected to find in such a record, such as Rahab, Barak, and Jephthae. We shall have great surprises in days to come and in *the Day* to come. The prominent now may be obscure then, and the obscure here may be prominent there.

Now turn to the primeval period, in vv. 4-7. I want you to notice that of the millions of persons who lived during this period, only three are named. But, as we shall see, they are representative persons : Abel, Enoch and Noah. Let us discover for what great truths these three persons respectively stand, and then observe the relation of these truths to one another, and our relation to them. Of course I can only be brief on such a theme, within our limits of time.

I. THE GREAT TRUTHS FOR WHICH THESE THREE PERSONS RESPECTIVELY STAND.

Abel stands for the truth of salvation. " By faith Abel offered unto God a more excellent sacrifice than Cain, by which he obtained witness that he was righteous, God testifying of his gifts, and he being dead yet speaketh." In Genesis 3 we read of the fall of man and of the race in man, and of the human remedy : " They sewed together fig leaves and made themselves aprons." Then we read, at the end of that chapter, of the appointed way of salvation ; the fig leaves had to be abandoned, and coats of skin were made for the covering of our first parents. But, of course, in order to get coats of skin, innocent creatures had to die. Adam and Eve must have taught their children this truth ; must have told them what had happened, and what they themselves had learned. So we are brought to chapter 4, where we read of two sons in the family and of a day when they came to present their offerings to God. Cain brought an offering of fruit, in recognition of the greatness and goodness of God. Abel brought fruit " also," and a blood offering, in recognition of God, but also in recognition of his own personal need of a Saviour. What was the difference between Cain and Abel ? This. Cain was religious, but Abel was Christian. You can be religious without any Cross, but you cannot be Christian without the Cross. The Cross is the starting point of spiritual life, the " A " in the divine alphabet, the keystone in the arch of truth, the foundation of the living temple. Abel therefore stands for the truth of salvation by blood shedding.

Enoch stands for the truth of fellowship. His is the shortest, but perhaps the fullest, of all Bible biographies, in Genesis 5 : 18-24, only 52 words in our Version. Read them carefully, and note that there were three stages in Enoch's life : 65 years during which he was vegetating rather than living, 300 years during which he walked with God, and endless years by deathless transference to the fuller life and fellowship of God. Enoch's life, of course, as Abel's, was based on redemption by blood, but what we are told of him carries the experience a stage further. Salvation tells of union with Christ, but fellowship tells of communion with Christ, and one may have the one experience and not the other. Every child is related to his father, but not every child is taken into his father's confidence and allowed to share his secrets. In wedded life there is union, but is there always communion ? Walking with God implies and involves surrender to God, and obedience, and not all Christians give this. For Enoch the supreme fact was God. He had not to go out of the world to get to God, for God was always where he was. His fellowship with God did not destroy his natural relations, he continued to live under human conditions, but he lived the common life in an uncommon way. Religion is not a change of space, but a change of spirit.

In the next place, *Noah stands for the truth of testimony.* For 120 years both by words and works Noah bore witness for God, warning men of certain judgment and pointing them to the only way of escape. Like Abel, Noah relied on blood-shedding for salvation, and like Enoch, Noah " walked with God," but the thing for which he pre-eminently stood and stands is testimony for God. He was salt in the surrounding corruption, and light in the prevailing darkness.

So much for the great truth for which these persons respectively stand : salvation, fellowship, testimony. Consider, in the next place,

II. THE RELATION OF THESE TRUTHS TO ONE ANOTHER AND OUR RELATION TO THEM.

I would say, first of all, that *these three truths are of the very essence of Bible teaching.* Salvation by blood is the key-note of divine revelation, struck first of all in the Paradise which the first Adam lost, and resounding through all the ages till it swells in glorious triumph in the Paradise which the last Adam has regained. The truth of fellowship with God also runs throughout all Scripture, and is set forth specially in the Epistles.

207

In a great variety of ways it is shown that by fellowship, by communion with God, is meant walking in harmony with His will, and in the enjoyment of His love. Anyone who is not walking in harmony with God's will, and not living in the enjoyment of His love, does not know the meaning of that for which Enoch stands. This is Christian maturity. Testimony before men is the expression of experience and conviction, and is the appointed and effective means of communicating to men the message of God. If from the Bible were taken all references to spiritual testimony, our loss would be incalculable.

In the next place, *these three truths are presented in the order of progressive Christian experience.* There is, and can be, no Christian experience at all where the soul has not come under the spell and power of Christ's salvation. We must begin, therefore, where Abel began. But consequent upon salvation in the primary sense, it is God's design that we shall live in fellowship with Himself, " walking in the light " by being well-pleasing to Him ; and so we must go on from Abel to Enoch. Wherever this is done the result will be that testimony is borne, both by words and works, to God's " goodness and severity."

Incidentally, these are the themes of the Epistle to the Romans. Salvation is the subject of chapters 1-5 ; fellowship is the subject of chapters 6-8 ; in chapters 9-11 there is a parenthesis on Israel, and then testimony is the subject of chapters 12-16, so that in this Epistle we have an extended exposition of these verses in Hebrews 11.

Finally, *these three truths constitute the test and standard of spiritual life.* The life of a true Christian originates in salvation, develops in fellowship, and issues in testimony. If these three things are not present, there is no true Christian experience. Let us distinguish between Christian experience and the experience of Christians. Many Christians need to get away from their experience to Christian experience. One may have the life of God, and yet have no knowledge of fellowship with God, and where there is no fellowship with God, there will be no testimony for Him. How is it that so many who profess Christ's name scarcely ever, perhaps never, bear witness, give testimony ? You ask them about it and they say, " Oh no, I could not do that, I am much too nervous "— not always when talking about other subjects ! I remember an athlete who declined to go to Church with his father and mother, because he said their pew was in front, and he did not like walking down the aisle to be looked at by all the people. But he did not mind 70,000 people looking at him the previous afternoon at a football match !

Now, let us get down to the facts, the realities, in this matter. Are you bearing testimony for Christ where you are, in the home, at the club, in the shop, at your recreation, everywhere, tactfully of course, and by your life first of all ? If not, why not ? The reason why not is that there is a want of fellowship, for no one can live in fellowship with Christ and not bear testimony. Again I say, you may be converted, regenerated, justified, come into the blessings of redemption, and yet be a stranger to this fellowship, and so neglect testimony.

You say—how can we go all the way ? How can we know in ourselves the truths for which these three men stood, salvation, fellowship and testimony ? The answer is, " by faith." " By faith, Abel. . . ." " By faith, Enoch. . . ." " By faith, Noah. . . ." The same faculty whereby we apprehended Christ for our salvation, for the reception of eternal life, is the faculty whereby we enter, on conditions, into fellowship with Him, and the faculty whereby we are given power and courage to bear Christian testimony. If every saved soul in this tent just now was living in fellowship with Christ and bearing testimony everywhere, it would affect the whole of Christendom, and the entire world. Are we not here at this time to see that the conditions are met, the blessings apprehended and held, and to go out to promulgate and propagate this three-fold divine truth ?

Spending our Inheritance.

By Dr. DONALD G. BARNHOUSE.

IT is very difficult to attempt the inventory of the universe. Ephesians 1 : 3 says that we have been blessed with all spiritual blessings in the Heavens in Christ. How shall we start to list them ? Where shall we find our categories ?

When I was in the theological seminary we had one professor who read from his manuscript, with an infinite detail of order and arrangement. His whole text, with heads and sub-heads, classifications and sub-classifications, was a masterpiece of interlocking argument. One of our more waggish theologues took the professor off at a dinner party. The student made a rather wild statement, knowingly far from the facts, and someone asked him for his evidence for such a statement. He replied, with a twinkle in his eye and with a perfect imitation of our professor's tones, " My authority for the remark is under Roman numeral III, section Capital F., sub-section Arabic 1, sub-sub-section Gamma, sub-sub-sub-section Gimel, complete with vowel points most in use in the Massoretic text of Codex Aleph and the palympsests." What ramifications of sections and sub-sections might I fall into if I should attempt to catalogue the blessings which God declares to be ours now—all . . . *all* spiritual blessings. It is clearly impossible to treat it properly, since the theme of our whole life-time, and the glory of eternity, are bound up in it.

> Wonderful grace of Jesus,
> Greater than all my sin !
> How shall my tongue describe it ?
> Where shall my praise begin ?

We may begin with the Cross of Jesus Christ. Immediately someone objects, " But the Cross of Christ is not in Heaven." Yes, it is. Not the literal wood that the Romanists have multiplied from many varieties of tree as a fetish, but the value of that sacrificial death is in the Heavens. That is why we read that the Heavenly things themselves had to be purified with better sacrifices than these of the object-lessons slain on the altar of tabernacle and temple (Heb. 9 : 23). Our assurance of salvation is in the Heavens. How do I know that I am most surely saved and never can be lost ? Because I am able to look away, through the Word of God, and see my surety in the Heavens. The leper, when he was to be cleansed, brought two doves to the priest. The one was killed and its blood was caught in a bowl. The other was dipped, alive, into the crimson tide and then released into the sky. If someone had challenged the former leper as to his right to walk among men without the cringing cry, " Unclean ! unclean ! " he would have had every right to reply, " See yonder flash of scarlet, winging against the white of the cloud and the blue of the dome above ? There flies my guarantee."

> Arise, my soul, arise,
> Shake off thy guilty fears,
> The bleeding sacrifice in my behalf appears,
> Before the Throne my Surety stands
> My name is written on His hands.

It would be possible to continue with this cateogry of spiritual blessings, which might be called positional blessings, but there is another category of blessings which bring us right down to earth. These are the blessings of the graces of the Christian life. You will never have them apart from Heaven. You may get a little of their mist and spray, but to be drenched in them, to be plunged in them until you are dyed in their hues, you must make the journey to Heaven. If you are to have love, joy, peace, long-suffering, gentleness, goodness, faith, meekness, self-control, you must get them in Heaven. Wait a minute, says a Bible student. Are you not mistaken ? These are the fruits of the Spirit. I admit that they are, as one cluster on the stem, the fruit of the Spirit ; but I ask a question. Where did the Holy Spirit pluck that cluster which we are to receive from His hand ? I shall show you that He got it in Heaven. And, further, did He go to Heaven and pluck it and bring it down to us here and begin feeding it to us while we were far from Heaven ? Not He. For it is the Holy Spirit who has brought us to our Mount Pisgah where we first saw the promised land of present Heaven. It was He, the Holy Spirit, who took us by the hand and led us into the Heavenly places. It was He who was a wall of fire about us that we might pass unscathed through the territory held by the enemy.

In fact, the Scripture teaches that the Holy Spirit Himself is the first of the blessings which is given to us from the Heavenly places. At Pentecost Peter linked the discussion of the power that came with the work of the Holy Spirit on that day with the ascension of our Lord Jesus Christ. He says, " This Jesus hath God raised up, whereof we all are witnesses. Therefore, being by the right hand of God exalted, and having received of the Father the promise of the Holy Spirit, He hath shed forth this, which ye now see and hear " (Acts 2 : 32, 33). So when our Lord went up, the first blessing came down, and it was the Holy Spirit who is both blessing and the Blesser for our further blessings. And the Holy Spirit, even though He is the Blesser, is not the source of blessings. They do not originate in Him, we are told. For when He comes He does not speak of Himself. Our Lord said, " He shall glorify Me ; for He shall receive of Mine, and shall show it unto you . . ." (John 16 : 14). So it is out of the treasure round the throne where Christ is seated in glory, that the Holy Spirit takes all the blessings that are ours in the Heavenly places and ministers them to our hearts.

211

But there are two ways of having the blessings of Heaven from Christ, through the Holy Spirit. You may have them in sample or in plenitude. You may have an occasional whiff or perfume, or you may dwell in the flower garden. You may have a few ounces of brown bread a day on short rations, or you may have a full loaf from the finest of the wheat. You may have saccharine, or you may have sugar. You may have desert fare, or you may have Canaan's milk and honey. I hope I give you an appetite for Heaven! " Ho! every one that thirsteth, come ye to the waters, and he that hath no money; come ye, buy, and eat; yea, come, buy wine and milk without money and without price. Wherefore do ye spend money for that which is not bread? and your labour for that which satisfieth not? hearken diligently unto Me, and eat ye that which is good, and let your soul delight itself in fatness " (Isa. 55 : 1, 2). It is all there for you in Heaven.

And there is more. We have spoken of positional blessings, and the blessing of the graces. May I point out that there are also the blessings of life and duty and service. Someone may think that these blessings are earthly. Too often they are. What there is of misspent labour in Christian work ! How many of us have been given the divine restlessness that was meant to shake us loose from ourselves and lead us into Heaven, and have sought to escape it by rushing into some form of " Christian work ! " The Lord begins to strike us gently, as you strike a bottle when you want a heavy, clinging stuff to come free, and we rush from under His hand, and take refuge in activity. How many an offshoot " faith " mission has been established in this way ! How many a " movement " " campaign," " tract work "—and you can fill in the blank for your own runaway efforts—has been formed without being born in Heaven ! And a year or so later there is a deficit to meet, and a duplicating, competing work. God was never in it from the beginning. True labour and duty and service for God are Heavenly blessings, to be obtained only in Heaven. When work is done for its effect in the world, even for its effect upon souls, it is out of the primary purpose for which God intended it. For at this point we come to the statement that God's purpose in choosing us before the foundation of the world, of making us accepted in the beloved, of making us the fullness of Him that filleth all in all, is, first, that we should be to the praise of His glory; and, second, that we might be the means whereby He gives to Satan a mouthful of dust.

Both of these things are to be accomplished in Heaven. In the highest Heaven, the far-above Heaven, we are to be to the praise of His glory (Ephes. 1 : 12). In the lower Heaven we are to manifest to Satan's hosts the manifold wisdom of God (3 : 10). We shall take the two aspects together, for the purpose of God in choosing us and taking us to Heaven now is visible from above, and gives praise to His glory, and is felt below in the embarrassment and discomfiture of the enemy. In order to understand this, we must go back a moment and sketch a frame for this picture. I have dealt with it at considerable length in my forthcoming book, " The Invisible War," and refer to the truth briefly, here, as it is necessary to the development of our thought.

212

When God created Lucifer it was to step into the position of prophet, priest and king under God, that he might be mouthpiece for God's orders, channel for universal worship, and instrument of God's government. He was so wonderful that he wanted to speak in his own name, take worship to himself, and rule in his own right. He said, " I will be like the Most High . . ." (Isa. 14 : 14). The hosts of all the angels split vertically, some of every rank following him, so that he has in his train (like an army with privates, corporals, sergeants, lieutenants, captains, majors, colonels and generals) demons, fallen angels, principalities, powers and himself of the order of the cherubs. Since he had aspired to be like God he was given a first problem, to demonstrate to the universe the utter worthlessness of any will that opposes the will of God. The earth was touched in judgment and made without form and void, waste and desolate, and darkness covered the face of the deep. We do not know how long he had to brood in that sinister silence of the world's first night, but in it he learned his powerlessness, but gained a gnawing hatred against God that made him for ever the arch-enemy. God then moved, and by His simple Word in six brief days reformed and refashioned the earth. Satan got his first terrible mouthful of dust. But when he saw man created—not on a rank above his own ; not on a rank equal to that of his principalities ; not even on a rank with his lowest angels—but on a rank a little lower than the angels (Psa. 8 : 5), he was incensed against God anew, and moved to destroy this man. For to Adam had been given the offices which Satan had held. He was prophet, and spoke for God, naming the animals. He was priest, to bring the worship of himself and his own. He was king, given dominion over the cattle and every creeping thing. This feeble man was soon seduced, and left the place of blessing for the place of his own way. There are evidences in the Scripture, which we cannot take time to bring forth here, that Satan thought he had outplayed God. Was not God holy ? Was not man moved into a place of sin ? Surely a holy God could do nothing about that. The whole of the human race was corrupt, and Satan had the potentialities of an increasing following. But he reckoned without God. God had planned His work of redemption in Christ. He was the Lamb slain from the foundation of the world (Rev. 13 : 8). We were chosen in Christ before the foundation of the world (Ephes. 1 : 4). Oftentimes people who know my very strong belief in the doctrine of election ask me why God chose us. The answer is before us.

Christ, the great Prophet, Priest and King, Himself was made lower than the angels, came forth from the grave bringing with Himself a great company of sons into glory (Heb. 2 : 9, 10). He did not save us for eternity merely, though we shall be with Him for ever. He saved us for this battle. The statement of it is here in our text. The third chapter of Ephesians tells of the formation and composition of the Church, and continues that the object was " to make all see (and I would omit the italicised word *men*), what is the fellowship of the mystery, which from the beginning of the world hath been hid in God, who created all things by Jesus Christ "—and now watch it closely—" to the intent that

213

now unto the principalities and powers in the Heavens might be known by the Church the manifold wisdom of God " (3 : 9, 10).

Let us examine certain features of this declaration. God's purpose is a present purpose—now. The instrument of God's purpose is the Church. The object of the purpose is to manifest His wisdom. The sphere of the manifestation is the Heavens. The audience of the manifestation is the principalities and powers. For you to fail to see what God has for you to do now, and to remain occupied with earthly lusts and pleasures when God is calling you to a Heavenly battle, is as treasonable as if the Royal Air Force had wanted to stay on the ground in 1940 and play with model aeroplanes instead of going aloft to meet the *Luftwaffe*. The sphere of our warfare is in the Heavenlies. God wants us, there, to be the instruments of exhibiting His wisdom before the forces of Satan.

If we analyse the Scriptures and examine this passage closely, I believe we can find the spiritual significance behind it. How can we manifest the wisdom of God ? The answer lies in what we replace. Satan and his hosts began the rebellion with the idea that brightness and beauty and creature wisdom were sufficient to run the universe. They were wonderful ; they would take a try at it. God answers, through us, that He can stoop to instruments far beneath the angels in wisdom, beauty or power, and that when these instruments are yielded to Him, He can pour Himself through them and do what creature power and creature wisdom could never accomplish. Herein lies the secret of an oft-misunderstood verse. In the upper room our Lord announced His departure, and with the announcement expressed certain principles that were now to come into effect. He was going to Heaven to represent the disciples in the presence of the Father. They would stay on earth and represent Him to the world. He would send the Holy Spirit to represent Himself within the disciples. With this new arrangement, and under the management of the Holy Spirit, the work would be carried on even better than when He was here in person. He said that it was advantageous for them, for such is the real force of the word, that He should go to the Father, for if this did not happen the Strengthener would not come (John 16 : 7). So they were to gain by His departure. But He, also, was to gain. He had work to be done, and He said that it would be better done by the disciples than by Himself. There is a problem for you. But there it is : " Verily, verily, I say unto you, He that believeth in Me, the works that I do shall He do also ; and greater works than these shall He do ; because I go unto My Father " (John 14 : 12). There have been fanatics and cultists who have tried to explain that their miracles duplicated and surpassed the miracles of the Lord, but this is seen to be ridiculous upon any thoughtful examination. The supposed miracles of Lourdes or of Christian Science (falsely so-called) fall into two categories. There are those cures of neurotic people who, having imagined themselves to be ill, now imagine themselves to be well, all to the glory of the Virgin of Lourdes or of Mrs. Eddy. The other type contains the infinitesimally small minority where there might be some reality to the healing. These must be seen in the light of the book of Job, where Satan, when he had received permission from God, put his hand upon Job and brought the boils that afflicted him so terribly. Satan, we thus see, has the power to bring human ills. The Word tells us that the unsaved masses are " taken captive by him at his will " (2 Tim. 2 : 26), and that the whole world lieth in the wicked one (1 John 5 : 19)—rests supinely in his embrace. The stage is thus set for the Satanic miracles. Satan puts his hand on one of his creatures and afflicts him, and then takes his hand off and makes him well, taking the glory to himself through one of his religious counterfeits such as those we have mentioned.

The greater works that we are to do are in a different realm altogether. Thank God, we do not have to look to healings, tongues and physical miracles. Our warfare is on a higher level, our works are greater works, and they are wrought in Heaven, and not on earth, though they have their repercussions here.

What was the greatest work which Christ did on earth ? Cleansing lepers ? Raising the dead ? And we are to do greater ? I have not seen or heard of anyone bringing a Lazarus back from the dead ; and if someone comes to tell me the story of a resurrection done in the corner, I frankly do not believe it. And even if it were true it could not be compared with Christ's raising of Lazarus, performed on a body that was corrupt, and in the sight of the whole town of Bethany. We do no greater works than these physical miracles, simply because there are no greater to be done. Yet the Word of God is true, and we have greater works that are for us to do.

Once more we ask the question, What was the greatest work which Christ did on earth ? Without doubt Christ's greatest work was to reach into the dead heart of man and plant a new life there, bringing a man out of darkness into light, out from the power of Satan and into the power of God. And in this realm we are to perform—I make bold to say that hundreds of us have performed—greater works than the Lord Jesus Christ ever did in this sphere of work ; and I shall demonstrate the truth of my seemingly presumptuous statement. The explanation lies in the difference between Christ's perfect nature and my sinful nature. For Christ to reach into the kingdom of Satan and lay hold on a child of Adam, communicate new life to him in such a way that the man shall be enabled to lay hold upon Christ as Saviour—what a wonderful thing ! Surely this is the greatest work that He ever did among men. Now, you and I are to do the same thing. When God the Father reached through Christ to men He had the God-man to work through. When He reaches through us to men He has the transformed sons of Adam to work through. Christ on earth was all holiness. I on earth am not all holiness. When Christ took a subject of Satan and turned him into an object of grace and then a subject of Christ, Satan might whine that he could not do anything about it ; that a much greater power than himself had come into his realm and stolen one of his citizens. But when the Lord reaches down and does it through us, there is indeed a mouthful of dust for Satan.

215

Let me illustrate my thesis by a story. During the war there was a United States submarine that sailed out of Pearl Harbour and turned westward toward Japanese home waters. The crews that took these boats to the coasts of China and Japan knew that they were to be gone for sixty or ninety days at a time. They could never radio their position for fear of drawing the enemy to them. From the moment that Diamond Head dropped below the horizon, they were cut off from all communication with their fellows until they came home with all their torpedoes gone. On the particular vessel of which I speak, there was a fine crew of men who had been out time and again on such expeditions, and had many a Japanese flag with the setting sun painted on their hull as symbols of the number of victims they had sent to the bottom. Suddenly a tragedy occurred on board when they were near the enemy coast, almost two thousand miles from their base. One of the crew was taken desperately ill with a ruptured appendix. If he were not operated upon within a matter of hours, he would surely die. There was no doctor on board. The only man with any medical training was a pharmacist's mate, who could wash out wounds, apply tourniquets and give a few pills, but who had never held a scalpel in his hand. He had worked in a naval hospital and had seen some operations. It was life or death for the sick man, and the sailor offered to operate. The captain took the boat down to depths where it would be perfectly still without the surface movements. A scalpel was fashioned from a razor blade. An insufficient supply of ether was drawn from a torpedo head, if I am not in error. The towels of the ship were gathered together, and one or two of the officers stood by to help. The operation took almost four hours, and finished when the sailor had sewed the incision with cat-gut from a violin string. But the operation was successful, the patient lived, and when the ship had sunk two more Japanese vessels it returned to Pearl Harbour with all its crew on board, and the convalescent sailor walked off the ship. Now, I declare, without fear of contradiction, that such an operation was a far greater triumph of surgery than if a Harley-street surgeon, with all his degrees and experience, had walked into an operating theatre, surrounded by assistants, anæsthetists, and nurses, and had performed the same operation.

Here is the illustration of our text. Now, to-day, in this age of grace, we are to manifest to the principalities and powers that God is able to stoop below the level of the angels and take men who were fallen, lift them to the throne of Heaven, unlock the storehouse of grace, equip them with divine power, enable them to speak the Word of life which will bring life to others. We do not need to be as beautiful as Satan ; we do not have to have the fire of a seraph or the might of a cherub ; we need not the speed of an angel or the cleverness of a demon ; we need not the subtlety of Satan, the acumen of the accuser, the education of the enemy. In fact, we do not have to have the wisdom of men, or the strength of men, or the best in human personality. What a triumph for God, and what dust for the serpent, when one of the foolish, the weak, the base, the despised, reaches out to Heaven and lays hold on the power of God and brings to naught the things that are ! The Lord God gets all the glory. If Mr. Churchill preached the Gospel over the wireless and there was a revival, worldly men could say that it was by the power of his eloquence and the dynamic of his diction. But when a Cockney street-preacher lifts up a cracked voice and calls men to Christ, then Satan is indeed chagrined.

Out in Africa, recently, I met a man and some of his converts, and the meeting gave me a thrill of joy. The Lord tells us in Luke that there is joy in the presence of the angels of God over one sinner that repenteth (Luke 15 : 10). It does not say the angels have the joy, and we may ask ourselves who has the joy in the presence of the angels. Out there in Africa, that day, I had some of it. I was in the presence of the angels, living in the Heavenlies, and saw a token of God's grace and power through a black African—and what an African ! We had driven west from Jos, in Nigeria, through Bauchi, and on to the Tangale country of the former cannibals. After a night at Biliri we were driven on toward Tula, and stopped for an hour to see the mission station at Kaltungo. The venerable pastor came to meet us. My translator told me that here was a man who, in his youth, had eaten human flesh. He had come from the lowest in the scale of humanity that a man might come. His gods were birds and beasts and creeping things. But the Spirit of God reached him and brought him out of death and into life. He became a power for God, and now is surrounded by a Church of which he is the pastor, and many of his spiritual children are the members. What a mouthful of dust for Satan ! What a manifestation to the principalities and powers in the Heavenlies through these frail members of our Lord's Church, of the manifold widsom of God.

Do we want to manifest that wisdom in the presence of the enemy ? We must have, first, the life of God. When we have been made partakers of the divine nature we are able to hold forth the Word of life and bring others out of darkness and into light. Then we shall know the droplets of His blessings. But hundreds of you would confess that you have the life of God, yet have never been used to win a soul. What, then, do we lack ?

We must have, second, a yieldedness to God and a willingness to be emptied of self and filled with Him. Then we shall know the showers of His blessing. But are we to be caught in the power of the Holy Spirit, and borne along by His mighty winds ? Then we must first be taken into Heaven where the winds originate, and we shall know the torrents of His blessing. And when this happens it will be seen in the highest Heaven that some have come through to the source of power and are, even now, to the praise of His glory. It shall be seen in the lower Heavens that God works not by might or by power, but by His Holy Spirit taking men from beneath the angels to the throne of God, and leaving dust for the devil as we go back and forth. And on earth we shall be seen triumphant, and men shall take knowledge that we have been with Christ.

Dust for Satan to-day, while tomorrow the scoffers round about us who laugh at us, and those who choose the mess of pottage rather than the birthright of sonship, shall be brought forcibly to acknowledge the worth of Christ, bowing before His feet, in our presence (Rev. 3 : 9).

There remains one phase of this truth to discuss. What happens when we pull the lever and start the blessings from Heaven earthward, passing through enemy-held territory ? We wrestle. And it is no human wrestling. But there is absolute victory and blessing poured out. Possess your possessions. Enter the Heavens. Live on the throne.

The All-Sufficient Answer to All Our Need.

By the Rev. Prebendary COLIN C. KERR, M.A.

IN Luke 1 : 30 we read the question of Mary, " How shall this be ? "
and the reply of the angel, " The Holy Ghost . . ." I want for
a moment to pass by that sacred mystery about which we ever speak
quietly and in measured terms. Sufficient is it to say that we are not
surprised at the question of Mary. She had been told that the Eternal
God would step out of the invisible world into time and sight ; that the
long-promised one was about to appear. She had been told the greatest
mystery that should ever fall upon a woman's ears, that she was to be the
mother of a child for which there was no earthly father. We are not
surprised, therefore, that she should address such a question to that heavenly
visitant who came with a message so clear yet mysterious. " How shall
this thing be ? " It is a question of awe-struck enquiry, not of unbelief.
Zacharias had been visited, and to him had been given the promise of a
supernatural happening, and his question contained doubt, a doubt
which was to breed dumbness, as ever doubt does. But that is not the
character of Mary's question. Mary's question is the question of awe-
struck enquiry begotten of an unquestioning faith : " *How* shall this be ? "
There is no rebuke, however loving, in the angel's reply ; there is no
reminder of the consequences of doubt, but there is that which is nearly
always given immediately in response to honest inquiry—an adequate
explanation. Mary said, " How shall this thing be ? " The angel
replied, " The Holy Ghost."

Some years ago a young clergyman, in his first ministry, came to
me and said, " I want to thank you for preaching my ordination sermon."
That caused great surprise, for I had never preached, and I assume I
never shall, a sermon at an ordination service. " What do you mean ? "
I asked. " Well, when I went for the ' quiet days ' preceding my ordination, I found myself in a foreign atmosphere. The things I heard did
not help me very much, but there was one thing that kept ringing in my
heart. It came to me as my ordination sermon. It was just the one
thing for that retreat." With gladness of heart I asked him what I had
said, and when and where. " Do you remember taking a quiet day at
—— theological college, and in the course of one of your talks saying :
' Now men, do not worry too much about definitions and doctrines of
the Holy Spirit, different ideas of holiness. They may have their place,
and they do ; but do not worry too much about them. Remember

219

this : the secret of the Holy Spirit is—the Holy Spirit, He is the secret.' "
He, a living personal God, He is the secret. And Mary said to the angel,
in effect, " You have brought to me a message too wonderful to believe,
yet I believe it, but it is so mysterious that I cannot understand it—How
shall this be ? " And the answer all-sufficient, can be summed up in
three words : " You want to know how it shall be, who shall bring it to
pass, who will be responsible for the formation of the Son of God within
you—Oh, mystery of mysteries—you want to know ? Well, the Holy
Ghost. He will be responsible."

This is to-night, I suggest, a very solemn meeting for all of us. When
you come to the end of a week such as this, with a sense of thankfulness,
there is just a sense of solemnity. It is the closing of a chapter for some,
it may be the closing of the book for a few, and one cannot speak without
mingled feelings of great thankfulness to a wonderful God, and feelings
of great solemnity. I would say to-night, whatever else you forget as
you listen, remember this : the secret of the Christian experience is the
Holy Spirit, for the Holy Spirit seeks so to relate you to Jesus Christ,
" in whom dwelleth all the fullness of the Godhead bodily," that if you
are pliable in His hands, responsive to His terms, and heeding of His
tones, you will go from glory to glory, transformed, until with others you
meet in His adorable presence and praise Him throughout eternity.
The secret is—the Holy Spirit.

Now, I cannot but feel that Mary's question of old is being asked by
most in this tent, who roughly speaking fall into two classes. There is
that glad, happy band whose name is legion, praise God, who have come
into some experience of the working of the Holy Spirit, who not speaking
of Himself nor drawing attention to Himself, has been throwing rays of
light upon the great centre and circumference of salvation, Jesus Christ ;
and perhaps He has been doing it for years in your life. Maybe it is only
recently that you have been aware of it, but to-night you are rejoicing,
you are a happy people. You are using Mary's question just as Mary
did, and saying, in effect :

> He cannot fail, for He is God ;
> He cannot fail, He's pledged His Word ;
> He cannot fail, He'll see me through.
> It's God with whom I have to do.

I do not doubt the result not for a moment, but it is too wonderful
for me to understand. Can you tell me the secret of the process whereby
there shall be a realisation of the promise ? The answer comes to you—
Yes, I can tell you how it is that your fondest hopes will be realised, and
the assurance you have will be maintained, how it is you will enter into
the land promised to you which has been already taken by faith. The
Holy Ghost is going day by day so to relate you mystically in your being,
consciously in your experience, to Jesus Christ, that you will find in Him
all that you need day by day, week by week, month by month, year in
year out until you stand in His glorious presence to give Him the praise.

But our story would be a happier one if all folk to-night were found in that glad class. Alas, it is not so. There is a great body of people who are asking Mary's question with a different tone ; there is no major key in their song, there is a psalm in a minor key. They are saying with a sigh all but despairing, " How shall these things be ? " As though it were impossible. Last Tuesday night I watched nearly 4,000 faces turned with unmistakeable longing to the speaker as he said his subject was going to be deliverance from sin, and I could read in the faces an intensity of desire, a confession of failure, and mingled fears and hopes. There was a one-ness of desire which was far too apparent to be missed by any sensitive soul. The cry, unarticulated by the lips, was going up from 4,000 hearts, "How shall this thing be ? " As I looked I realised what a variety of experience lay behind that common cry. There were missionaries going back to their field with love and thankfulness. There were the young students going back to their Universities, faces aglow with laudable ambitions, with castles in the air, but feeling there was hardly a hutch built upon earth. I looked at that company I am privileged to represent, ministers, knowing something of what is behind the scenes of ministerial life—and how many a minister is far more spiritually tired than his congregation knows !—how many a minister is carrying on the routine work in a regular way, seeking to be faithful at the drive of conscience, but no longer at the constraint of the Holy Ghost. I thought of many young people, some attending their first Keswick, and others who have come saying, " If I do not get something this year, this is the last time." So my imagination played, as I think it had a right to play, as I looked into the faces of intensity of desire, longing and passion. I believe there are many here to-night who are asking Mary's question, and saying, "You speakers have told us that there is this life, there is this experience ; that God means us to be rejoicing in victory, to know a life of blessing and fruitfulness even in a world of atomic bombs and bread rationing—God means us to be rejoicing in Christ Jesus, but tell us how shall these things be ? " To them I say the same thing. The answer is— the Holy Ghost. He wants so to relate you to Him who is justification, who is righteousness, who is wisdom, who is redemption, who is sancti- fication, that you shall know experimentally and not merely theoretically a full salvation. The secret is the Holy Ghost. The Holy Ghost is the answer.

If I may be allowed just for a moment to touch upon a subject which may be regarded as too doctrinal or even mystical for an evening meeting when the tent is hot and crowded, I think it will help some of you later. Do remember that God in the Trinity of His Being is a Community, a Society of Persons, and each brings to the soul the wholeness, that is the completeness, of God. It is not a question of the three Persons each contributing a third, making together a composite unity which we call God. If that were so, in worshipping the Son, or the Spirit, or the Father, we should be worshipping something less than God, which would be idolatry. In some mysterious way we shall never understand in this world, in the Trinity of His Being is a Community of Living, a Society of Persons, and each brings to us the wholeness of Deity. That is why it is that as touching Deistic characteristics, what is predicated of one Person is predicated of the other, and is predicated of the third Person. If you go through your Bibles carefully you will find that as touching the attributes of Deity everything said of the Father is applied to the Son, and everything said of the Father is definitely applied to the Holy Spirit, and everything said of the Spirit is said of the Father. All that is predicated of one is predicated of all, because each is God. You may say, is this practical ? Most intensely so, if you would understand the way in which God wants to lead you into the fulness of salvation. Each Person of the Blessed Trinity is God. As we think of the Father so we think of the Son, what we think of the Son, so we think of the Holy Spirit. Yet have we not three Gods, but one God. Three Persons, and each Person brings to us the wholeness of Deity. Though that is true, each comes to the soul with a different emphasis. God : Father, Son and Spirit, but each with a special emphasis, or we might even say, each to emphasise a special ministry.

God the Holy Spirit, what is His emphasis ? The ministry of the Holy Spirit which He emphasises is to reveal Jesus Christ in such terms that mystically the soul of the sinner and Saviour become one. That is why—I say it with reservation but without hesitancy—we are unwise, I think, when we talk as though Christ saved us from the judgment of sin and the Holy Spirit sanctifies us from its power. *The Holy Spirit is not sanctification*, the Holy Spirit is the Sanctifier, and He sanctifies us by relating us to Christ who is both justification and sanctification. It is as the Holy Spirit reveals the altogether blessed One that the soul opens up and opens out and finds itself mysteriously one with the Christ revealed by the Holy Ghost. So I say the emphasis with which the approach of each Person of the Trinity is made, is characteristic of His ministry : the Father approaches us, speaking in general terms, with a ministry of provision, of spiritual supply and sovereign purpose. He tells us that it is His own blessed will to vest in Jesus Christ, as in a great depository, all the things He has provided for the soul, and the finality of truth. Jesus Christ comes to us with a ministry. His ministry is one of self-revelation ; to speak of Himself ; a holy egotism ; a sublime egotism which we love in association with Him, but which we would never tolerate in association with anybody less than God. His whole ministry is—" I AM." May I sum it up in a single one of His divine utterances when He said to the crowds that they came because they had eaten of the loaves and were filled, but not because they understood the sign (John's word for miracle). They had never realised that if there was someone in their midst who could turn a few loaves into a supply for many hundreds, that someone must be Creator, God Himself. They had followed Him because they hoped for a similar experience. You remember how He urged them to labour for the bread that perishes not, and then came the promise to which I have referred, " He that cometh to Me shall never hunger, and he that believeth on Me shall never thirst." Notice the present tense in each case. He that *keeps on coming* to Me, as the Holy Spirit relates him to Me, shall never hunger ; and he that *keeps on believing* on Me shall never thirst. I am the provision for the soul in its entirety and for all eternity. When it comes to God the Holy Ghost, His special ministry is a ministry of spiritual attachment, of creative relationship, of mystical union. He knows no more holy task than to point men continuously to Jesus Christ. He does not speak of Himself, He ever points away to the Lord Jesus. No wonder Paul said, " In whom dwelleth all the fulness of the Godhead in bodily form." He had become incarnate. And " we are complete in Him," not in the Holy Spirit. The Holy Spirit leads us to the great depository of divine provision and shows us all we need there, and creates the faith to appropriate it.

So when it comes to this glad moment to-night, I humbly would claim some small share, if so be enabling grace will be given, in a ministry on earth which, relying upon the sovereign Spirit, would seek to point you this last night of the Convention to Him in whom we all are complete, in whom dwelleth all the fulness of the Godhead bodily. We are complete in Him. I have taken a rather mystical line—I make no apology— I hope as you think things over you may find some little help. But to come to something less deep, a little illustration may help.

When I was over in Ireland some while ago, I came into touch with a minister of the Gospel away in a remote, isolated spot, who told me of a discovery he had made which interested me quite a lot. He said, " For years I have had to take a watercart some distance three or four times every week to bring back water for washing and cooking and cleaning purposes generally. There is no water laid on to my manse ; it was so with my predecessor, and has always been the same. But I had an idea that I might make a discovery "—I think he had a scientific bent— " I started digging about, and would you believe it, just at my back door I discovered a well," and he added, " We have been going all this time week after week to collect water from a distance, and there has been a well at my door the whole time." I need not apply it. Beloved, there is a well of living, bubbling water. That well of water is not the Holy Spirit. The Holy Spirit leads you to the well and enables you to draw its precious waters, and bids you come and come again. Jesus Christ said, " I am the water of life." " If thou knewest the gift of God, and who it is that saith to thee, Give me to drink ; thou wouldest have asked of Him, and He would have given thee living water." " The water that I shall give him shall be in him a well of water springing up into ever-lasting life." " In you a well," " out of you rivers of living water." I believe to the very core of my being that it is possible for all of us to go home having within us a well of ever-living water, and because it bubbles up it is bound to bubble over. In us a well, from us *rivers*, not even a river. If that does not speak of freshness, of fruitfulness, of perennial satisfaction, then words have no meaning.

Now, where is this experience to be found ? When St. Paul was writing to the Philippians, in the third chapter he contrasted the old covenant and the new, and he said by implication, there was a sign for the old covenant and there is a sign for new covenant. The sign for the old covenant was circumcision, and no Hebrew missed its significance. But he goes on to say, We are of the real circumcision; we have our covenant sign; it is a threefold one. "We are of the circumcision who worship God by the Spirit, rejoice in Jesus Christ, and have no confidence in the flesh." I believe that just as the Holy Spirit has led you into a healthy salvation, your whole being will go out in worship to God by the Spirit. You will be rejoicing, not in Keswick primarily, not in some experience basically, not in some victory in the immediate past, you will be rejoicing in Jesus Christ. But more than that, to the degree that you have entered into that salvation, there will be "no confidence in the flesh," and you at Keswick know the real meaning of that word "flesh"— as we have said for young people, knock the last letter off and spell it backwards, and you find "self." The word "flesh" nearly always in the New Testament refers to that selfish principle with which we were born, and which is as a virus of sin. Just to the degree with which the Holy Spirit makes the Lord Jesus plain and personal to you, you will be worshipping God by the Spirit. You will rejoice in Jesus Christ, you will find yourself singing such a hymn as "Jesus, I am resting, resting" in fact of who Thou art (as well as "in the joy of what Thou art"), "I am finding out the greatness of Thy loving heart." People will say, "You seem to speak with a great deal of self-assurance." You will reply, "That is not quite right; I speak with a great deal of assurance, but not self-assurance, for I have no confidence in the flesh. I know that if I start to-morrow out of touch with my risen Lord, I shall be where I was a year ago, perhaps worse." We, the covenant children of God, worship God by the Spirit. That will alter a good deal of your behaviour; a good deal of the lightness that creeps into missions and conventions would go out very quickly. Worship God by the Spirit, rejoice in Christ Jesus, and have no confidence in the flesh.

I should like to pursue that thought, the second part of the new covenant. We rejoice in Christ Jesus because it is the sublime task, the great joy of the Holy Spirit, so to relate us to Christ that we come to know some of those things which He is prepared to do and indeed ever does for *the rightly related soul*. The Holy Spirit delights to cause men and women to rejoice in the wonder of Christ's atonement. Christ is made unto us justification. God is just, and the Justifier of him that believeth in Jesus. Why? Because, for such, Jesus the Christ has met all the liability and settled all accountability, Jesus Christ has met the debt, paid it, settled it and has become in His own bleeding body both the receipt and payment. God is well pleased. Did you not hear the words this morning—how my heart leapt as Mr. King was speaking about it—" Who shall lay any thing to the charge of God's elect? Shall God who justifieth?" What an absurdity! Why, He justifieth. Shall Christ who died? What an absurdity! He died to meet my liability! " Who shall lay any thing to the charge of God's elect?" No accusation, no condemnation, no separation. The results of the Fall are met in redemption. Man was accused, judged and cast out. In Christ no accusation, we fear no condemnation, we fear no separation. Thanks be unto God for His wonderful plan of salvation ! I believe it is the happiness and delight of the Holy Spirit as we talk and read about these things, to make it all closely personal and real until two things have happened : mentally we have received it, and experimentally we have become mystically united to the Christ who died. He is our justifier.

You want to know, when it comes to principles of sanctification, how does the work of God the Spirit come into operation ? You want to know how to be sanctified. I do not think that it is along the line of addition and subtraction. Taking A.B.C.D., things that are wrong and saying " these must go " and then taking E.F.G.H., things that are right and saying " these must be added." Oh no. We are never told, so far as I am aware, in the New Testament—do not misunderstand me—not to be conformed to *worldly things*, else should we cease to live, but rather not to be conformed to the *world*. Were this not the case, since the world, for example, eats, and drinks, and breathes and dresses, we should, refusing these things simply because the world does them, just die ! We are told not to be conformed to the world. That is very different. This means that I refuse to do, or not to do, things just because the world says so. I will not be the servant of the world and conform to it. I belong to Jesus Christ and am His servant, and what things soever I do or do not, I do or do not because of His dictation over my life. I conform to Him *not* to the world. He shows us the beauty of Jesus, the wonder of that altogether lovely One. As we behold the glory of the Lord as in a mirror, something is taking place, indeed two things. The Holy Spirit is creating faith in the picture we see, and we become one with Christ, in His beauty.

As Mr. King reminded us, the greatest exhibition of love was Jesus Christ. I should like to have a little reverie. I am sitting back in my chair and just thinking quietly, and the Holy Spirit leads my mind, as sooner or later He leads the mind, to the altogether satisfying and sufficient One, Jesus Christ. I look at Him as He is conjured up before my mind. How long He suffered ; how kind He was ; I cannot think of Him envying anyone : He had no palace, not even a humble home, save the one at Bethany. He never vaunts Himself, pushing Himself to the front, almost treading somebody under-foot in so doing. As for being puffed up or conceited, you can never associate the thought of conceit with Jesus Christ ; and as for behaving Himself in an unseemly fashion, one cannot imagine it. Similarly, you cannot think of Jesus Christ seeking His own comfort. Though He were God, yet He sought not to please Himself. When one was brought into His presence by rough hands, though the sin was hateful, He thought no evil of her. Though He judged most honestly the act, He could ever separate the sinner from the sin. Just to the degree a person is holy, to that degree a person will be slow to be critical. Real holiness realises the price of sin and is sorry for the sinner. I awake from my reverie, I rise from my chair—I have had just a glimpse of the divine, and I go out of my house and meet somebody, and I feel so well

P
225

disposed toward that one that I am even impressed with it myself, and I say, I felt differently toward that one. I get to my office and telephone calls come, and other disturbances, and I find that somehow my reaction is different. Two things have happened. Faith has been created in the vision, it is true, and I have been united to the One, to Jesus Christ by the Holy Spirit.

I will close with one other thought—the *sufficiency of His grace* : " My grace is sufficient for you." I was looking out of my window one day and saw a young man walking up and down, pacing the street with a look of anxiety on his face, the reason for which I thought I knew. I went out and called in a friendly manner his nickname, " Patsy, what is the matter ? " He said, " I want to be a Christian, but I dare not." "Why not ? " "Do you know where I work and what I have to do where I work ? How can a man be a Christian there and doing that ? " I had my own way of treating him. Looking into his face I laughed a merry laugh. " Poor old Patsy," said I, " You have got such a little tiny Jesus, He is not even able to keep poor old Patsy. My Jesus is the eternal Son of God, raised from the dead, and able to look after me and everybody else as well." "Oh," said he, " I never thought of it like that." He came into my house, and on his knees the great transaction was registered in the Lamb's book of life, and he got up one with Christ, who is justification ; one with Christ, who is sanctification ; one with Christ who has sufficiency of grace ; one with Christ who is beauty personified ; and went on his way back to the old firm and the old temptations, but a new man in Christ. He had asked the question, "How shall this be ? " and had heard the reply, " The Holy Ghost."

FRIDAY,
July 19th, 1946.

10 a.m. **Missionary Meeting.**

THE REV. W. H. ALDIS (*Chairman*) and MISSIONARIES.

3 p.m. **Afternoon Meeting.**

THE STRUGGLE AND THE REST OF LIFE.
DR. DONALD G. BARNHOUSE.

8.30 p.m. **Communion Service.**

AFTER THE SUPPER, THE SERVICE.
THE REV. GUY H. KING.

Saved to Serve.

FOR the "last great day of the feast" the theme is ever the same—Christian service. The Keswick Convention does not teach sanctification and holiness as an end in themselves, but rather that His people might be fit for the Master's use. Therefore, the instructional and hortatory messages of the Convention having reached their climax on Thursday, Friday morning is always devoted to the great missionary meeting, and the evening to the united communion service.

Both these unique meetings elude description ; a spirit characterises them that only those who have been present can really appreciate. The missionary meeting is athrill with the interplay of mingled emotions, as missionaries from various parts of the world tell of the need of the peoples among whom they work, and of the triumphs of the Gospel as it goes forth to them. The communion service is one of the most remarkable expressions of fellowship in Christ Jesus which the Church has ever witnessed, as clergy and ministers and lay-folk of numerous Churches and denominations and movements join together in " remembering the Lord's death, till He come."

No one is better fitted to preside over the missionary meeting than the Rev. W. H. Aldis, whose life has been spent as a missionary and in the service of missions ; and he did so once more with his customary graciousness, introducing the missionary speakers with a kindly word, and at the close, presenting most effectively the appeal of the Lord's last Commission, in its application to the lives of all present.

A spirit of deep reverence and worship marked the communion service. There was no stirring of the emotions, no call to sacrificial venture : withal there was the same wondrous consciousness of the divine presence in the midst, as in the morning, as more than 3,000 people bowed in quiet adoration. That a meeting of the same congregation, in the same place, later in the same day, could be so different from the missionary meeting, yet equally moving and satisfying, is beyond the power of words to convey.

The very wind and rain were hushed to silence, and a solemn stillness, which seemed almost awesome, laid its spell upon every heart. The service, which was conducted by the Rev. Guy H. King, began with the singing of " Jesus, Thou joy of loving hearts." Mr. F. Mitchell led in prayer, and a brief and most appropriate address was given by Mr. King. Then, after the giving of thanks, the elements were distributed—first to the servers, and then by them to the vast congregation. Leaders and speakers of the Convention, clergy, ministers, missionaries, well-known Christian workers, and laymen in varied walks of life, joined in this ministry of taking the bread and the wine, quietly and efficiently, to the thousands of people bowed in worship.

Then, in a final act of thanksgiving, the Convention ended with the exultant singing of " Crown Him with many crowns ! " That was the true note upon which to end, for it was—as it ever has been—the keynote of the Convention.

Set apart for Jesus !
Is not this enough,
Though the desert prospect,
Open wild and rough ?
Set apart for His delight,
Chosen for His holy pleasure,
Sealed to be His special treasure !
Could we choose a nobler joy ?—and would we if we might ?

Set apart to serve Him,
Ministers of light,
Standing in His presence,
Ready day or night !
Chosen for His service blest
He would have us always willing
Like the angel-hosts fulfilling
Swiftly and rejoicingly each recognised behest.

Set apart to praise Him,
Set apart for this !
Have the blessed angels
Any truer bliss ?
Soft the prelude, though so clear :
Isolated tones are trembling,
But the chosen choir, assembling,
Soon shall sing together, while the universe shall hear.

Set apart to love Him,
And His love to know !
Not to waste affection
On a passing show.
Called to give Him life and heart,
Called to pour the hidden treasure,
That none other claims to measure,
Into His beloved hand ! thrice-blessed 'set apart ! '

Set apart for ever
For Himself alone !
Now we see our calling
Gloriously shown !
Owning, with no secret dread,
This our holy separation,
Now the crown of consecration
Of the Lord our God shall rest upon our willing head !

—FRANCES RIDLEY HAVERGAL.

230

World-Wide Opportunity.

THE missionary meeting, to which the whole of Friday morning was devoted, was as always, the climax of the Convention. A spirit of keen expectancy prevailed, and the brief addresses of the eleven chosen missionaries were listened to with closest attention. The Rev. W. H. ALDIS, who presided, introduced them as representing, not any particular missionary societies, but the world and its need of the Gospel. He suggested that the Church was, on the whole, complaisant about the situation on the mission field, while, in his opinion, there was not the slightest justification for complaiscency. A similar thought was expressed in prayer by the Rev. W. W. MARTIN, that God would " open the hearts of His people to the sob and sorrow of a distracted world, so that they might take their share in its evangelization."

THE CALL OF CHINA.

China was represented by two speakers, and it fell to the lot of Miss ANNA CHRISTENSEN, of Denmark, to sketch the first scene in the panorama of world-wide opportunity. She described the beginnings of her thirty years' missionary work in China, in a girls' school and in the villages ; and how later she was led into an itinerant Bible teaching ministry in all parts of China, from Manchuria to the borders of Burma. Throughout eighteen years of such work she had seen lives transformed through response to the Gospel message. To-day, after six years of Japanese terrorism, the political situation was dark, but the spiritual prospect bright : there was a hunger for the Word of God, such as never before existed in China.

The Rt. Rev. H. A. MAXWELL, Assistant Bishop of Western Szechwan, gave as one of the reasons for the improved prospects of the Church in China, the fact that so many missionaries had gone to Japanese concentration camps rather than desert their posts and friends. Many critics at home considered this action a waste of personnel, but the Chinese people said, " Now we know that your missionaries love us." The war had effected a great change in all classes of the community ; it had been no uncommon sight to see eminent Chinese Christians doing lowly tasks in tending wounded and dying soldiers. Another factor in the new situation was that Christians had been scattered far and wide through the country, and had spread the Gospel message to many untouched rural areas, and schools and colleges had been established. It was the hope of the Chinese Government that within the next ten years, 75 per cent. of the population would be literate. What an opportunity for the Christian publishers of China ! In closing, Bishop Maxwell emphasized that the

Church in China was totally inadequate for its opportunities, and needed consecrated men and women, with gifts of friendship, to help it in its hard, but immensely worth-while work.

A Cry from India.

India, also, was represented by two speakers. The Rev. J. E. Woodward, illustrating the vastness of the problem of evangelizing that great land, said the population of 400 millions were living in 650,000 villages (the majority of them never yet reached by the Gospel), speaking 75 different languages, 200 main dialects, and following six Indian religions. An aged pilgrim, on his way to a holy city, groaning with fever and parched with thirst, refused to drink water during a long railway journey, for fear of defilement. Religion ruled the lives of the educated with its philosophies, and of the uneducated with the shackles of caste ; religion also governed political life. Fear of impending political changes should not impede the preaching of the Gospel, Mr. Woodward urged. Pandit Nehru had said the religious rights of citizens must be recognised, and this should include Indian Christians. In certain States laws against Hindu apostasy had been passed, yet in spite of all obstacles Christ was gathering out of India a people for Himself.

What may be accomplished by India's own sons, when constrained by the love of Christ, was strikingly exemplified when Mr. Bakh Singh, an Indian evangelist, described some conversations he has had with Hindus, Mohammedans and Sikhs. He began by exclaiming, " Sirs, we would see Jesus," and declared that that cry expresses the deepest need of India to-day. Among instances he cited was the quest for peace of a Hindu Sadhu, a doctor of philosophy, who had visited eighty-four "holy " cities in a seven-year pilgrimage ; and ultimately found that for which he yearned, in the Christian faith. Another indication of India's unsatisfied longing, was the unprecedented demand for Scriptures.

Stricken Japan.

A graphic picture of the devastation in Japan, almost inconceivable to those who have not seen it, was given by Miss M. A. Burnett, who has spent many years there. Although interned during the war, she and her colleagues were allowed to keep in touch with Japanese Christians, who were wonderfully good to them—as were also their non-Christian neighbours, and even the police. To-day, amid the prevailing desolation, Church life was shattered and Christian communities were scattered. But the Emperor of Japan was known to be reading the Bible, and all Japanese Christians were praying for his conversion. In a moving appeal for more missionary recruits, Miss Burnett said, " During my twenty-eight and a half years in Japan, I have hardly seen any young men from universities coming to evangelize Japan. God grant that some may seize this glorious opportunity."

Emerging into the Light.

Long known as " the dark continent," Africa is now no longer rightly so called. As Mr. Kenneth Richardson said, whereas it was once like a darkened prison, now all the doors were opening and Africans were pressing out into the light of Christianity and of modern civilization. Many were dazed by their freedom, and needed guidance, not only from animism, which still held seventy million Africans in its grip, but from the temptations of modern life; false ideals, propaganda, agitation, discontent, and racial hatred had to be met with the truth and power of the Christian Gospel. Hundreds of Africans had gone into the Forces and worked side by side with Europeans; they were now going back to their mud huts tainted with sin and disease, through strong drink having been supplied under a mistaken idea of social service. In face of this unprecedented need and opportunity, missions were understaffed in every way; now was the critical hour, and the Church of God should mobilize its forces and go into the great land of Africa.

At this point Mr. F. MITCHELL led the meeting in fervent prayer for missionary work in all parts of the world. Then, while Dr. W. N. Fullerton's magnificent missionary hymn, " I cannot tell why He, whom angels worship " was sung, the offering was taken, and afterwards dedicated by the Chairman to the Lord's service in the extension of His kindgom.

SOUTH AMERICA'S ROMANIST REPUBLICS.

The ten progressive Republics of South America, with their 100 million people, felt that after coming through the war unscathed they had nothing to learn from Europe, said Mr. HORACE BANNER. Recalling the religious background of these Republics, he said that when Europe sent the Gospel to America, North America got the Pilgrim Fathers but South America got the Romish Fathers, and for over 400 years Rome had held almost unchallenged sway. It would rejoice the heart of the early pioneers that now Roman Catholics were being converted to the Gospel on a scale without parallel in any other part of the world. The Bible was being read, and one Christian sold 750 Bibles to men working on the banks of the Amazon producing rubber for the Allies. The speaker appealed to his audience to pray that God would raise up South American nationals " to help us finish the job."

WAR-SCARRED ASIA.

Miss M. E. F. STILEMAN, representing S.E. Asia, dealt with the modern problems of repatriation and rehabilitation and their application to Burma, Singapore, Malaya, Siam, Indo-China, Java, Sumatra, and the islands of the sea. The people from these lands scattered about in refugee camps and orphanages all passionately wanted to return to their homes, even when told that their dwellings had been destroyed and that no food was available. A great work lay before Christian people in the vast corridors that had been fought over during the war, if the sick souls and bodies of these unfortunate folk in these far-off places were to be healed.

MOSLEM LANDS.

Deprecating the use of the adjectives " hard " and " difficult " in connection with missionary work in Moslem lands, Mr. GEORGE SWAN said that they inculcated a defeatist attitude toward evangelistic activity

233

among Mohammedans. There was much room for optimism in regard to the present situation. Although people at home sometimes despised mission schools, the Mohammedans considered them most important; and although, in Egypt, they had tried repeatedly to secure the passing of a law which would close the schools, they had not succeeded. Again, although they built schools and hospitals near to those of the missions, the people seemed to prefer the missionary ones; and in one case the Mohammedans had to ask the Christians to take over one of their orphanages! It was important to remember, in connection with work among the Moslems, that " nothing is too hard for the Lord."

PALESTINE AND THE JEWS.

Recently returned home after long experience in Palestine, the Rev. H. W. L. MARTIN drew a graphic picture of the Jewish population of the Holy Land. They presented an amazing and bewildering variety. They came from every nation, from a hundred different backgrounds, cultural, political, social and religious; among them were orthodox and liberal Jews, also many atheists; and artists, musicians and professional men all jostled each other for a livelihood in the urban centres. The majority of these people were adrift from their moorings, and their restless longing for spiritual peace had led the Jewish leaders to call conferences of young Jews to consider the urgent need for a revival of religious observances. Recently a Christian missionary had been invited to tell this assembly the reasons for his own faith. The New Testament was in great demand—was, indeed, a " best seller "; but it was not easy for a Jew to confess Christ.

EUROPE'S DISILLUSIONED LANDS.

The last of the missionary speakers was Mr. JAMES STEWART, who described the countries of central Europe as distracted, disillusioned, war-weary and sin-ridden. Europe was a great mission field, and many countries were in almost pagan darkness. One could search all Belgium, Luxembourg, France, Spain, Portugal, Italy, Austria, Czechoslovakia, Yugoslavia, Albania, Greece, Turkey, Bulgaria, Rumania, Poland, Lithuania, Latvia and Estonia, without finding a Protestant town of any size. Apart from the Protestant cities of Germany one Protestant city existed in the heart of Europe, Debrecen, the Geneva of Hungary. Millions of people in these countries had never seen a Bible or heard the glorious message of redeeming love.

CHALLENGE OF THE GREAT COMMISSION.

After these moving cameos from all parts of the globe, the Chairman observed that they had a strange resemblance one to another, in that most told of wide open doors; but in some cases the doors were beginning to swing to, some already seemed to be partially closing, and no one could tell how long they would remain open. Now was the day of opportunity for the Christian Church.

Then, before calling for response to the Master's great commission, Mr. Aldis invited various groups to rise—first, retired missionaries;

next, missionaries on furlough ; and finally, accepted recruits. It was both stirring and humbling to see that band of veteran heralds of the Cross, and the large number who are spending and being spent in the service of the Kingdom, and the group of young people whose lives have been gladly laid at His feet, for the fulfilling of His commands. All these have given their lives, their all, to Him ; small wonder that many in the tent were painfully conscious of how little they do, and how little they give, for His dear sake. They had an opportunity of making response to the missionary call, however, for Mr. Aldis proceeded to invite those to rise who would pledge themselves to increase their gifts to missions ; and a very large number did so. Then, parents who would be willing to give their children, if the Lord should call them to His service overseas ; and again there was an excellent response—not easily made ; the sacrifice involved in the readiness to rise, was very manifest in the wave of deep emotion which stirred every heart present. Finally, the Chairman invited those young people to stand who would be ready to go wherever the Lord might send them. This was the hardest test of all ; and to it a considerable number made their unreserved response. They were in the goodly succession of countless hundreds who in such missionary meetings in years gone by have pledged their lives to their Lord's service ; the mission field has no better recruiting ground than Keswick. So it proved once again this year. These surrendered lives were lovingly committed to God's directing care ; and out of full hearts all joined in the reverent singing of :—

> Were the whole realm of Nature mine,
> That were an offering far too small ;
> Love so amazing, so divine,
> Shall have my soul, my life, my all.

The Struggle and the Rest of Life.

By Dr. DONALD G. BARNHOUSE.

IN one of the Keswick Conventions before the war I had a conversation with a gentleman concerning one of the hymns frequently sung here. He questioned whether the hymn was merely idealism, or whether there was real practicality in it. The hymn that he mentioned was :—

> Like a river glorious
> Is God's perfect peace,
> Over all victorious
> In its bright increase ;
> Perfect, yet it floweth
> Fuller every day ;
> Perfect, yet it groweth
> Deeper all the way.

We discussed it at length, and I admitted, readily, that there were lines in the hymn that I thought foreign to my Christian experience and foreign to the experience of any Christian I had ever known. I referred to the lines

> Not a surge of worry,
> Not a shade of care.

and especially

> Not a blast of hurry
> Touch the spirit there.

But now I have found, on earth, a glorious river that I think can be used to illustrate the Christian life. It is Africa's great Congo. I first saw it when the aeroplane on which we were flying from Libreville, in French Equatorial Africa, to Leopoldville, in the Belgian Congo, came swooping down out of the clouds to fly at two or three hundred feet above some of the greatest rapids on earth. It was a marvellous sight from the air, and a few days later we set out to see the Congo at closer range. At and above the city of Leopoldville the Congo river is as calm and placid as a mill pond. The Stanley pool swells out until it is almost forty miles across. We crossed the river to Brazzaville on the lower edge of that pool, and could hardly see a ripple. It was necessary to look closely in order to see the direction of the river's flow. Then we took a car and drove ten miles down the river, walked a mile or so under the tropical sun, crossed a small, swinging bridge, high above a tributary, and came, at last, to the rocks on the edge of the rapids. The vast flood of the

236

Stanley pool and the waters of half a continent, push down through a narrow place between the rocks, scarcely half a mile wide. The roar of the water is like thunder. The pressure is so tremendous that at times waves fifty feet high are tossed into the air. Then I understood the hymn. The Congo is a glorious river, and I could sing

> Like the glorious Congo
> Is God's perfect peace.

The river is chocolate brown from the erosion of a million square miles and more ; it flows in a still basin forty miles across, and churns through rapids that are tearing in their torment. Up the river, calm and placid ; down the river, rapids.

So is the life of the Christian as it is revealed to us in the Word of God as it has been spread before you in these chapters. In the highest Heavens, seated with our Lord in the throne of His Father, we have a peace that passeth all understanding. In the lower Heavens and on the earth, we have a turbulent, roaring conflict. And since the Holy Spirit describes it in terms of wrestling, let us say, simply, that we have a wrestling match with unfair opponents who will stoop to any trick, for whom there are no rules and no holds are barred.

At this point I can imagine one of the dear ladies that fill Christian meetings the world over, and whose life is bounded on the north by the mission meeting, on the south by the Sunday-school, on the east by the library, and on the west by the vicar's tea (with an occasional trip to foreign parts, such as Keswick), looking around rather dazedly and saying, " Oh, my ! " Or perhaps even " Dear me ! " Yes, my good soul, the Christian life is a downright wrestling match, not with human beings our own size and weight, flesh and blood that we might compass, but we wrestle against principalities and powers, against the world rulers of this darkness, against spiritual hosts of wickedness in the Heavens (Ephes. 6 : 12).

Someone may ask me if I know what the Keswick message really is. Yes, I do. And if you turn to the contents of the Keswick Hymn Book you will discover that, after forty-one hymns on the subject of " Longing for Holiness," there are forty on " Consecration," forty-three on " Faith," thirty-five on " The Fullness of the Holy Spirit," twenty-seven on " The Overcoming Life," fifty-nine on " Union with Christ," and then a section with nineteen hymns on " Conflict." But a cursory glance shows that outside of the heading on " Conflict," you will find such hymns as " Will your anchor hold in the storms of life ? " " Through the night of doubt and sorrow," " Awake, my soul . . . ," and many others. One hymn I found while glancing at the first lines in this book, which is classified under " General Hymns," but which is certainly a masterpiece for " Conflict." Listen :—

> Lift up your head, ye gates of brass ;
> Ye bars of iron, yield,
> And let the King of Glory pass ;
> The Cross is in the field.

The banner, brighter than the star
   That leads the train of night,
Shines on the march, and guides from far
   His servants to the fight.

A holy war those servants wage
   In that mysterious strife,
The powers of heav'n and hell engage
   For more than death or life.

Ye armies of the living God,
   Sworn warriors of Christ's host,
Where hallow'd footsteps never trod,
   Take your appointed rest . . .

But I need not appeal to the hymn-book for my authority. Hymns reflect the experience of the saints, but some might hold that the experience of Christians is not always Christian experience. So let us go to the Word of God. " Ye have not yet resisted unto blood, striving against sin " (Heb. 12 : 4). " This charge I commit unto thee, son Timothy, according to the prophecies which went before on thee, that thou by them mightest war a good warfare " (1 Tim. 1 : 18). " Thou, therefore, endure hardness, as a good soldier of Jesus Christ " (2 Tim. 2 : 3). " I therefore so run, not as uncertainly ; so fight I, not as one that beateth the air " (1 Cor. 9 : 26). " Fight the good fight of faith . . ." (1 Tim. 6 : 12). All these are direct utterances, and there is a great body of typical truth in addition to these statements, in which the Christian life is seen as an uncompromising fight : slaying the Amalekites, hewing Agag in pieces before the Lord, choosing the smooth stones to see Goliath fall, taking the hammer and nail and driving it through the head of our sin until, like Sisera, it lies dead on the tent floor ; and all the other conflicts with the Philistines, who, though they were but flesh and blood, exemplify the forces with which we have to deal in the spiritual realm. All of this is very consistent with the Keswick message. In fact, it *is* the Keswick message, for the word that has been associated with this place through the years is the word *life*—life abundant ; fullness of life ; life in the Holy Spirit ; life in union with our risen Head ; life on the throne ; life in .every part, down to the day-by-day humdrum living. There is the glorious paradox that in every part of it there is perfect peace and there is absolute conflict. In abundant life there is peace, but in abundant life there is the pressure that sends us forth to work. In fullness of life there is peace, but in fullness of life there is the compelling of *noblesse oblige.* In the life in the Holy Spirit there is peace, but in the life in the Holy Spirit there is a Leader taking us forth to work and witness. In the life in union with our risen Head there is peace, but in that life there is arming for conflict, but in the life on the throne there is the finding of the supplies that enable us to go forth to battle. We must not emphasise the peace without the conflict, for that makes for flabbiness. We must not emphasise the conflict without the peace, for that makes for despair.

238

Alexander Whyte told the young Scot who had returned from Keswick with only half the message, that he had misunderstood it, and that life was " a sair fecht to the end." Yes, a sore fight to the end, but victory in every part.

Years ago, at a conference for the deepening of the Christian life which was held at Princetown I was asked to give a word of testimony. I was introduced by the late Charles G. Trumbull, editor of the *Sunday School Times*, and in his remarks his tongue slipped and he spoke of the battle that is won and fought, caught himself and said, " I mean that is fought and won." When I spoke I took the phrase, and pointed out that for the Christian the battle was indeed won and fought. The Lord won it on Calvary, and then gave it to us to fight. In our own experience the battle is won in the Heavenlies, far above all, and then is fought with the principalities and powers in their realm and ours. The fight in our realm is in every phase of our being and will differ with each person in detail, though the principles are always the same. One man's temptation will be to steal a penny, another man would be tempted to steal a pound, still another, ten thousand pounds. The nature of the fight is the same in each case. One individual will be tempted to escape into a constant reading of novels, whether of shilling shockers or those that will take one into a dream world of romance. Another person will be tempted to spend his life in the British Record Office poring over old documents to find what one fourth-rate official wrote to another fourth-rate official in the seventeenth century, and in his antiquarianism slowly becoming himself an antique. The nature of the fight is the same in both cases. " Be sure your sin will find you out " does not mean that you may be certain your sin will be discovered before the world, for we all know that God in His grace sees to it that most of our sins do not see the light of day. " Be sure your sin will find you out " means that the enemy who knows human personality only less well than God will discover the one door you have not fully guarded, and will bring the fight to that portal of your being. The fight can be in the realm of your athletic prowess, young man, or it can be, dear lady, a matter of your pride over your knitting. This does not mean that you must abstain either from athletics or knitting. It means that the Lord must run with you and be master of your pride—and your tongue—while your needles click.

The war will be in the field of our pleasures and in the field of our pain. Let me give an illustration from each. Take, first of all, our sense of humour. I told Dr. Scroggie one day, when we were laughing together, that if my sense of humour were amputated my spine would go with it. He said, " What would you be then ? " and I replied, " A jelly-fish." It is to the glory of God and to the defeat of Satan that a dour Scot like Dr. Scroggie has such an amazing sense of humour. Thank God for it. And Bishop Taylor Smith ! Some of the best jokes I know were learned from him. And his humour was one of the factors that made Christ so winsome to souls through him. Let me tell you a story about Bishop Taylor Smith. Here at Keswick, several years ago, we were on the platform together. The Holy Spirit took that great man and searched our hearts through him, and filled us afresh with the divine love. The Bishop and I walked up the hill to the speakers' hotel and something reminded the Bishop of a funny story, and he told it to me. We reached the hotel, and there were biscuits and squash, and good fellowship, and the Bishop regaled us with his brilliant wit. The laughter subsided and gave way to chuckles, and the chuckles to a moment of silence. Mr. Aldis looked at his watch, and said that some might wish to retire and we would go to prayer. We all were on our knees and the Spirit of God bathed us once more before we parted for the night. There is the glory of the Christian life. Introduce the thought of prayer in the Name of the Lord Jesus into the world's humour, and there would be a horrified gasp at the incongruity of it. But you can go from laughter to prayer in an instant when you know the Holy Spirit is in both, as He can be. After the prayer we walked out into the hall, and were the last to go up the stairs. He was before me, and I said, " You know, we Americans are not used to bishops, and you are totally unlike what I thought a bishop would be." He stopped short and turned around. We were two steps apart, but my height brought me to a dead level with his keen eyes, which had turned to steel in that moment. " What do you mean ? " he said, with a touch of sternness. " Well," I replied, " you are so . . . so human, and yet . . . so divine." The winter in his face turned to spring, and he said, " Come to my room, I want to tell you a story." We went along the corridor to room number three—I went there the other day and stood at the door, remembering him and thanking God for the memory —he stopped and made me go in first. The maid had turned down the bed for the night, and laid out his pyjamas—flaming scarlet silk pyjamas. I said nothing, but thanked God again that the Bishop had let no sanctimoniousness rob him of his love of colour. He told me the following story.

" A few months ago I went to a military hospital to see a soldier who was dying. He was my former batman. As I talked with him he asked me if I would like to hear how he found Christ. Of course I wanted to hear it, and he said, ' It was my first days with you, sir. Do you remember them ? ' I had quite forgotten them, and he talked on about them. ' The troopship loaded at Portsmouth for India. I found orders that I was to be batman to the Chaplain-General. I was scared to death. And then I saw that not only was I to serve the Chaplain-General, but a bishop. I came along to your cabin, saluted, reported for duty, and stood stiffly at attention, hardly daring to look at you. You had me come in and close the door. You inquired my name, and then the following conversation took place.'

" ' Do you know the Siamese national anthem ? '

" ' No, sir.'

" ' You know the tune of *God save the King* ? '

" ' Yes, sir.'

" ' Well, the words are these ; repeat them after me. " Oh, wha ta goo Siam . . . Oh, wha ta goo Siam." You had me repeat them more rapidly until I was saying, " Oh, what a goose I am." Then I knew how human you were.' " The Bishop laughed at the memory of it, and then went on with the dying man's story. " The next day you were shaving, and you had laid the razor blade down on top of the sponge. You reached out to grasp the sponge, and I thought you were going to be cut terribly. But you stopped, saw it, and said, ' How kind of the Lord to keep me from cutting myself ! ' Then I knew how divine you were, and I wanted to be like you from that moment. Soon I realised that it was Christ in you, in every part of you, and I came to Christ." There was the Bishop, a living embodiment of the Keswick message, meeting a man as a man must be met, because he had first of all met the principalities and powers as they must be met. He had wrestled with them in the power of Christ, and had the victory in every part of his radiant being.

Let us turn, now, to another phase of the battle. Mr. Churchill said, " We shall fight them on the beaches, we shall fight them in the fields, we shall fight them in the cities, we shall fight them in the ruins of St. Paul's." The Christian must learn that our wrestling is like that. Satan and his hosts will come. They will not balk at the invasion. And we must fight them in our bodies, we must fight them in our sense of humour, we must fight them in our affections, we must fight them in our emotions, we must fight them in our work, we must fight them in our play, we must fight them in our drawing-rooms, we must fight them in our dining-rooms, we must fight them in our bedrooms. Thank God for the noble host of warriors who are winning the battle of the bedrooms— who lie racked in pain, yet glorifying God.

I remember so well my visit to the most beautiful mission station in the world, Dohnavur, and Amy Carmichael. That mission station has probably cost ten thousand pounds more than it could have been put up for had it been built without beauty and line and colour. Some Judas may say, " To what purpose is this waste ? " But the Lord will answer, " Let her alone. She has poured it upon My feet and on the feet of India." . When I was about to go into Miss Carmichael's room I was told to be careful and not to press her hand too strongly, lest I hurt her. I found her lying in her bed, in a large room reflecting her surpassing love of beauty. I held out my hand, and she laid her hand in mine, misshapen and knotted with arthritis, and she said, " I am so glad you have come. I have wanted to meet you ever since I saw the first copies of *Revelation* magazine. I looked at it and said, ' A coloured cover on a religious magazine ! Beauty of type and lay-out.' " And she continued, " God never made an ugly thing. The entrance of sin brought ugliness. Oh, if Christians would only realise that their gardens must be the most beautiful, their dress the neatest . . ." I quote from the memory of ten years gone by, but it was delightful to meet the human soul of Dohnavur, and realise that its beauty had been won through Christ wrestling in a soul against the principalities and the powers. And there on a bed of pain she was not laid aside. She says it in one of her books with proper scorn. Someone wrote her a letter and said, " I am so sorry that you have been laid aside . . ." Laid aside ! When a soldier is transferred from the rear where he has become dead tired unloading supplies, and is put into the front lines where the shells are falling and men are dying, has he been laid aside ? Never. He has been transferred to another front, and there he fights, perhaps more than he ever fought before. And when a child of God is transferred from the activity of preaching to the activity of pain, let no one say he has been laid aside. You lie in the night with every nerve become a broad avenue along which the cavalry of pain come galloping, and you wrestle. You look at the time and see that it is eleven o'clock. You turn out the light and wrestle, and toss for hours and hours. You look at the time and it is eleven-twenty. And so the night passes . . . or does it ? And to the glory of God and the discomfiture of Satan and his hosts, we lie and remember that the river glorious is flowing, and that the tossing rapids which bear us along and dash us against the rocks were in the quiet of the great pool above not long ago, and that it is His current that bears us on.

Some of us will never know some of the wrestling that saints are called upon to do for God. I learned the meaning of the word *in* from a missionary, and learning that meaning learned a great many more things. A man from China told of fleeing before the Japanese. The Chinese Christians crowded into the mission compound, and a bomb fell near. The Japanese came, and fortunately there was a Christian Japanese officer who spoke to them and told them to remain quietly within the compound. The Chinese surged forward and pushed the Japanese back, and the compound was freed. The runners came in a few days later, telling of the great strength of the new drive that was coming, and the missionary and his wife and small child started out with scores of the Christians to flee before the enemy. For hundreds of miles they walked across country in that land of no roads. They followed the paths along the edges of the fields. At times they threw themselves into ditches to escape the fire of machine-guns from low-flying planes. They subsisted on roots and grass and the bark of trees. Then the missionary said, " Who shall separate us from the love of Christ ? Shall tribulation, or distress, or persecution, or famine, or nakedness, or peril, or sword ? As it is written, For Thy sake we are killed all the day long ; we are accounted as sheep for the slaughter." (I realised that few of us knew the actual reality of such tribulation, distress, famine, and other calamities.) And then the missionary said quietly, with just one word ringing out above the rest of the quiet sentence, " Nay, *in* all these things we are more than conquerors through Him that loved us " (Rom. 8 : 35-37). More than conquerors . . . and the glory of Christian living is that we know it in the midst of the fight. There is no doubt as to the outcome, and there is no doubt as to the present calm in the midst of tempest, joy in the midst of sorrow, strength in the time of weakness, light in the time of night, life in the midst of death. Yet, in, *in* all these things we are more than conquerors.

It has been asked what is meant by being more than conquerors. We none of us know what it means in its fullness. But let me make a suggestion concerning what it means to be more than conquerors.

Compare the conquest of the Allies in the world war with that of the Lord's troops in the invisible war. The Allies are conquerors, but question the the permanence of their victory. We are more than conquerors, for we know our victory is certain and eternal. The Allies are conquerors, but are worn and weary. We are more than conquerors, for though the outward man perish, the inward man is renewed day by day. The Allies are conquerors, but have lost many of their sons. We are more than conquerors for we shall doubtless come with rejoicing bringing our sheaves with us. The Allies are conquerors, but are on short rations. We are more than conquerors, because we are blessed with all spiritual blessings in the Heavenlies. The Allies are conquerors, but fear that the enemy will rise again. We are more than conquerors, for we know that the God of peace will bruise Satan under our feet shortly.

And, finally, we are more than conquerors because of the nature of our victory. It is not in ourselves. One of the grandest hymns of the Christian life is one that is not to be found in the Keswick book. It is Luther's great battle cry of the Protestant Reformation :—

> A mighty fortress is our God,
> A bulwark never failing.
> A shelter He amidst the flood
> Of mortal ills prevailing ;
> For still our ancient foe
> Doth seek to work us woe ;
> His craft and power are great,
> And armed with cruel hate :
> On earth is not his equal.

How, then, are we to meet such a foe ? Luther understood. Listen :—

> Did we in our own strength confide,
> Our striving would be losing,
> Were not the right Man on our side,
> The Man of God's own choosing.
> Dost ask whom that may be ?
> Christ Jesus, it is He !
> Lord Sabaoth is His Name,
> From age to age the same,
> And He must win the battle.

That is why we are more than conquerors. For we are more than conquerors through Him who loved us.

"Finally, my brethren, be strong in the Lord, and in the power of His might. Put on the whole armour of God, that ye may be able to stand against the wiles of the devil. For we wrestle not against flesh and blood, but against principalities, against powers, against the world-rulers of this darkness, against the hosts of spiritual wickedness in the Heavens. Wherefore take unto you the whole armour of God, that ye may be able to withstand in the evil day, and having done all, to stand. Stand, therefore, having your loins girt about with truth, and having on the breastplate of righteousness; and your feet shod with the preparation of the Gospel of peace; above all, taking the shield of faith, wherewith ye shall be able to quench all the fiery darts of the wicked one. And take the helmet of salvation, and the sword of the Spirit, which is the Word of God; praying always with all prayer and supplication in the Spirit, and watching thereunto with all perseverance and supplication for all saints; and for me . . ." If we had another chapter together it would be possible to spend it all on examining the armour. I love beautiful armour. One of the delights of going to Madrid is to spend some time in the most wonderful collection of armour in all the world. What artisans they had for making the panoplies that clothed the kings and princes and noble knights of feudal times. But none of them, not even the golden armour of Charles V of Spain, can touch that which is provided for us.

Here we are told to put on the whole armour of God, and the various pieces are described. In Romans we are told to put on the Lord Jesus Christ. The latter is the short form of what we have in Ephesians. Be girded with truth. But Christ answers, I am the truth. Then, put ye on the Lord Jesus Christ. Have on the breastplate of righteousness. The Spirit answers, Christ Jesus is made unto you, righteousness. Then, put ye on the Lord Jesus Christ. Be shod with the preparation of the Gospel of peace. But the Spirit tells us, He is our peace. Then, put ye on the Lord Jesus Christ. Take the shield of faith. The Spirit answers, We live by the faith of the Son of God. Then, put ye on the Lord Jesus Christ. Take the helmet of salvation. But the Spirit tells us, The Lord is my rock and my salvation. Then, put ye on the Lord Jesus Christ. The command comes again, Take the sword of the Word of God. But the Spirit answers, In the beginning was the Word, and the Word was made flesh and dwelt among us. Then, put ye on the Lord Jesus Christ.

There is our answer, and there must be the last word of these addresses. Christ. CHRIST. CHRIST.

The Sun of Righteousness on me
Hath risen, with healing in His wings ;
Wither'd my nature's strength, from Thee
My soul its life and succour brings ;
My help is all laid up above ;
Thy Nature, and Thy Name, is Love.
CHARLES WESLEY.

After the Supper, the Service.

By the Rev. GUY H. KING.

ONLY a very brief message is called for to-night; and it shall be on the words of John 13 : 4, " He riseth from supper, and . . . girded Himself." The Master Himself made clear the lesson of this story, in telling us that it was all to be an example to us : we, in our turn, were to do as He had done. Therefore, not even the most exact expositor will quarrel with me for taking our text and applying it to ourselves.

Quite a number of times during this week of holy convocation various speakers have described the truths of the convention as a spiritual " feast " ; not a few of us have felt that, indeed, He has brought us into His banqueting house, and His banner over us was love. Well, that feast is now over ; and we rise from supper, to go out again into ordinary life. But it is a feast of another sort, a Feast of Remembrance, that is in our minds this evening, as we—nearly four thousand of us—gather, from so many different sections of His Church, around the common Table of the Lord, for this sweet, and strangely moving, Communion Service. At the end of this hour of fellowship, with Him, and with one another, we shall rise from Supper, and, please God, it shall be to gird ourselves for His service. Come back with me to our Gospel story, and see how the Master girded Himself:—

For Lowly Service.

In the light of that incident, there is surely no task too humble for us Christians to undertake. We do not forget that it was at a moment when our Lord was peculiarly aware of the high dignity of His Deity, " knowing that the Father had given all things into His hands, and that He was come from God, and went to God," that He stooped to this menial ministry. So not even the loftiest is exempt from the lowliest tasks for Him. As we rise from supper, some of you will find awaiting you work that is accounted great among men—great privileges, great opportunities, great responsibilities ; but most of us will be called to smaller spheres. Whether, in human estimation, we figure large or small, the remembrance of the Master at the disciples' feet will assuredly bring us down humbly at His feet, ready to gird ourselves for any service, however lowly. And shall we not also prepare ourselves—

For Earnest Combat.

He went forth from that Supper to engage the mightiest foe of all good, and to wage the greatest battle in all history : the battle of Calvary.

There are not many prophecies that we can safely make concerning the future of those who meet here at His Table ; but one of the few things that we do know for certain about one another is this, that, as we rise from supper, the devil will be waiting for us. The three intimates discovered it as they descended the Transfiguration Mount ; and we, too, shall find it out—so we had better gird ourselves for the fight. The broken bread of this Remembrance is the token of the cost He paid, the reminder of the victory He won ; and the recollection of His triumph that this Supper brings us will accoutre us for that wrestling against the principalities and powers in the Heavenlies that was described for us so powerfully this afternoon, and will encourage us to lay hold on the victory of faith which His conquest has made so gloriously possible for us all. Combat there assuredly will be, as we go down to-morrow from Keswick ; but conquest will as certainly be ours as we gird ourselves with the realities of which the blessed Symbols speak. And lastly, the Supper will spur us on to a readiness—

For Uttermost Devotion.

Think how the Saviour went from the communion of that Upper Room, to the other communion of the Garden—from handing the cup to the disciples, to handling the other cup for Himself : the former a symbol, for all time, of the latter. How moving it is to hear Him say, out from the midst of His agony, " Not as I will, but as Thou wilt." Later, on the Cross, just before He breathed out His Spirit to the Father's care, He said a final word of fundamental importance. The first three Gospels tell us that He shouted it out, but do not tell us what it was ; the fourth Gospel says that it was just one word (in the Greek) " Finished ! " He had taken the cup, and drunk it, yea, to the last bitter dregs, and handed it back, " finished," to His Father's hand. The cup of poured-out wine that we shall presently take and taste is His own appointed memorial of His outpoured Blood—the sign of His uttermost devotion to His Father's will. And ours ? Shall we not, under this blest shadow of the price of our redemption from sin's bondage, and unto His glad service, rise from supper, and gird ourselves for a life's devotion—anything, anywhere, any cost ?

Early Morning Prayer.

IT speaks eloquently of the purposeful spirit which prevails throughout the Convention, that several hundred people rise in the mornings in time to attend one or other of the two prayer meetings at 7 a.m. This is especially appreciated when it is realised that for the majority this week is half of their annual fortnight's holiday. Instead of the leisurely rising which most people regard as one of the pleasurable indulgences of a holiday, they prefer to keep tryst with the Lord.

A rather larger number gathered this year in the small tent, for the general prayer meetings, than in the Pavilion ; and the size of the congregations grew steadily as the week progressed. The Rev. E. L. Langston, who was to have presided, was prevented by illness from attending the Convention, so his place was taken by Prebendary Colin C. Kerr, except on the last day, when Mr. F. Mitchell was chairman. Prebendary Kerr suggested a plan of prayer for the week, beginning on the Sunday with intercession for all Evangelical witness throughout the earth that day ; on Monday, for our own lives, character, conduct, recreation—that all might be to God's glory ; on Tuesday, for our homes—children, young people, parents, the observance of Sunday, and kindred aspects of home life ; on Wednesday, for business life, that it might be conducted according to Christian principles ; on Thursday, for our nation, and especially for those in authority in Church and State ; and finally on Friday, for the British Commonwealth and the whole world—" beginning at Jerusalem," with a united act of prayer for our own unsaved relations. Brief addresses, fitting in with the subjects for each day, were given by Convention speakers.

On several mornings it was raining heavily while the prayer meetings were in progress, and the noise of the rain on the tent was somewhat distracting ; but it did not affect the liberty of the Spirit in prayer, and one after another voiced the petitions upon the hearts of all—briefly and concisely, in obedience to the chairman's behest.

> When morning gilds the skies,
> My heart awaking cries,
>   May Jesus Christ be praised !
> Alike at work and prayer
> To Jesus I repair :
>   May Jesus Christ be praised !

Prayer for the Mission Fields.

THERE is quite a marked distinction between the general prayer meeting and that for the mission fields of the world. For one thing, the Pavilion is, in unfavourable weather, much quieter than the small tent ; and it is attended by such a large number of missionaries and those closely connected with missions, that the visitor is struck by the fact that the majority of the prayers indicate a first-hand knowledge of the mission field. There is thus a definiteness in petition which is most heart-warming.

This year the meetings were led by the Rev. A. T. Houghton, a former missionary and now secretary of a large missionary society. He presided graciously and firmly, guiding intercession along the line of thought for the day. On Sunday, petition was offered for Europe and the Jewish world ; on Monday, for Africa, including Madagascar and Mauritius ; on Tuesday, India, Ceylon and Central Asia were specially mentioned ; Wednesday, China, S.E. Asia and Japan ; Thursday, South America and the islands of the Pacific ; and Friday, Moslem lands and " The Unfinished Task."

A feature of the meetings was that each was closed with a number of one-sentence petitions, in which missionaries or stations, native Christians or specific needs in the areas named, were mentioned ; and all were gathered up in the final prayer of the chairman.

Thus, within the week, the whole earth was encompassed by the prayer of faith ; both the vastness of its need and the personal requirements of many hundreds of its heralds of the Cross, were uplifted to the throne of grace, in the assurance that He who is able to meet the immensity of world problems delights also to undertake for the smallest details of the lives of His children.

> The love of Christ constraineth ;
> Oh, let the watchword ring,
> Till all the world adoring
> To Jesus' feet it bring.
> Till north and south the kingdoms
> Shall own His glorious sway,
> And east and west the nations
> Rejoice to see His Day.

The Missionary Reception.

PERHAPS more missionaries attended the Convention this year than ever before, because larger numbers are in the Homeland than in ordinary times, as they have come from every field, for long-overdue furlough, and not a few from ex-enemy concentration camps. It was inspiring to see, at the reception to them, on the Wednesday afternoon, so vast a throng of those who have made the supreme response to the Master's call, and gone forth at His command whithersoever He has led, not counting the cost. They enjoyed a time of informal, happy fellowship, meeting others from different spheres of witness, exchanging news and comparing points of view.

Then followed a brief meeting, which torrential rain did its best to "drown." It succeeded, by the noise it made on the canvas of the tent, in rendering the greater part of the proceedings practically inaudible to all except those immediately in front of the platform ; but it could not rob the roll-call of its thrill, as the Rev. W. H. Aldis, the gracious chairman of the Convention, and missionary statesman, called upon the missionaries from various continents, lands and islands, to stand. Two groups held especial interest for all : the retired missionaries—who, Mr. Aldis said, do not like to regard themselves as "retired," but "re-tyred" for further service, especially in prayer ; and the new recruits. The latter were a small group ; tragically small, in view of the vastness of the need on the mission field to-day.

Two solos were beautifully sung by the Rev. Geoffrey Lester, and a message of encouragement was given to the missionaries by Dr. W. Graham Scroggie, on the parable of the sower, who sowed his seed and *rested until the harvest* (Matt. 13 : 24-30). Our responsibility is to sow the seed, Dr. Scroggie said, and to leave the growing of it to God. All too often we harass ourselves with worry over what is not our responsibility. If we are faithful in the sowing, the harvest will be sure.

Sow in the morn thy seed,
　At eve hold not thy hand ;
To doubt and fear give thou no heed,
　Broadcast it o'er the land.

Thou know'st not which may thrive,
　The late or early sown ;
Grace keeps the chosen germ alive,
　When and wherever strown.

And duly shall appear
　In verdure, beauty, strength,
The tender blade, the stalk, the ear,
　And the full corn at length.

The Ministers' Meeting.

PERHAPS one of the greatest influences of Keswick throughout the years has been that exercised through ministers who there have entered into a deeper experience of submission to the Lord, and have gone forth with lives transformed to declare, in all parts of the land, and overseas, the message which was the means of leading them from spiritual defeat to victory. The number of ministers at the Convention has, therefore, the profoundest significance: and this year they practically filled the Methodist Church, for the service held specially for them. The Rev. W. H. Aldis presided, and addresses were given by both Dr. W. Graham Scroggie and Prebendary Colin C. Kerr—two more contrasting personalities than whom it would be impossible to find ; but both one in heart and message " in Christ Jesus." Dr. Scroggie spoke on the distinction between consecration and sanctification—consecration being the work of God alone ; while in sanctification we are called upon to act. He then recalled his first visit to Keswick, and said that two ideas remained from it—the Saviourship and the Lordship of Christ. He urged upon his brethren in the ministry the claims of Christ to be truly Lord.

Prebendary Kerr also was very practical in his message, as he spoke of the difference between the interior and the external life. The life lived deep down inside is the real man ; that presented to the world is an assumed life—a mask. Like Dr. Scroggie, the Prebendary illustrated his point from his own experience, and described how as a young man he had faced up to the true implications of Christian discipleship—that he should be what, go where, and go when, Christ wanted. He passed on that challenge to his hearers.

Young People's Instructional Meetings,

YOUNG people's meetings have long been a feature of the Convention, and it is a sign of the virility of the movement that they should be so. This year, however, they took on a rather different character than in the past, because it was realised by the Council that a new generation has grown up during the war which knows not Keswick. The long interval since the last Convention in 1939 has left its mark upon the young Christians of to-day, in that for the most part they do not really know what Keswick is and for what it stands. To meet this manifest need, it was decided that the young people's meetings should be instructional in character. This was appropriate also to the mood of present-day youth. They are growing up in a world overshadowed by uncertainty and pessimism. They are alive to the stern realities of this atomic age, and seek for the answer to the prevailing sense of instability, if such an answer is to be found. It can be found, many of them realise, in the Christian Faith, and in that alone ; and supremely in the message of full salvation as proclaimed at Keswick. It was in the spirit of earnest inquiry therefore, that they attended the meetings held specially for them.

For manifest reasons, there were not quite so many young people at Keswick as in the years preceding the war ; and the four meetings were all held at times when there were counter-attractions—the first, on the Sunday evening, while the broadcast hymn-singing was beginning, in the large tent ; on Tuesday and Thursday mornings, while the Convention meetings were proceeding ; and on Wednesday evening, at the hour of the open-air meeting—so it was evidence of real singleness of purpose that the small tent was about half full on each occasion. The Rev. Kenneth Hooker presided over them all, and the addresses were given by the Rev. Gordon M. Guinness, on the Holy Spirit ; Mr. F. Mitchell, on New Testament teaching regarding the clean heart ; the Rev. H. W. Cragg, on full surrender; and the Rev. J. Dunlop, on practical Christianity. Space does not allow more than the briefest indication of how these themes were developed. Mr. Guinness pointed out that the baptism, anointing and sealing of the Holy Spirit are all aspects of one initial experience, at conversion ; while the filling of the Spirit may be given at the same time, or later. Those not baptised with the Spirit, are resisting Him ; those not filled with the Spirit, are grieving Him. We may grieve Him through pride, self-will or carelessness. Anything in the life unlike Christ, grieves the Spirit.

On the controversial subject of the " clean heart," Mr. Mitchell had some very illuminating things to say. He emphasised that, rightly used, the phrase does not indicate a state of sinless perfection, but rather is relative and progressive in meaning. A clean heart is one steadily responding to the Spirit of God in the twofold process of revealing sin and revealing the Saviour. When we speak of clean water we do not mean that it must be filtered, distilled, and sterilized ; we mean that it is wholesome. So a clean heart is a healthy heart, in which sin is hated, and God loved—progressively.

Mr. Cragg's plea for full surrender was based upon Paul's appeal to the Romans, " Present your bodies a living sacrifice " ; and Mr. Dunlop, in the final address of the series, showed that practical Christianity issues from a true identification with Christ in His death and in His resurrection life, as stated by Paul in Galatians 2 : 20. There are, he made clear, two conditions to be fulfilled before we can enter into this experience— a frank and full reckoning with sin ; and acceptance of the will of God for us. Then all that remains is, that we must claim, and trust. That is the only secret of fruitfulness, victory and service.

There was nothing in the nature of an appeal, and certainly nothing emotional about these meetings ; but a deep impression was made, and many of the young people came to the leaders and speakers for personal talks, while goodly numbers asked for " Morning Watch " cards, signifying their intention of observing their quiet time with God, regularly at the beginning of each day.

Rise ! for the day is passing,
And you lie dreaming on ;
The others have buckled their armour,
And forth to the fight have gone.
A place in the ranks awaits you,
Each man has some part to play ;
The Past and the Future are nothing,
In the face of the stern To-day.

Rise from your dreams of the future,
Of gaining some hard-fought field,
Of storming some airy fortress,
Of bidding some giant yield ;
Your future has deeds of glory,
Of honour (God grant it may !),
But your arm will never be stronger,
Or the need so great as To-day.

ADELAIDE ANNE PROCTOR.

Open-Air Meetings.

KESWICK Convention has one supreme objective : the deepening of the spiritual life of Christian believers. It is impossible, however, for thousands of Evangelical Christians, gathered together for fellowship in the Word of God, to experience spiritual blessing and victory in their personal lives, without there being some expression in evangelistic witness. So, almost inevitably, every day of the Convention, except the Friday (when the United Communion Service was held), was brought to a close with a great open-air meeting in the Market Place. If it had not been included in the official programme, it would have been held spontaneously !

The weather, which was, on the whole, singularly unfriendly to the Convention this year, did not prevent or spoil one of the open-air meetings : the rain had stopped every day by the time they began, at 9 p.m. They opened, of course, with the singing of well-known Convention and evangelistic hymns and choruses, for which the Rev. Geoffrey Lester—who served the Convention so well as pianist at most of the gatherings—played the portable organ. Great crowds were attracted, and the square in front of the picturesque little Town Hall, which stands in the middle of the market-place, was so densely thronged that the police had to make a way through for passing cars. In the midst, of course, was a solid phalanx of several hundreds of Convention visitors ; but large numbers of townspeople and holiday-makers stood on the fringes, in climbing, walking and boating attire ; and they listened with keen interest. It is notoriously difficult, in these days, to get people to listen to open-air meetings, but the gatherings at Keswick were so manifestly out of the ordinary, that nearly all who were coming and going through the town stood and listened, and the great majority of them stayed until the meetings ended.

Ringing testimonies were given by distinctive groups of speakers each night—on the Sunday, by Army Scripture Readers ; on Monday, by visitors from overseas ; on Tuesday, by undergraduates of Oxford and Cambridge ; on Wednesday, by members of H.M. Forces ; and finally, on Thursday, by former prisoners-of-war. All these, in differing style and with differing emphases, proclaimed the same glorious Gospel and bore the same glad testimony to the transforming power and grace of Christ our Lord. The former prisoners-of-war, of course, made a deep impression, and were listened to with intense attention, as they told their stories of ordeals at enemy hands, and of long weary months in concentration camps, during all which they proved the sustaining grace of God indeed to be their strength.

The whole proceedings were guided skilfully and unobtrusively by the Rev. W. H. Rowdon, who was in charge of the meetings, and who, in a brief concluding address each night, pressed home the messages which had been given, and sought to bring the hearers to a place of decision and of personal trust in the Lord Jesus Christ as Saviour.

While the meetings were proceeding and after they had concluded, personal work was conducted among the crowds; in this ministry missionaries, Christian workers of all ages and from many spheres of witness, and laymen of all Church associations, had a part, as they availed themselves of opportunities presented to them, and commended their Saviour to those whom they perceived to be ready to receive a word in season. The little township of Keswick was left in no doubt concerning the Gospel message, and what it meant to those who attended the Convention.

The distinctive message of the Keswick Convention is contained every week in *The Life of Faith*, a weekly paper for the deepening of spiritual life, which has been closely associated with Keswick from the beginning, and is the recognised organ of the Convention Movement. Its regular features include devotional and Bible study articles on various aspects of Keswick teaching, news of Evangelical activity at home and abroad, discussion of topics of interest to all Christian people, the answering of readers' questions, and reviewing of books. It is published on Wednesdays, at 2d., by MARSHALL, MORGAN & SCOTT, LTD., and is obtainable from any newsagent provided a regular order for it is given.

I cannot tell why He, whom angels worship,
  Should set His love upon the sons of men,
Or why, as Shepherd, He should seek the wanderers,
  To bring them back, they know not how or when.
But this I know, that He was born of Mary,
  When Bethlehem's manger was His only home,
And that He lived at Nazareth and laboured,
  And so the Saviour, Saviour of the world, is come.

I cannot tell how silently He suffered,
  As with His peace He graced this place of tears,
Or how His heart upon the Cross was broken,
  The crown of pain to three and thirty years.
But this I know, He heals the broken-hearted,
  And stays our sin, and calms our lurking fear,
And lifts the burden from the heavy laden,
  For yet the Saviour, Saviour of the world, is here.

I cannot tell how He will win the nations,
  How He will claim His earthly heritage,
How satisfy the needs and aspirations
  Of east and west, of sinner and of sage.
But this I know, all flesh shall see His glory,
  And He shall reap the harvest He has sown,
And some glad day His sun shall shine in splendour
  When He the Saviour, Saviour of the world, is known.

I cannot tell how all the lands shall worship,
  When, at His bidding, every storm is stilled,
Or who can say how great the jubilation
  When all the hearts of men with love are filled.
But this I know, the skies will thrill with rapture,
  And myriad, myriad human voices sing,
And earth to heaven, and heaven to earth, will answer ;
  At last the Saviour, Saviour of the world, is King.

W. Y. FULLERTON.